The Sardinian-Piedmontese Army in the War of the Austrian Succession 1740–1748

Organisation, Uniforms & Equipment Including Flags, Standards & Guidons

David A. Wilson

Helion & Company Ltd

Helion & Company Limited
Unit 8 Amherst Business Centre
Budbrooke Road
Warwick
CV34 5WE
England
Tel. 01926 499619
Email: info@helion.co.uk
Website: www.helion.co.uk
X (formerly Twitter): @Helionbooks
Facebook: @HelionBooks
Visit our blog at http://blog.helion.co.uk/

Published by Helion & Company 2024
Designed and typeset by Mach 3 Solutions (www.mach3solutions.co.uk)
Cover designed by Paul Hewitt, Battlefield Design (www.battlefield-design.co.uk)

ISBN 978-1-804515-39-6

British Library Cataloguing-in-Publication Data.
A catalogue record for this book is available from the British Library.

To my wife Josette for many years of patience.

To my late friend and Professor, Teddy Suren (Willie) for his original inspiration and 'joie de vivre'.

To Jean François Blanc for his constant encouragement.

Contents

In memory of Mr Pierre Charrié 1923–2021

Charles Emanuel III, King of Sardinia, Prince of Piedmont. *Carlo-Emanuele III Re di Sardegna, Prince de Piemonte.* (Author's Illustration)

Foreword

It is difficult to appreciate in a few words the enthusiasm and the competence with which David Wilson has been able to gather and develop the information for this study and present us with, along with his schematic illustrations, the real state of the Sabaudian army during the turbulent events of the Austrian Succession War in Northern Italy. David has accomplished a careful and complete picture of the organisation and uniforms of this army, as well as presenting the most important personalities that characterized the Piedmontese army of those times.

I met David for the first time at the end of the 1980's in Briançon, where he was standing guard at the entrance of the Citadel in the uniform of *Royal Ecossais*, and we immediately became firm friends. I remember us discussing French army uniforms of Louis XIV's period together.

Since then, we have remained in contact exchanging information and our research on military organisation and uniforms of the XVII and XVIII centuries.

It is therefore with an immense pleasure that I welcome this new and valuable work covering an army and a period that is not usually studied in English that will decisively contribute to the knowledge of that war and the events that occurred in Italy.

Giancarlo Boeri

Preface

This book is the first what I hope will be a series covering the uniforms and equipment of the different armies who fought in the War of the Austrian Succession. Although principally dedicated to the uniforms, I have added some historical notes to put everything into context.

The style of the iconography will be a mix of schematic and figurative illustrations together with separate colour plates for equipment, arms including artillery, colours, standards and guidons. I have been inspired by the style of Lucien Rousselot, Eugene Leliepvre and Albert Rigondaud 'Rigo' amongst others as well as some contemporary and modern illustrations. This would not be complete without mentioning the late Spanish military artist José María Bueno Carrera whose illustrations have also influenced my work.

Living in the region of Nice for over 40 years inspired me to start with the 'local' army of this period first, this will be followed by the principal opposition, the French army.

If the uniforms, colours, standards and equipment of the fighting regiments are the essential interest, I thought it would be interesting to add some colour with some details of the Court Guard Companies. Although I have shown the officers in powdered wigs, it is highly unlikely that they were worn on campaign, except for some of the senior officers.

I hope that both students of history as well as wargamers and military modellers will find this work of interest.

David A. Wilson
La Trinité, France 2023

Acknowledgements

I would like to thank the following researchers for the aid and encouragement that they have given me over the years and without their dedication this book would never have been so complete. To Giancarlo Boeri for his precious help with this work and without his aide this work would never have seen the light of day. To Enrico Ricchiardi for his kind help and guidance and providing additional information and verifying the manuscript. To Giovanni Cerino Badone for his kind help and providing additional information, in particular his help with the Artillery research and reading through the final text. To the late Roberto Gobetti and Sergio Masini of the Accademia di San Marciano of Turin Italy, who provided me with extracts from the researches published in their 'Armi Antiche' Bollettino dell'Accademia San Marciano. To Pier Franco Chillin della Ministero della Cultura, Musei Reali – Biblioteca Reale and the Staff of the Biblioteca Reale di Torino for the kind help and patience with my poor Italian and showing me so many original works. To Gilles Carrier-Dalbion of the Guides du Patrimoine Savoie Mont Blanc for his help with old Savoyard texts. To Jean François Blanc for his help in my research and to have opened many doors for me, and his constant encouragement & constructive criticism. To Dr Andrew Bamford for his constant encouragement & guidance.

Piedmontese Army Ranks and Appointments

Alfiere	Ensign (a junior infantry officer)
Aiutante Maggiore	Adjutant Major
Appuntati	Lance Corporal
Arciera	Archer (an assistant to a Provost)
Armaioli	Armourer
Artigliere	Gunner
Bombardiere	Bombardier
Brigadier Generale	Brigadier General
Brigadiere	Cavalry Corporal
Caporale	Corporal
Capitano	Captain
Carpentiere	Carpenter
Cappellano	Chaplain
Carabiniere	Carabinier
Carrettiere	Waggoner
Cavaliere	Cavalryman
Chirurgo	Surgeon
Chirurgo Maggiore	Surgeon Major
Colonnello	Colonel
Cornetta	Cornet (a junior cavalry officer)
Cornisti	Hornist
Dragone	Dragoon
Fanteria	Soldier/Private
Foriere portastendardo	Quartermaster with the rank of standard bearer
Frater	Chaplain
Fuciliere	Fusilier
Furieri	Quartermaster
Generale di Fanteria	General of Infantry
Generale di Cavalleria	General of Cavalry
Granatiere	Grenadier
Guardie	Guards
Ingegnere /Ingenieur	Engineer
Luogotenente	Lieutenant
Luogotenente Colonnello	Lieutenant Colonel
Luogotenente Generale	Lieutenant-General
Maggiore	Major
Maggiore Generale	Major-General
Maniscalco	Farrier/Blacksmith
Maresciallo d'alloggio/ Maresciale di Logis	Cavalry Sergeant
Minatore	Miner
Nominato	Appointee (a private selected to be a corporal but not yet promoted)
Oboista	Oboist
Piffero	Fifer
Portastendardo	Standard bearer (This appears to be a junior NCO rank in the *Guardie del Corpo* only)
Preposto	Provost
Sellaio	Saddler
Sergente	Sergeant
Sergente Maggiore	Sergeant Major
Soldato	Soldier/Private
Sottobrigadieri	Cavalry Lance Corporal
Sottoluogotenente	Second Lieutenant
Stato maggiore	Regimental Staff
Tamburo	Drummer
Tamburo maggiore	Drum Major
Timballiere	Kettle Drummer
Trombettiere	Trumpeter
Zappatori	Sapper

1

Introduction

'Je atans mon astre' (I await my star)
Device of Amedeo VI of Savoy, nicknamed the Green Count

The War of the Austrian Succession was fought during the reign of Charles Emmanuel III. This war was a particularly hard test for the new Sabaudian army. Due to its unique but difficult geographic location, surrounded by mountains on three sides, whose passes were blocked by snow for several months a year, and hills and plains to the east. The only major maritime access was the port of Nice, much coveted by other nations, in particular the French, who had already invaded the region twice during the reign of Louis XIV, and who also demolished the citadel and most of the fortifications of Nice built by the Hospitalliers.

In the 1860's, the French finally acquired this much coveted country by a vote, which was a rather doubtful one, at least by modern standards, the women and the working classes being excluded, and only after the King of Sardinia had modernised the port of Nice at his own expense. The decision was also helped by a vast number of veterans of the French army of Napoleon who had been settled in the region and their descendants as well as by a large group of new troops introduced before the vote by Napoleon III, who voted as residents. The importance of the rich mines of Savoy (iron, silver and lead) were also much coveted by the French and were an added incentive. Also, to a lesser degree, so was the valley of Aoste.

Being the privileged point of land passage east-west on the Mediterranean coast had obliged the Dukes of Savoy, later the Kings of Sardinia, to adopt a policy of swaying with the wind to survive, and they were quite good at it, the King ended up by gaining new territory in Italy from the Duchy of Milan in the peace treaties at the end of the War of the Austrian Succession, even during the conflict they were negotiating with France to change sides, survival being the watchword for the nation.

The Sabaudian army stood the test and won most of its battles against the French and their allies (Spain), in particular the Battle of Casteldelfino/Chateau Dauphin in October 1743 and the Battle of the Assietta, on 19 July 1747. They also lost a few, such as the Battle of Pierre Longue (Pietralunga) on 18 July 1744, an epic and bloody defence in the mountains, particularly around Mount Cavallo and the Battle of Bassignana on 27 September 1745, where they were totally outnumbered and the Spanish light infantry decisively defeated their Piedmontese adversaries. They were fully aware of the numerical superiority of their enemies and tried to compensate for this with their strategy. Their idea was to try to block the enemy in the valleys with strategically placed fortresses, of which Fenestrelle is a prime example, and then take them in the flank which would nullify their superior numbers and most importantly stop them from getting down into the plains. The campaign of 1744 was based on this strategy.

The geographic situation also had an influence on the composition of the army, which by necessity, was mainly based on infantry, with only two cavalry regiments and a small unit of lifeguards, the most important part of the mounted troops were the dragoons, who still fought as frequently on foot as on horseback, effectively still being very much mounted infantry.

In this small study we have the chance to show that the Piedmontese were quite well organised and kept fairly complete records of both uniforms and colours in coloured manuscripts – they were regularly updated giving us a good and accurate guide. We are also helped by the fact that they standardised the manufacture of military clothing and centralised their suppliers for a lot of their needs, and many of these administrative papers survived to our times.

On a strategic level, Carlo Emanuele III now had to rely on other people. The War of the Austrian Succession represented not only the shift of command functions from the sovereign to trained senior officers, but at the same time the predominance of the Foreign Secretariat during this war. In 1742 it was still the Marquis Ferrero d'Ormea (Gran cancelliere, the equivalent to a prime minister) who was pulling the strings of military politics.

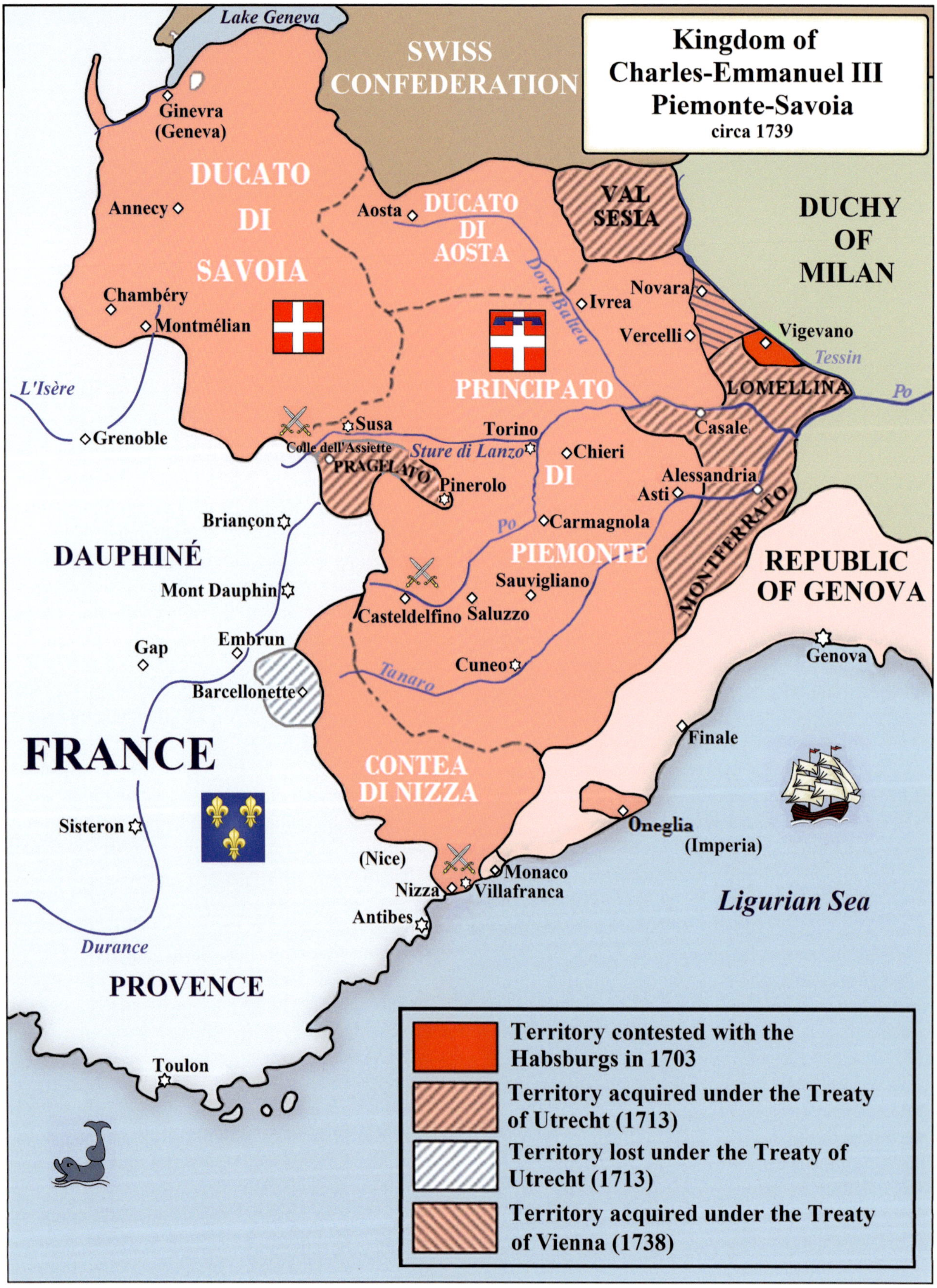

Map of the Continental Kingdom of Sardinia. Note that the only access to the sea was Nice, the commercial maritime port and Villefranche sur Mer (*Villafranca*) the naval base. Imperia (*Oneglia*) was also a port but was not connected to the rest of the country so was isolated. (Author's Illustration)

The Olezetti album of 1744 and another manuscript dated to 1747,[1] give us a fairly clear image of the dress of the Piedmontese troops who fought in the war of the Austrian Succession.[2] The magnificent Royal Library in Turin and the Palace Museum together with the State Archives provides a beautiful and compact site for researchers with a vast collection of original artifacts. One important detail is that we do not know for sure exactly when these colours were really issued, probably fairly promptly, but this insinuates that they commenced the war with the previous stands of colours as shown in the Lauro album of 1736.[3]

I have redrawn the infantry colours as the illustrations in original albums (Ozelletti of 1744 in particular) were rather small and not symmetrical, so slightly false compared the real colours. Also note the break in the staffs which is to suggest they were much longer.

Another tradition was following an incident in 1734 at the Battle of Guastalla that the war cry 'Savoia!' was born and it continued to be used throughout the army until June 1946. The *colonnello* of the Savoy cavalry regiment, in the act of ordering the charge against the Spanish, shouted 'Savoia' to encourage his men and received, in reply, a similar cry in chorus from all the soldiers of the regiment.

Cesare Balbo once described the character of the Piedmontese, when compared to other Italians as 'less ferocious, but of greater military value, originally feudal, then military in the correct term, with fewer changes, therefore less variability, more constant and with greater fidelity'.[4]

1 Archivio di stato, Torino. JB III 16. Livre de l'Uniforme des Regimens d'Infanterie au service de S.M. le Roi de Sardaigne selon l'Établissemen qui en a eté fait en dernier lieu 1744.

2 Archivio di stato, Torino. H VIII 53. Livre de l'uniforme des Troupes regleès de S.M. avec les Drapeaux, Étendards ou Guidons de chaque Corps 1747.

3 Biblioteca Reale, Torino, Ms mil. 431. Nicolas Lauro, Tapissier (circa 1734–1736) Livre Desquis des Drapaux de tous les Regiments d'Infanterie au service de S.M. Charles Emanuel II (sic) Roy de Sardaigne.

4 Cesare Balbo, count of Vinadio 1789–1853, Historian, ex-Prime Minister of the Kingdom of Sardegna and military theodicean and responsible for the 'Risorgimento'.

2

The Composition of the Army

Firstly, a few clarifications; both the French and Italian regimental names are used; as French was the language of the court in Turin and frequently used by the officers, and the regiments' names were in written in Italian, but with a Piedmontese influence, as this was the language spoken by the national soldiers (often by the Swiss and German soldiers as well who had spent a certain time in the country). The regimental names were frequently written the same in French. It should also be noted that a large number of the King's officers were nobles from Savoy, then part of the country, who spoke French and their region had been repeatedly attacked and partly occupied by France, as well as a large number of persecuted French protestants who had found refuge in the kingdom ever since the revocation of the Edict of Nantes in 1686 and most fought for the King of Sardinia, Duke of Savoy. In the county of Nice another similar language (Niçois) was spoken. Most of the regiments were raised before 1730 except where indicated. The foreign regiments, changed their names on the death or retirement of their previous *colonnellos*, taking the name of the new commander. Where known, the names and the years of these changes are noted in the text. As noted, although most regiments spoke and were commanded in Italian, some regiments were French speaking and some foreign regiments used German.

In the Kingdom of Sardinia there were several different forms of service:

The Royal household troops – The recruits of the Guards were raised from national volunteers, with a majority of young nobles who formed the Officers class.

The eight national ordnance regiments – The recruits of these regular regiments (including infantry and artillery) were raised from national volunteers and were maintained on a permanent basis, if somewhat reduced in peacetime, but were quickly augmented in times of conflict. Their grenadiers had a permanent establishment.

The 10 regiments of provincial infantry – These regiments were raised from men of the continental provinces of the kingdom (the island of Sardinia being excluded), aged between 18 and 40 years old, who had to assemble twice a year for training. In peacetime, only the cadre and an administrative company were kept on a permanent basis. Their grenadier companies were only formed in wartime. This was closer to a militia style of service, if somewhat better organised than in most countries of this time. The period of service was generally 20 years, but known regional variations were the Savoyards only had to do 18 years and the Niçois only 12. Due to the duration of the war, some of them could be considered as regular soldiers by 1741.

The 14 regiments of foreign infantry – The foreign regiments (Swiss, German and Italian, plus one 'mixed' regiment) were raised with the usual system of the capitulations, the regiments were not raised for a single campaign and they had a permanent existence, but the numbers of men in each company fluctuated between periods of peace and war. Their grenadiers had a permanent establishment. Of the Italian regiments, Sardegna became a national regiment after 1750 and Corsica was eventually disbanded.

Regiment of invalids – This corps was officially raised in 1710 (although some companies had been in existence much earlier, since 1685 in fact) and they were based and garrisoned in the fortresses or strong points. There were 17 companies in 1747.

Mounted troops – This was not the most efficient part of the army. The greatest difficulties for the Kingdom of Sardinia in keeping this corps efficient were not so much in equipment but in mounts, as there was no effective remount structure within the kingdom. The horses had to be imported, mainly from Germany (Friesland, Oldenburg, Limburg, Holstein, Bremen). Only bays without stars or blazes were selected, between four and six years old, and sixth of them were mares. Another lacune was their tactics, which were obsolescent at this time, and they lacked light cavalry. A hussar company was raised on 20 July 20 1734, but it was converted to the *Reggimento La Regina Dragoni* on 28 November 1736. The regiments fought in ad hoc brigades. The two cavalry regiments were permanent organisations, but with the number of effectives varying between peace and war. The four dragoon regiments were also permanent organisations with the number of effectives varying between peace and war. A fifth weak regiment was raised in 1726 in Sardinia, but they remained based on the island performing police and customs duties.

The artillery regiment – The cadre of Officers and senior NCOs were of a permanent organisation. The men were contingents of temporary servicemen. A number of other specialists were also retained in peacetime. These included the miners and the engineers who conducted sieges, constructed field works and bridges. In peacetime they worked on civilian projects including bridges and public buildings as well as consolidating and improving the fortresses.

The light/mountain troops – There were a number of such units, in particular the Vaudois, who were a semi-permanent Protestant militia of French Huguenot origin, they were in reality part of militia and they were considered as one of the best and most dangerous units of the army. The other, much smaller, short-lived company of Micheletti, who came from Sardinia, was prone to desertion and was quickly disbanded as being useless.

The *Milizia* (militia) – This was an ancient corps, created before the provincial infantry and they did not have a firm ordnance, and they were only mobilised in times of national emergencies and disbanded at the end of hostilities. While some were simple garrison troops, others could take the field. In reality the provincial infantry regiments were descended from the original *Milizia*; there were standing orders for the militia that they were to defend their provincial territory and were very rarely called to serve outside the boundaries of their region.

The Company of Pardoned Deserters – A fairly small unit raised from enemy deserters, considered at best as unreliable if not completely useless.

Logistics – The army's logistics functioned in a similar manner to the French system, even if the *Ufficio Generale del Sold*o was a much more effective bureau. Field commanders and governors had direct access active a logistic chain with intendants and commissaires, and they had in their staff specific officers to do so. It was divided into two departments, one which was responsible for munitions and one for rations but was run by one office which improved their efficiency. Everything was centralised, including the acquisition and manufacture of arms and uniforms.

The navy – This service is not covered in this book, only the naval infantry, the galley company.

3

The Generals and High Command

Luogotenente Generale Giovanni Battista Cacherano di Bricherasio (1706–1782)

Giovanni Battista Cacherano was born in Bricherasio (Pinerolo) November 14, 1706, the son of Theodore III, a *capitano* of the Monferrato regiment. He embraced a career of arms, as did his brothers Filiberto, Charles and Gianmatteo. In April 1734 he raised, partly at his own expense, a regiment of national infantry. He was appointed *colonnello* of this regiment, which was called the *La Regina* (the Queen's) in honour of Polyxena Christina of Hesse, the first wife of King Carlo Emanuel III.

The regiment participated in the final stages of the war of the Polish Succession in Italy. But only later, in the course of military operations in defence of Savoy and the valleys of Casteldelfino, during the first phase of the War of the Austrian Succession, did he come to the King's attention, obtaining the rank of *brigadier generale* on 22 January 1744.

He led his regiment at the disastrous Battle of Madonna dell'Olmo (30 September 1744), near Cuneo, where he fought honourably and was wounded on the field along with his two brothers, Charles and Gianmatteo. Carlo Emanuele III promoted him to *maggiore generale* of the infantry at Asti on 9 May 1745. He transferred the following year to Piacenza. From Piacenza, where had held the military command for a few months, he moved in January 1747 to Savona to be reunited with *La Regina* who had taken part in the siege of the castle in December 1746 under the command of his brother Gianmatteo, the *luogotenente colonnello* of the regiment.

He was recalled from Savona by a direct order from the King who promoted him to the rank of *luogotenente generale* of infantry on June 20, 1747; he then assumed the command of the troops moving through the valleys of Susa and Fenestrelle to defend the frontiers against the French incursions. His selection by Charles Emmanuel III was justified during the last phase of the conflict, marked by the famous Battle of l'Assietta.

This campaign decided the fate of the last Franco-Spanish offensive in Piedmont, when at last the conflict turned in favour of the Austro-Piedmontese. As soon as news was heard of some movement from the region of the Dauphiné towards the passes of Exilles and Fenestrelle, the French army under the command of *maréchal* Belle-Isle with his brother Charles-Armand de Fouquet, chevalier de Belle-Isle, the Austro-Sardinians deployed 10 battalions on the Alpine border of Piedmont to confront the French, and they were supported by four battalions of Austrian infantry commanded by Count Colloredo, to which Charles Emmanuel III added a further 12 battalions of infantry to the dispositions at the last minute.

The chevalier de Belle-Isle, with 29 battalions and seven pieces of artillery crossed the Pass of Monginevro and arrived on 18 July at Côte-Plane in front of l'Assietta, the day after he moved with two large columns, while the third column would move down in the valley of l'Assietta, then up towards the Grand Serin, to outflank the Piedmontese and cut off their retreat.

Against this column di Bricherasio lined up his Austro-Sardinian forces – 5,400 men, (3,784 regular infantry plus 1,500 militiamen). The Piedmontese troops were in prepared redoubts on the summits of l'Assietta and 1,076 Austrians placed immediately behind them. The combat was in doubt for some time, and the French seemed about to overwhelm the small head of the Assietta pass, but by nightfall the Piedmontese were masters of the field while the French had to retreat down the valley on the central track, after suffering heavy losses, including their commander, the chevalier de Belle-Isle.

The positive outcome of the battle should probably be attributed to Count Paul Novarina of San Sebastian,[1] commander of the first battalion of *Guardie*, but present with their grenadier company. Hit by repeated and massive enemy assaults the count refused three times to execute

1 The Count of San Sebastiano actually disobeyed an order, both verbal and written, even though it was issued not by Bricherasio but by Alciati. In any case, his tactical appreciation of the battle was incorrect, as the French intended to pin him down, and he fell for the deception splendidly. Afterwards, the high command could not punish him, as the battle had been won anyway. So, instead he received awards and promotions, but ended up being offered the command of a second-rate regiment. So, eventually, he decided to resign and retired to his domains.

an order, sent to him by di Bricherasio, to retreat from the angles of the head of the pass and the western side of the plateau, to the Grand Serin (this commanded the access to the whole of the line), whose defence was considered by di Bricherasio of paramount importance for the safety of his troops. It would appear, due to the virtue of this 'extraordinary disobedience'[2] the Count of San Sebastian was able to drive back the French assault, and the positions of l'Assietta were held. The French were forced to retire and victory finally went to the Piedmontese.

San Sebastian proved that regardless of the opportunity to retreat towards the main forces of the Grand Serin, where the situation was threatened , and given the delay in receiving orders, that no order of concentration had been given to him, as was confirmed in other respects by the official report given to Carlo Emmanuel III a few days after the battle by Count Giuseppe Damiano Priocca, and all of the contemporary Austrian and Piedmontese officers, who had ignored the disobedience of the Count of San Sebastian.

On 17 November 1748, Charles Emmanuel III awarded di Bricherasio the Grand Cross and Collar of the Order of Saints Maurice and Lazarus some 19 weeks later, and, he was awarded the title of the Holy Faith of Vercelli with an annual pension of 1,200 Piedmontese *Livres*. On 11 May 1750 he assumed the post of tutor to the Duke of Chablais, the king's son and the following year, in 1751, di Bricherasio was appointed representative of the sovereign, with the title of Viceroy and Captain General on the island of Sardinia, from which he returned four years later to take over, on 16 July 1755, the governorship of the city and county of Tortona.

But it is only some three years later, on 24 April 1758 that he was able to consolidate the political and administrative power of Carlo Emmanuel III's bureaucratic-military government, with his promotion to the governorate of Alexandria. He then strengthened the central institutions of the administration, limited the privileges of the clergy and some other religious orders, as well as combating the smuggling and other abuses of the local communities on the basis of new mercantilist laws of Piedmont. However, di Bricherasio's political activity ended in 1763 when he was appointed governor of the citadel of Turin. His final honours came on 4 December, when he was awarded the Collar of the Supreme Order of the Annunciation and promoted on 4 March 1771, to *Maestro Generale di Fanteria e Artiglieria*. Di Bricherasio died in 1782, leaving nine children behind.

2 Vicomte Paul De Choulot, Gabriel Maximilien Ferrero, *Histoire de L'Armee Sarde* (Turin, Chez Bocca, Libraire du Roi, 1845), *Part 1-3*.

Marquis Cesare Alberico Balbiano (1687–1765)

The Marquis Cesare Alberico Balbiano of the second line of Viale had been a *luogotenente* in the *Guardie* regiment from 12 March 1704, but was then discharged. He became the *luogotenente colonnello* of the provincial regiment of Turin (7 September 1713), he participated in the campaign in Sicily (1718–1720), later becoming a Gentleman of the Chamber, reaching the rank of *colonnello* on 28 March 1730. He left the command of the regiment in 1739 having obtained the command of the *Novarese*. He became the Governor of Susa, was a skilful defender of Valenza in 1745, and commanded the Piedmontese troops the following year during the invasion of Provence.

On 17 January 1747 he was promoted to *luogotenente generale*. He could count among his descendants both squires and knights of honour who were welcomed at court, notably his eldest son Carlo Gerolamo Gaetano, who became a cornet in the *Guardie del corpo* and *luogotenente colonnello* of cavalry by 1763, *colonnello* in 1768, to major general in 1774, *capitano* of the *Guardie del corpo* in 1775, *luogotenente generale* in 1780 and became a *generale di cavalleria* in 1789.

Victor-Amé de Seyssel d'Aix (1679–1754)

Victor-Aimé de Seyssel; nineteenth Seigneur d'Aix, seventh marquis de la Serra et de Sommariva del Bosco, baron de Châtillon and de Meillonas, was born December 29, 1679, with the signal honour of having Victor-Amadeus, Duke of Savoy as his godfather. He was probably brought up at the Turin academy, as his father specifically requested this in his will.

He started his military career in 1706. As a *maggiore* in the regiment of Savoie he took part in the defence of Turin while it was besieged by the French and where he was grievously wounded.

In 1710 he married Henriette-Marguerite, the daughter of the Prince Del Pozzo de la Cisterna, one of the most distinguished families in the Piedmont. Between 1711 and 1720 he was with the Duke's army as the *colonnello* commanding the *Savoie* regiment.

On 29 July 1721, the Marquis returned to Turin following a mission to the King of Denmark. In October 1729, he was on a diplomatic mission to Britain, at the same time he was named as *capitano* of the first company of the Kings' *Guardia del Corpo*.

In 1731, on 28 of September, he was named as the Governor of the Citadel of Turin. And it was in this capacity that he assisted in the famous meeting of the state council, presided over by the king, Charles-Emmanuel III, where the decision was taken to arrest and imprison the former king, Victor-Amadeus II, who after abdicating tried to take back the crown from his son. The marquis d'Aix was a close friend of Ferrero, marquis d'Orméa, *Gran Cancelliere* of King Charles-Emmanuel III who ran the kingdom for a while.

In October 1731, the marquis was promoted to *luogotenente generale*, and with that rank he fought in the war against the Imperialists. In 1733, the King having defeated the Milanese, named the marquis as the Governor of the Citadel of Milan until 1736, when peace was signed, he returned the citadel to the Austrian general, Wachtendonc.

At the same time, he was also the Governor of Cremona and he bought from the crown of Savoy, the marquisate of Sommariva, previously belonging to the house of Urfe of Poitou with all the titles, fiefs, rents and all other attached dependencies.

On 14 October 1736 patent letters were issued in favour of Victor-Amé de Seyssel, marquis d'Aix and of Sommariva as Grand Master of the Artillery. In 1737 and he was created Knight of the Supreme Order of the Annonciade.

In October 1742, he took part in the counter attacks against the Spanish, when he was with the King. After crossing the Mont-Cenis the king advised him to attack the Maurienne. In 1743 *Capitán General* de Las Minas, the commander of the Spanish army in Savoy, was trying to invade Piedmont via the valley of the Queyras, but the marquis d'Aix, at the head of a corps, advanced and placed his general headquarters at Sainte Pierre, positioning his troops on the flanks of a mountain called the Bois de la Lévée.

The army of Las Minas, composed of French and Spanish troops, started by attacking the fortifications and trenches, but the Piedmontese pushed them back, they then took the fort at Punto. The next day, 8 October 1743, the enemy recommenced a general attack, but their efforts were in vain, the Franco-Spanish army, beaten at all points was obliged to retreat back to the Dauphiné.

The marquis d'Aix distinguished himself again the following year (1744) in defending the Alps, which earned him the rank of *generale di fanteria*. During this conflict, one of his sons, Francois-Joseph-Octave, an aide de camp to King Charles-Emmanuel III, was killed at the Battle of Pierre Longue, where he had been ordered, along with *Generale di Cavalleria* du Verger de Thomas, to defend the lines of the Chateau Dauphin. Both officers carried out their orders and both were killed with their swords in hand trying to re-take a gun battery.

In 1749, he was confirmed as the Grand Master of the Artillery, *generale di fanteria* and Governor of the town and province of Turin. He died in Chambery in 1754 and was buried in the church of Saint Francis; his wife and only two of his sons survived him out of his seven children.

François Louis d'Allinges, Count D'Apremont (1682–1743)

François Louis d'Allinges, Count d'Apremont, knight and commander Grand Cross of the Order of Saint Maurice,was a *luogotenente generale*, governor of Nice, General of the Galleys, and commanding general for the King of Sardinia in Lombardy (1733–1736). In 1721 he became *luogotenente colonnello* of the *Genevois* dragoon regiment. He was in the assault on the heights of Vico. As a volunteer he was ordered to go to the aid of Pisa. It was with this detachment that he later entered Castel Alfiere.

At Cirié, he was with the rearguard; in the affair of Saluzzo, he was commanded by the King to reconnoitre the enemy, and had a horse killed under him. He was also present at the Battle of Turin, at the siege of Pizzighettone, and at the affair of Verzolo, where he was the first who assailed the enemy. He later became successively Governor of Valenza in 1735, of Novara the same year and finally Viceroy of Sardinia and *luogotenente generale* of the County of Nice. Although he was called courageous, energetic and competent by his superiors, he was seen by his subordinates as domineering, suspicious and abusive.

In 1742 he was promoted to *luogotenente generale* and commanded the cavalry. He was in command of the army of Savoy at the Battle of Camposanto on 8 February 1743 where he received a fatal wound in the right side at the level of his groin from which he died four days later, on 12 February in Modena.

Karl Sigismond Friedrick Wilhelm Leutrum von Ertingen, 1692–1755

Born in Karlhaunsen, Baden, on 27 June 1692, Karl Sigismond was the son of the second marriage of the Baron Friedrick Sigismond, and he had spent the first years of his life inside the family's castle at Karlhaunsen, built by his grandfather in 1650. He arrived in Piedmont at the age of 14, together with his half-brother Karl Magnus, attached to the escort of Prinz Eugen. Leutrum decided to enter in the Sabaudian army. Promoted *capitano* in the infantry, he was trained by *Capitano* Johann Hernst Wahren. In 1725 he became *luogotenente colonnello* of the *Rehbinder* regiment; eventually he became the *colonnello* of the regiment in 1749, fighting with what was now his regiment during the War of the Polish Succession, in particular during the siege of Gera-Pizzighettone in the winter of 1733. Towards the end of 1735 he was promoted to *brigadier generale*.

He was sometimes known as 'Baron Litron', but this was simply a mispronunciation of his German name, not a reference to him drinking, because the 'litre' as a measure for wine was still unknown in the eighteenth century (in fact the word 'pinta' was used). This was a rumour, affectionately cultivated by the people of Cuneo. That he was a prodigious drinker and lover during his lifetime is only partially true, as he was not a drinker. However, his reputation as an unrepentant womaniser is well deserved, as the parish registers of the time testify – Leutrum, unlike many contemporary noblemen, recognised all the children he had with the young ladies of Cuneo, and he provided financial support for them all.

When the War of the Austrian Succession began, Leutrum was marching to the lower Padanian plain. The *Rehbinder* was one of the few Piedmontese army units ready to take the field in that sector of the front. With the first battalion, he moved from the camp of Parma and fought at the Battle of Camposanto, 8 February 1743. During the second phase of the battle, three Spanish infantry brigades (the *Guardias*, *Irlanda* and *Flandres*) smashed through the first line of the right wing of the Austro-Piedmontese army. From the second line, the generals D'Apremont and Leutrum led a counterattack with three battalions from *Savoye*, *Piemont* and *Rehbinder*. The right wing of the Spanish line was broken and compelled to withdraw. During this action the Spanish *Guadalaxara* regiment was cut off from the main body of the army and compelled to surrender. Leutrum was badly wounded, but he was comforted by his new rank of *maggiore generale*. Before the end of the year Leutrum had reached Turin, and then Orbassano and the camp of San Colombano in the Susa Valley, while his regiment fought in Varaita Valley.

In the spring 1744 Leutrum arrived at the entrenched camp of the port of Villafranca (nowadays called Villefranche sur Mer). On 20 April he faced, under the command of the Comte de Cinzano, the Franco-Spanish offensive. With the grenadiers of the *Bourgsdorff* regiment (previously *Rehbinder*) he was able to recapture the lost redoubts on Mont Gros and the Col de Villefranche with an enveloping manoeuvre in co-ordination with grenadiers of the *Saluce*, *Tarentaise* and *Guibert* regiments.

They were eventually outnumbered and beaten back, and he was forced to surrender the positions. He left for the port of Oneglia, after which he returned to Piedmont.

The key to southern Piedmont, the city-fortress of Cuneo, was in danger of an immediate siege by the composite French-Spanish army under Prince de Conti. Charles Emmanuel III immediately changed the governor of the place. The old Ottavio Pallio, Comte de Rinco was replaced by Baron Leutrum. An officer of the garrison, De la Fléchère, once wrote of him:

> Baron Leutrum reached Cuneo in the night, between August 18 and 19 with the first battalion of Regiment Kalbermatten and some pieces of light artillery. Everybody knew him for his merits, prudence, ability, resoluteness and of the military virtues. So, it is not the case for me to speak any more about him, since I should say to everybody how good he is.[3]

The new governor prepared the city to resist the siege by raising the morale of the garrison (eight battered battalions, about 3,244 men). He raised three free companies, together with 11 companies of citizen militia. The houses of Cuneo became quarters, all the combustible materials were transferred to safety, the streets were unpaved, and large quantities of water and food supplies and other necessities were brought into the city. They stored enough supplies to be able to withstand at least five months of siege.

More importantly, Leutrum ordered the construction of three new redoubts on the glacis, about 300 meters from the covered way. He wanted to defend the glacis as long as possible. He had at his command two able officers, an officer of the engineers, Bernardino Pinto Comte di Barri and a *Luogotenente* Bussolino of the miners. The enemy opened the trenches on 12 September. On 22 October the three detached redoubts were still in the hands of the Piedmontese.

> So ended the siege of Cuneo, during which Leutrum, thanks to his courage and ability, together with his tireless care, won the honour and the respect of both the garrison and that of the citizens. The troops had sustained with fervour and courage the siege and obeyed all the dispositions and the orders of their Governor. The citizens did all the things you could hope for in such an occasion, since they all worked at every moment for the safety and resistance of the Place.[4]

In May 1745 Leutrum was promoted to *luogotenente generale*, just in time to face the new great French-Spanish offensive under *maréchal* Maillebois. The Baron fought a minor battle on 26 August, near the Fortress of Ceva, one of the few Piedmontese victories in that campaign. On 28 October, the defeated Sabaudian army retreated to Turin, the Citadel of Alessandria was under siege and Asti, between them, was occupied by the enemy. Leutrum, with a small force, stopped a French offensive, led by *maréchal* de Mirepoix, against Ceva. During the winter of 1745–1746, minister Bogino and the chief of the engineers, Ignazio Bertola, the country's strategic thinkers, planned a counter offensive.

The commander had to be Baron Leutrum. He assembled his forces near Trino and spent the winter

3 Mons de la Flechère de Chatillon, *Défense de la Ville de Coni assiégé par l'Armée Française et Espagnolle en 1744*, manuscript in the Biblioteca Civica di Cuneo.

4 Mons de la Flechère de Chatillon, *Défense de la Ville de Coni assiégé par l'Armée Française et Espagnolle en 1744*, manuscript in the Biblioteca Civica di Cuneo.

clearing the way from Turin to the occupied city of Asti, liberating Castigliole on 29 November 1745. For the first time, since the end of 1744, a Piedmontese force had taken a considerable number of prisoners in a military action.

By February 1746, the fortresses of Balangero and Castagnole Lanze surrendered to him.

Then the main offensive against Asti was launched, in the middle of a storm. For the first time, Leutrum had at his command a strong army of about 30,000 men – 31 infantry battalions and a number of cavalry regiments.

Beginning the assault to the east was not the best situation the Sabaudian could have wished for, and the artillery siege train had many problems. During the night march from San Damiano to Asti, the artillery crews informed Leutrum that, since it was the bad season, it was not possible to ford the Borbore stream with the artillery. Leutrum simply said 'I want them to ford'. After many attempts, all unsuccessful, the crews again spoke to the general. He listened to them and again told to his men 'I want them to ford'.[5] By that night all the cannons had forded the stream.

The Piedmontese general cleared the way and on 7 March 1746 Asti was liberated after only two days of artillery bombardment. The French garrison (nine battalions, about 5,000 men), 27 flags and eight pieces of artillery were captured. On 10 March the Citadel of Alessandria was freed. Just in time since heavy snowfalls soon caused a breakdown of the Piedmontese logistics.

Leutrum, now *generale di fanteria*, could not move until April, so on 17 April he besieged the city of Valenza on the river Po. The city was taken on 4 May 1746 in a sea of mud. With the surrender of Tortona on 27 November, Piedmontese territory was now completely free of enemy forces.

Leutrum then faced the Franco-Spanish offensive of 1747. In the Ligurian theatre Leutrum, with a very small force was able to defend the Saorgio-Oneglia-Savona line until the arrival of the Austrian army from Genoa to face the enemy advance with over than 50 battalions.

At the end of the War of Austrian Succession, he became governor of Cuneo. A regiment of German infantry, *Burgsdorf*, became the *Leutrum*. As he was a Protestant, and he refused to become a Catholic, he could not receive the collar of the Supreme Order of the Annonciade, the greatest honour of the Kingdom of Sardinia.

He died on 16 May 1755 in Cuneo, of dropsy (oedema, due to congestive heart failure). His coffin was later transferred from Cuneo to Torre Pellice in the heart of the Waldesian Alps by the soldiers of his regiment. He was beloved by the citizens of Cuneo in particular, and by the Piedmontese people in general, but first of all, by his soldiers.

He was probably the best commanding field officer of the Sabaudian army in eighteenth century. Born June 1692, infantry *capitano* in 1706, *luogotenente colonnello* by 1725, *colonnello* in 1732, *brigadier generale* in 1735, Governor of Cuneo in August 1744 *luogotenente generale* in May 1745, *generale di fanteria* in February 1746.

Uniforms

In fact, there was not a uniform for *générale* as such at this time. Instead, they wore their regimental uniforms, but with more lace as befitted their rank. The general staff officer's lace was as follows: the *brigadiers* coat and waistcoat was to be richly embroidered or laced; the *colonnello*'s coat was to have laced borders, the coat cuffs and waistcoat were to be richly embroidered or laced; the *luogotenente colonnello*'s coat and waistcoat was to have simple lace borders and the cuffs two bands of lace; the *maggiore*'s to have a simple lace border on his coat, cuffs and waistcoat. All the coats were worn with riding boots and in some cases a breast plate and the officer's knightly orders and sashes.

5 Biagio Gho, *L'Agro Alessandrino durante le Guerre della Prammatica Sanzione* (Alessandria: Unione Tip. Editrice Ferrari, Occella & C. 1931).

1. *Luogotenente Generale* Giovanni Battista Cacherano di Bricherasio wearing the uniform of the infantry *Reggimento della Regina*. 2. *Brigadier Generale* Karl Sigismond Friedrick Wilhelm Leutrum von Ertingen wearing the uniform of the *Reggimento Alemano di Rehbinder*. 3. *Luogotenente Generale* Victor-Amé de Seyssel d'Aix wearing the uniform of the *Reggimento di Artiglieria*. 4. *Luogotenente Generale* Marquis Cesare Alberico Balbiano wearing the uniform of the infantry *Reggimento di Torino*. (Authors reconstructions based on the uniforms of their regiments, as there was not yet an official uniform for senior officers)

4

The Royal Household Regiments

Gardes du Corps de S.M. (*Guardie del Corpo di Sua Maestà*).

This corps served both as a household guard, on foot and mounted, and in times of war they had served as a heavy cavalry, but limited to bodyguard duties. Whenever the king went on campaign, he was escorted by a guard called the detachment of war, consisting of 30 Guards. When the king went out of the palace, the detachment took the following order: four Guards preceded the king, the commander walked beside him and the rest of the detachment closed the escort. They were present at the battle of Madonna dell'Olmo.

The *Guardie del Corpo* received their orders personally from the king and this constituted a prerogative that distinguished them from the other troops and the guards were extremely proud of this honour.

At the beginning of the reign of Charles Emmanuel III, the composition of the *Guardie del Corpo* did not undergo any significant changes. The first important changes took place in 1737, and the new organisation of the *Guardie del Corpo* can be obtained from that year's companies accounts.

There were 240 men divided into three companies of 80 men, each company rising to 130 guards in times of war, including officers and trumpeters. In 1737, they were organised as follows:

The Headquarters Staff,
An *aiutante maggiore*, a *sellaio*, a *furieri*, a *cappellano* and a *chirurgo*.

The First or 'The Savoyard Company' who were now termed *Guardie del Corpo di S.M. (Sua Maestà)*, originally called *Compagnia Gentiluomini Arcieri Guardie del Corpo di S.A.R.*
Capitano Barone di Blonay; *Luogotenente* Vassallo della Martiniera; *Cornetta* Conte St Denis; *Marechal de Logis*, Chevalier Giorgio Disonges and Chevalier de Blonay; a *foriere-portastendardo*, a *timballiere*; two *trombetti*; a *maniscalco*; four *brigadieri*, four *sottobrigadieri*, three *portastendardo* (this appears to be a junior NCO rank in the *Guardie del Corpo*), and 33 mounted *guardie* and 12 dismounted *guardie* rising to 54 guards. They had 67 cavalry horses.

The Second or 'The Piedmontese Company' *Compagnia Guardie del Corpo di S.M.*
Capitano Marchese di Tournon; *Luogotenente* Conte Coardi di Carpeneto; *Cornetta* Marchese di S. Germano; three *Marechal de Logis;* Chevalier Avogadro di Casanova, Conte San Martino di Baldissero and Conte Argentero di Bagnasco; A *timballiere*; two *trombetti*, four *brigadieri* and four *sottobrigadieri*, a *maniscalco* and 38 mounted *guardie* and 20 dismounted *guardie*. They had 67 cavalry horses.

The Third or 'Sardinian Company' *Compagnia Guardie del Corpo di S.AM.* Originally, they were called 'The Sicilian Company' as they had been raised in Palermo. They were renamed when Victor Amadeus II became the King of Sardinia in 1720.
Capitano D. Emanuele Valguarnera; *Luogotenente* Chevalier Requesens; *Cornetta* Cav. Orioles; three *Marechal de Logis* Chiaffaleone, Romeo e Chevalier Protto; two *trombetti*, three *brigadieri* and two *sottobrigadieri*, a *maniscalco* and 50 *guardie* rising to 60, the numbers of mounted and dismounted are not given. They had 67 cavalry horses.

Several changes occurred in the officers from 1737 to 1748, such as the appointment of the Marquis Francesco di Sales as *capitano* of the First company in place of the Baron of Blonay who had been appointed Vice King of Sardinia on first of September 1741. There was also an increase in the number of men in the companies between 1743 and 1748.

On 14 September 1748 a new organisation of the *Guardie del Corpo* was established following a Royal decree:

Stato maggiore (regimental staff)
Aiutante Maggiore (adjutant major) Conte di Bagnasco.

First or 'The Savoyard Company' *Guardie del Corpo di S.M. (Sua Maestà)*. *Capitano* Paolo Francesco, Marchese di

Guardie del Corpo. 1. Officer in full dress, loosely based on a portrait of Lionel de Blonay. 2. *Guardie* in full dress c. 1747. 3. *Guardie* in service dress c. 1747. Note that the service coat is deliberately shown a little duller when compared to the full dress and his hair is not powdered. Only six buttons on the coat, placed one, two and three. 4. *Timballiere* (kettle-drummer) in full dress c. 1747. Authors reconstruction based on a contemporary clothing order, 1736, (with the kind assistance of Enrico Ricchiardi and Giancarlo Boeri). 5. *Trombetti* in service dress c. 1744. After a contemporary painting by Peeter Jan Verdussen. (Author's Illustrations)

Sales; *Luogotenente* Barone di Blonay; *Cornetta* Conte di Chatillon; *Maresciale di Logis*, De Benernise, De La Tour and Chevalier de Blonay Marsighy.

Second or 'The Piedmontese Company' *Compagnia Guardie del Corpo di SM.*
Capitano Marchese di Tournon; *Luogotenente* Conte Solaro di Gavria; Cornetta Marchese Asinari di S. Marzano; *Maresciale di Logis* Chevalier Avogadro di Casanova, Marchese Reggiano di St Albano and Chevalier Carlo Balbis.

Third or 'The Sardinian Company' *Compagnia Guardie del Corpo di S.M.*
Capitano D. Emanuele Valguarnera; *Luogotenente* Chevalier Requesens; *Cornetta* Chevalier Orioles; *Maresciale di Logis* Chevalier Protto and Chevalier Saletti.

Note. The *Capitano* of the third Company, D. Emanuele Valguarnera 1737, was succeeded by Giovanni di Requesens e del Carretto in 1751 when he became the Grand Chamberlain.

Uniforms

Service Dress

The *guardie* wore a black tricorn with a blue (Savoy) cockade on the left brim with a black loop and a brass button and yellow/gilt lace border, gold lace and gilt button for the officers.

Theoretically, they were all of commissioned rank, so all the companies wore white cravats.

Their service dress uniform consisted of a collarless scarlet red coat lined dark blue with yellow/gold stitched button holes. The coat had six brass buttons on the coat, grouped from the top as one, two and three, and three buttons on their red cuffs. The coat had horizontal pockets, each with three buttons and yellow/gold stitched button holes, red cuffs with yellow/gold stitched button holes, red linings and turn backs. The waistcoat was scarlet red with yellow/gold stitched button holes down the front and on the pockets and their breeches were red. They wore black cavalry boots.

Full Dress

The full-dress version was similar but with additional gold lace buttonholes (eight) on the coat, gold lace down the edges of the coat and lace around the border of the cuffs as well as around the pockets. There were also three lace loops below the pocket. The troopers on dismounted palace guard duties sometimes wore blue stockings and black brass buckled shoes instead of riding boots depending on the occasion.

Campaign Dress

Earlier in the century for campaign wear they had a buff coat fastened with hooks and eyes, which was worn over the service dress coat with the coat cuffs turned back over the 'buffalo' coat giving the appearance of a buff coat with red cuffs and turn backs and buff leather breeches. But there is no specific mention of its use during this period, so it was possibly no longer worn.

NCOs

The *sottobrigadieri* had the same pockets as the *guardie*, but with a wide gold lace around it. The *brigadieri* had a gold lace around the border of the cuffs and a second wider one below as well as around the pockets. The button holes were laced as well on the full-dress coat.

Officers

The *colonnello*'s full-dress coat had larger gold laces to emphasise his rank and a waist sash with large gold tassels. The officers' coats had gold lace and gilt buttons. The officers wore a sash of blue and/or gold silk with two gold hanging tassels, one on each end of the sash; these were blue with a gold central stripe for *alfieri* and *luogotenenti*, gold with a blue stripe down the centre for *capitani*. They were armed with a pair of pistols and a sword. Officers only were expected to wear a steel breast plate, at least on campaign. The officers also had a simpler service dress with only two laces down the front of the coat, one large and one thinner with the buttons placed in between. And in the field they wore a laced buff waistcoat.

Trombetti

The *trombetti* and *timballiere* appear to have had two different uniforms, a simple gold laced red coat for everyday service and a heavily laced full-dress coat. Unfortunately, we have very little information on this service dress which consisted of a red coat lined and cuffed in a red. It had shoulder fringe, simple hanging sleeves, and gold lace on all leading edges, including two laces, one large and one thin, around the slash cuffs around the pockets.[1]

The full-dress livery coat appears to have had the royal lace down the sleeves, down the coat, two each side, four around the waist, four bands around the cuffs, and two bands around the lower edge. There was silver lace down

1 See the painting, A military encampment, depicting the Household Cavalry 'Guardia del Corpo' of the Duke of Savoy (1744-1745) with a standard bearer and horses by a tent, by Jan Peter Verdussen 1744. <https://www.sothebys.com/en/buy/auction/2020/the-rafael-valls-sale-online/jan-peeter-verdussen-a-military-encampment>. He shows a trumpeter in a simple red coat, with red cuffs and gold lace on all leading edges and seams, no blue or king's lace. Strangely, he also shows red housing and holster caps for the ensign. Location now unknown, sold by Sotheby's 2020. Ex collection of Lord James Butler of Dublin.

the front of the coat, and around the pockets. The button holes were stitched with silver thread. The buttons were covered in silver and blue lace. There was also some gold lace on the waistcoat, usually just down the front edge. The rest of the uniform was the same as the *guardie*.[2]

The *trombetti* were armed with a sword and a pair of pistols, the *timballiere* was only armed with a sword. Their leather waist belt and frog were covered with red cloth, edged gold and with a band of livery lace down the centre. The ball trumpet may have been silvered.

The *trombetti* had royal blue banners, of an unknown design, with silver or gold fringe edges and the trumpet cords and tassels were made of blue and white silk. The drum banners were embroidered with the king's crowned arms with supporters in the first company, the other two are thought just have the kings crowned cypher. The kettle drums were made of copper and the drumsticks (called mallets) were of made varnished wood.

Arms and Equipment

The *guardie*'s sword had a straight double-edged blade with a double shelled brass hilt and the grip was bound with brass wire, the length 102.7cm and was carried in a black leather scabbard with brass fittings suspended on a frog on a buff leather waist belt. They carried a pair of pistols, similar to the M 1726 dragoon model, but shorter with a better finish, carried in holsters on the saddle brow. The pistols had a rounded brass butt, with an overall length of 50.3cm and a calibre of 16 mm and weighed 1.2kg.

They carried a carbine specifically made for the *Guardie del Corpo*, different from the line cavalry model; the barrel was mounted with pins and not rings. The wide carbine belt was made of buff leather covered with blue velvet cloth and edged with a large gold lace and a zigzag of gold lace stitched down the centre and it had a steel swivel clip.

When they were on dismounted guard duty in the interior of the palace, they carried a short, broad bladed vouge called an *aguccia* with an upturned crows' beak on one side. It was originally designed around 1632–1637 and may have derived from a large iron hunting spear. The later sovereigns adopted slightly modified variants.

Carlo Emanuele III made an exception to his rule of frugality and adopted a new model, which had the profile of his father's model, but with the new coat of arms adopted in 1713, together with his own initials and now only the beak was gilded. It was engraved with royal insignia, a crowned eagle with the arms of Savoy on its breast in a baroque frame and stylised floral patterns. It probably had a blue tassel and fringe around the head. The haft was made of varnished beech wood and was studded with brass tacks. It measured 2.18m in length.

Horse Furniture

The saddle was a standard model for the period, made of buff leather. The harness was of blackened leather with steel fittings. The housings and holster caps were medium blue with yellow gold embroidery and border, including the crowned royal cypher, a crowned inter-twinned 'C & E' on the holster caps and in the corner of the housings, dated to sometime before 1747. Prior to this they appear to have been red, laced with silver and gold. The troop and *trombetti* carried a red cloak rolled up and attached behind the saddle.[3]

The officers' saddle cloth and holster lace was, for the three most senior officers – *colonnello*, *luogotenente colonnello* and *maggiore* – one thin lace and one broad metallic gold laces and gold fringes. *Capitani* had one broad metallic gold lace and fringe, junior officers – *luogotenenti* and *alfieri*– had just one thinner metallic gold lace border, with no fringe. The NCOs had a simpler metallic border, but with the crowned royal monogram on the holster caps and in the corner of the housings.

Horses

Although there were no official rules, contemporary illustrations show them mounted on what appears to be dark bay stallions.

The Standards

Each of the three companies had their own unique square standard, generally they are shown carried on red fluted jousting style lances (*asta da torneo*), as shown in the albums.[4] Some texts mention the interior of the fluting as being gilded. The lance had a leaf shaped gilded steel finial and gold cords and tassels, in the centre there was a rectangular steel carrying bracket painted the same colour

2 Authors reconstruction based on a clothing order; with descriptions of the galloons used by the Tailor Leonardo Marino. Reference AST Contratti_Mazzo 25_1736_096, State Archives Turin. Which does say how the lace was placed, but I have based reconstruction on the trumpeter's dress of the French Gendarmes de la Garde, the Spanish Garde du Corps and the British Lifeguards of the same period as a guide, which shows all these companies used a fairly standard model of applying the lace.

3 The texts also mention a white cloak, but contemporary iconography only shows rolled red cloaks.

4 This is probably due to a misinterpretation of one of the albums where the blue has faded to a pinkish mauve colour.

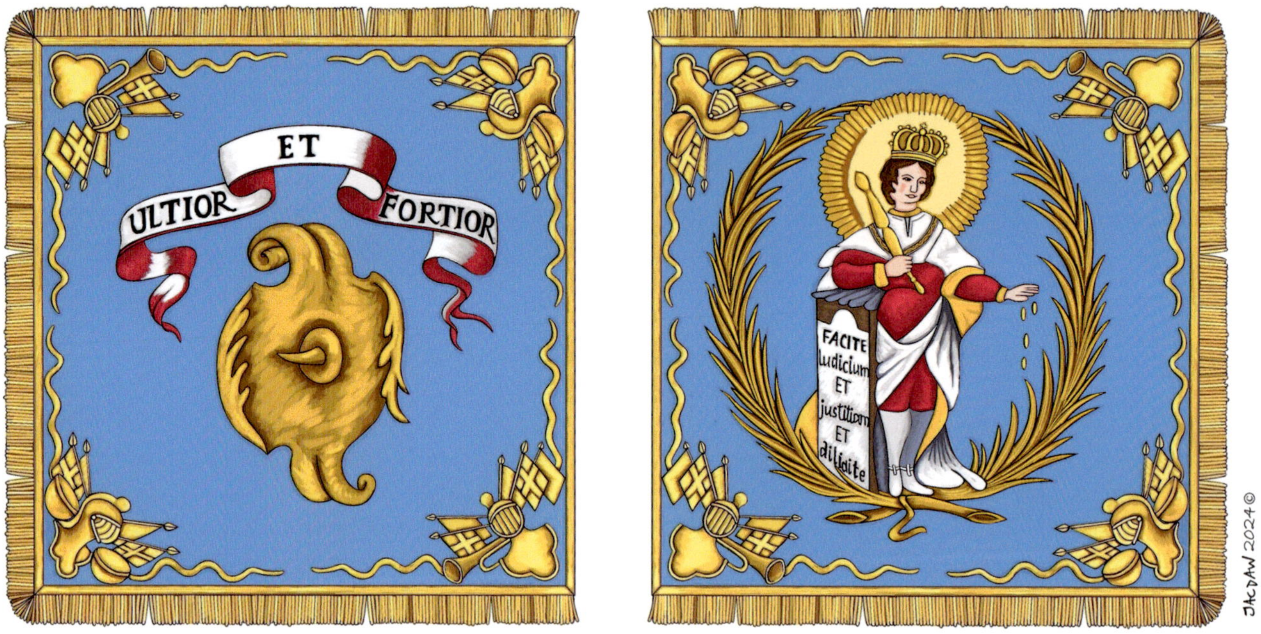

Standard of the First Company *Savoia*. On the obverse Blessed Amadeus and on the reverse a golden shield under a scroll bearing the motto 'ULTIOR ET FORTIOR'. (Author's Illustration)

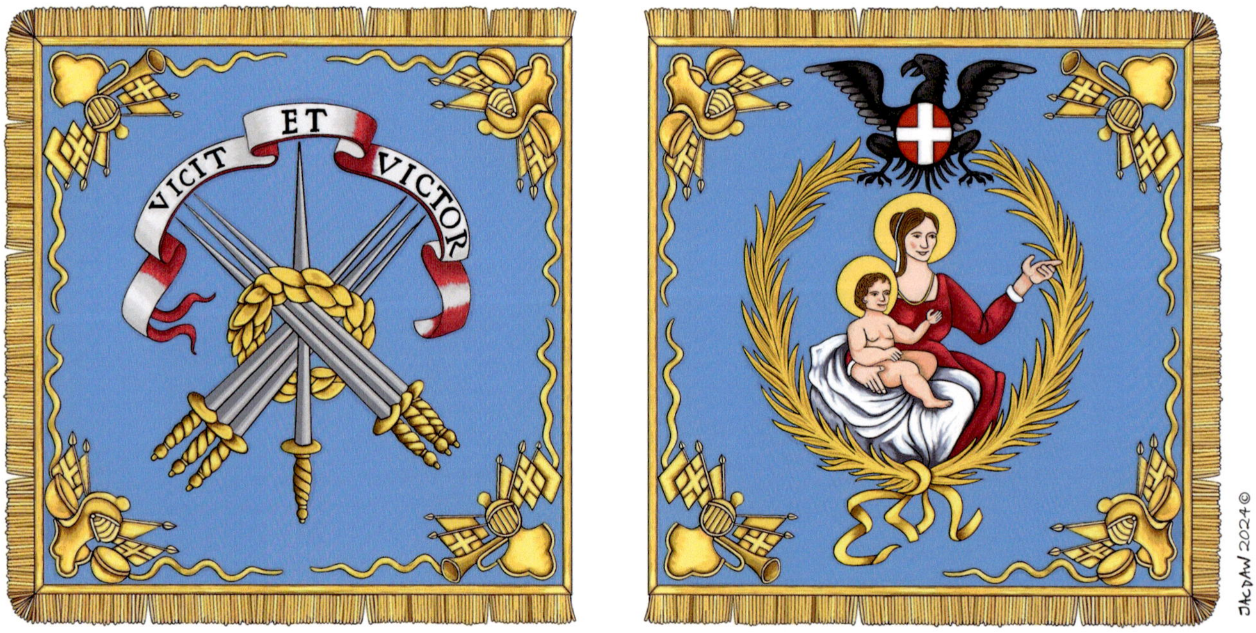

Standard of the Second Company *Piemonte*. On the obverse the Madonna and child under the eagle and cross of Savoy and on the reverse a trophy of crossed swords under a scroll bearing the motto 'VICIT ET VICTOR'. (Author's Illustration)

as the lance. The standard was carried with the aid of a shoulder belt. It was made of leather and probably covered in velvet, probably blue and edged and embroidered with gold lace. It was joined by a ring and a spring clip by two gilded metal plates.

The size of the standards was around 60cm by 60cm square, excluding the fringe. All the standards had a medium blue *(azzuro)* damask silk field with an embroidered golden trophy of arms including a helm and flags bearing crosses, in each corner, both obverse and reverse. The border of the standard had a thin gold laced border and gold fringes. Only the central motifs changed for each company.

The first company, *Savoia*, had on the obverse, in the centre, an image of Blessed Amadeus IX of Savoy wearing a crown with a golden aura around his head and wearing an ermine and red robe whilst leaning on a stele bearing the text 'Facite Judicium et Justiciam Deus dabite pacem in finibus vestry', which changed to 'Facite Judicium et Justiciam diligite pauperes et Deum' sometime before

Standard of the Third Company *Sardegna*. On the obverse a scene of the Annunciation and on the reverse, Saint Rosalie, patron saint of Palermo under the eagle and cross of Savoy. (Author's Illustration)

1745.[5] He is holding a golden sceptre in one hand and dispensing gold coins with the other, all within a wreath of golden palms, but, in fact the words 'pauperes et Deum' do not appear on the watercolour of the stele. On the reverse, in the centre, there was a stylised golden baroque shield with a central spike, above, a white banner or scroll bearing the motto 'ULTIOR ET FORTIOR' (farther and stronger). The lance had a gilt spear head and ferrule, the fringes, cords and knots were gold, and the cravat was probably blue with a gold fringe.

The second company, *Piemontese*, had on the obverse, a wreath of gold palms surmounted by a black eagle bearing the arms of Savoy upon its breast, in the centre the Madonna wearing a red dress and blue, grey white cloak sitting with the baby Jesus on her lap. Both with golden auras around their heads. On the reverse, in the centre there were seven crossed swords 3, 1 and 3, bound with a wreath of laurels around them, above, a white and red scroll with the motto 'VICIT ET VICTOR' painted in black. The lance had a gilt finial and ferrule, silver and gold fringes, red and silver cords and knots.

The third company, *Sarda*, had on the obverse, in the centre a scene of the Annunciation within a wreath of golden palms. On the reverse; in the centre of a green and gold floral wreath with white and red flowers (roses). In the centre; Saint Rosalie, patron saint of Palermo, wearing a red robe and a blue cloak holding an open book in her right hand and a flower with a long stalk in her left hand. Her head within a golden aura. The lance had a gilt finial and ferrule, silver and gold fringes, cords and knots.

This was the same standard which was originally presented to the *Sicilian* company in 1714 and this standard was retained when they became the Sardinian (*Sarda*) company. A specific Sardinian standard was only issued in 1750.

The above descriptions date to around 1744, but they appear to have replaced fairly frequently as there are some variations of the description of the motifs. In 1745 the first company had silver palm leaves and Blessed Amadeus was on a gold central medallion. The second company also had a gold central medallion bearing the Madonna and Child and a fringe of green palm leaves, the third also had a gold central medallion bearing the Annunciation with gold palm leaves around it. The reverse was the same for the first and second companies but on the third company's standard, Saint Rosalie was now shown on a gold medallion as well.

Arquebusiers Gardes de la Porte de S.M. (*Guardia della Porta*)

In 1740 there were 140 officers and men in two companies rising to 166 *gardes* in 1743. They were palace guards with no field service. They were never issued with any colours. At the end of the war, they were reduced to a single

5 One should remember that these mottos refer to the words spoken on the verge of death, on 30 March 1472, by Blessed Amadeus IX, Duke of Savoy: *Facite iudicium, et iustitiam, et diligite pauperes, et Dominus dabit pacem in finibus vestris* (quoted on page 37 in *La Real Chiesa Parrocchiale di Nostra Signora del Carmine e del Beato Amedeo IX di Savoia*, descritta dal teologo professore Maurizio Marocco, Torino 1871).

company of a *capitano*, four *luogotenente*, five *caporali*, five *appuntati*, two *tamburi*, a *piffero* and 80 *arquebusiers*.

The *capitani* of the *Gardes de la Porte* under Charles Emmanuel III were Conte Giuseppe Bologna di Sambuci from 1737 till 1746 when he was succeeded by Chevalier Vittorio di Castellinardo.

Uniforms

The *Arquebusiers* wore a black tricorn with a Savoy blue cockade on the left brim with a black loop and a brass/gilt button and lace border, the officers had gold lace and button.

The troop had white cravats in 1744 with dressed and powdered hair. They wore black cravats in 1747. They wore a scarlet red collarless coat. The coat had eight evenly spaced gilded brass buttons on both sides of the coat, and three on the cuffs. The coat had horizontal pockets, each with three buttons and had Savoy blue cuffs and lining. The cuffs also had gold buttons and loops. In 1747 the coat had had a gold button loops on both sides of the coat.

Their waistcoats were dark medium blue with gilded brass buttons and their breeches were also dark medium blue. They all wore medium dark blue stockings and black shoes with square brass buckles. They wore fine buff leather gloves. The stockings are shown worn over the breeches in 1747. They had a short cloak called a *mantello alla roquelaure*. This was worn slung over their left shoulder, and probably held in place by a loop and toggle. It was made of crimson red woollen cloth with a fall down collar edged in gold lace, lined with the same cloth, which was blue by 1747. The cloak had three parallel bands of gold lace around the edges, the front hems, the lower hems, the shoulder, and side seams. There was an opening in the centre for his arm.

The officers' coats had gold lace and buttons. The *tamburi* and the *piffero* wore a scarlet red coat, which had gold laced button holes in pairs, and gold lace edging on cuffs, seams, edges of their pockets and down the leading edges of the coat. They carried their swords on a leather waist belt covered with blue cloth and edged in gold lace.

Arms and Equipment

The *Arquebusiers* basic firearm was a musket. Their sword appears to have been carried on a clip and chain hooked to the breeches under the waistcoat, there is no evidence of a bayonet and scabbard. The NCOs carried stylised Spanish half pikes/spontoons with a steel blade which merged into a stylised gilded crowned cypher. Below the cypher there was a gold and blue fringe. The cyphers of at least two different monarchs were carried at the same time as that of Charles Emmanuel III, for at least two reasons, a mix of economy and respect for the previous monarchs.

Compagnie des gardes suisses (*Compagnia della Guardia Svizzera di S.M.*)

The company was made up of 114 officers and men. Again, this company were basically palace guards with no field service. They were under the command of a *capitano* with the rank of *colonnello* (this was an honorary title and this '*capitano*' was usually the *colonnello* of one of the regular Swiss regiments), a *luogotenente* with the rank of a *maggiore*, an *alfiere* with the rank of a *capitani* , four *sergenti*, four *caporali*, three *tamburi*, a *piffero* and a 100 *guardie*. They also had a priest, a secretary, a surgeon and six trabants. Even though there was an *alfiere* they did not have a colour.

The *capitani* of the Swiss Guard of Charles Emmanuel III were Conrad Henrich Ab Yberg of Schwitz, 1735–1740, and François-Joseph Frédéric Kydt (Ghidt/Kyd), also from Schwitz, from, 1740–1774.

Uniforms

The company wore a black tricorn with a dark blue cockade on the left brim with a black loop and a pewter button and white/silver lace border. They had their hair dressed, but not powdered and the guardsmen sported moustaches. The buttons and lace were in silver for the Officer's and NCOs.

The men's full-dress uniform consisted of a red coat without a collar. The coat, around the horizontal pockets and cuffs, was completely covered alternative bands Savoyard Royal Livery lace and the Great Livery lace. It appears to have been lined with off-white twill according to cloth samples conserved in the *Armeria Reale* in Turin, but the1744 manuscript appears to show blue as does the 1747 manuscript, but not very clearly, so when did the change occur? The coat had buttons covered in blue cloth, probably silk on the coat and on the cuffs. The horizontal pockets had three buttons, and the coat had a blue lining and thin silver lace on all leading edges. The troop had white cravats and wore buff leather gloves, not gauntlets.

Their waistcoats were blue with pewter buttons and a thin silver lace edging to the waist coat and pockets and their breeches were blue with a frill of livery lace around the knee. They all wore blue stockings in winter and white in summer.

They also had a service uniform which consisted of a red coat lined and cuffed blue, 10 pewter or silver buttons with white or silver laced buttonholes on both sides of the coat, three silver buttons and lace on cuffs and pockets.[6] The waistcoat was blue with silver/white stitching on all

6 See the previously cited painting, A military encampment, depicting the Household Cavalry 'Guardia del Corpo' of the Duke of Savoy (1744-1745)… On the left-hand side of the painting there is a soldier who resembles a French Garde Suisse but in reality, it is a Piedmontese Garde Suisse. This painting is the only indication of this uniform, all the other references only show the full dress. I must thank Enrico Ricchiardi for pointing this out to me

leading edges and button holes, silver buttons. They appear to have had ventral cartridge boxes.

For foul weather they had a short cloak called a *mantello alla roquelaure*. It was worn slung over their left shoulder. It was made of red woollen cloth with a fall down collar edged in the Great Livery lace.

NCOs

The *caporali* had the same uniform as the guardsmen, but their cuffs were made of blue velvet simply adorned with silver lace around the border. Their buttons were silver. The *sergente*'s tricorn had a larger silver lace than the guardsmen. The *sergenti* wore a collarless scarlet cloth coat lined with off-white twill with blue velvet cuffs. It was covered in silver lace on the seams, around their pockets, down the leading edges and cuffs. Specifically, it was bordered with 15m of thin silver lace and adorned with 9m large silver galloon. The buttons were silvered pewter. The waistcoat was blue laced silver as were their breeches.

Their stockings were blue in winter and white in summer, adorned with a coloured ribs or 'clocks', colour unknown, but probably silver. For foul weather, the *sergenti* also had a short *mantello alla roquelaure* cloak, worn slung over their left shoulder. It was made of scarlet woollen cloth with a fall down collar edged in silver lace.

Officers

The Officers were not obliged to wear a uniform, but their coats probably had silver lace and buttons. The only solid information we have concerning the officers are from 1717, these regulations required them to wear gold galloon instead of silver. These officers were also designated, like almost all of the officers of the military household as the '*Bacchette nere*' (black canes). This honorific title, gave them the right to carry short ebony canes at important ceremonies, decorated on both sides with a crown of ivory or gold, depending on their function.

Tamburi and Musicians

The *tamburi* and musicians wore the Royal Livery; a red coat lined blue. The 1739 regulations specified that the musicians of the *Guardia Svizzera* should wear a uniform identical to that of the troops, but with more silver galloon, over 46m was used. As there are no contemporary depictions of *tamburi* or *pifferi* of the *Guardia Svizzera*, the reconstruction of their distinctions is particularly difficult. The lace was probably applied transversally on the coat sleeves and vertically on the coat, following the seams as well as around the pockets, cuffs and collar, according to the fashion of the era for *tamburi* in the Sardinian army. The *pifferi* possibly had a swallow's nest of silver lace on the top of the sleeves, but probably not before 1750.

The drum was suspended on a leather drum belt decorated with livery lace. The drum could be painted either red, with blue hoops or blue, with red hoops, adorned with either with the Grand Arms of the Kingdom of Sardinia or simply with white/silver crosses.

Arms and Equipment

The guards carried a sword 'alla Svizzera', but in fact it was similar to those of the infantry officers with a gilded hilt, slung from a very wide leather baldric completely covered in red cloth, edged in silver with two bands of Savoyard Ducal Livery lace and a band of Sardinian Royal Livery lace down the centre in between the others.

The *sergenti* were armed with a standard pattern infantry partisan (*Sergentina*) and the staff was possibly covered with red velvet, and adorned with brass studs. The iron head was possibly gilded. It had a fringe of gold yarn mixed with blue silk tied under the iron shaft. It had a walnut staff decorated with brass studs and had a silvered steel ferrule and there was a gold and blue fringe below the axe head. The guard's sword had a brass hilt and was carried in a baldric covered in blue velvet, edged with a large silver lace.

Compagnie Dragon des gardes-chasse (*La Compagnia di Dragoni Guarda Caccia*)

The *Compagnie Dragon des gardes-chasse* (company of dragoon gamekeepers) was recruited from soldiers no longer fit enough to go on active campaign. They were drawn from the regiments of dragoons and were under the control of the Chief of the Court Hunt. The company was consisted of a *capitano*, two *luogotenente*, a *brigadiere* and a troop of 25 mounted dragoons and two *caporali* and 40 dragoons on foot, which rose to 88 in 1747. They were not destined for field service.

However, in wartime, even though they were not engaged in combat, the mounted *Dragoni Guarda Caccia* were in charge of the relays for delivering dispatches containing the king's orders and periodic situation reports written by the generals commanding the army, which were delivered directly to the capital (Turin).

The *capitani* of the *Dragoni Guarda Caccia* under Charles Emmanuel III were *Capitano* Giovanni Battista Cerutti from 1728, succeeded by Maurizio Amedeo Pellione on 1 May 1744. He commanded the company until 1754.

Uniforms

The company wore a black tricorn with a dark blue cockade on the left brim with a black loop and a pewter button and white/silver lace border; the officers had silver lace and a button on their hats. The troop wore black cravats and a red collarless dragoon coat. The coat had eight pewter buttons, grouped in twos on each side of the coat, and four

Royal Household Companies (Casa Reale). 1. *Guardie del Corpo* on Palace duty with his *Aggucia*. 2. *Guardia Svizzera* wearing his livery coat and armed with his special Swiss halberd. 3. *Sergente* of the *Guardia Svizzera* in full dress. 4. *Arquebusier* of the *Guardia della Porta* wearing his cloak slung over his shoulder. 5. *Sergente* of the *Guardia della Porta* with his partisan decorated with the Royal cypher, in fact that of the previous king, Victor Amadeus. 6. *La Compagnia di Dragoni Guarda Caccia*, mounted troop. (Author's Illustration)

on the cuffs, also grouped in twos. The coat had horizontal pockets, each with three buttons and had dark blue cuffs and linings and turn backs. Their waistcoats were blue with pewter buttons and their breeches were also blue. The mounted company wore black dragoon gaiters with brass buckles. Originally the foot company wore white gaiters, but around 1750 they adopted black grenadier gaiters with brass buttons. When they were not on service, they all wore white stockings. The *sergenti* had a silver lace around their cuff. The officer's coats had silver lace and buttons and the *tamburo* wore the Royal Livery.

Horse Furniture

The saddle was a standard model for the period, made of leather. The harness was of blackened leather with steel fittings. The saddle cloth and holster caps were red with a white lace edge which had a central blue stripe. Strapped behind the saddle they carried a red cloak trimmed blue. The '*Catalogato Saluzzo 341*' of 1752/1757 in the Biblioteca Reale di Torino, very clearly shows a *garde* mounted on a Piebald horse.

Arms and Equipment

The mounted dragoons carried a sabre which had a curved blade with a brass double barred hilt carried black leather scabbard with brass fittings on a leather waist belt. The carbine belt was made of buff leather. They carried a pair of pistols, similar to the dragoon model, in holsters on the saddle brow. Over their shoulder they carried a small buff leather cartridge pouch on a buff bandolier stamped 'D C' in gold letters. The foot dragoons also carried the sabre and were armed with a musket. Over their shoulder they carried a small buff leather cartridge pouch on a buff bandolier. The carbine/musket belt was made of buff leather.

La Compagnie des Hallebardiers du Vice-roi de Sardaigne (*Alabardieri del Vicerè di Sardegna*)

This was a small company which consisted of only 23 officers and men, raised in 1722 to guard the palace in the town of Cagliari. The company was composed of a *capitano*, a *luogotenente*, a *corporale*, and 20 halberdiers. They were again basically palace guards with no field service. They were stationed in Cagliari. In practice they performed the same functions of the bodyguards, and they were recruited from the Invalid Company. They appear to have armed with halberds for service inside and outside the palace.

Uniforms

The company wore a black tricorn with a dark blue cockade on the left brim with a black loop and a pewter button and a white lace border, the officers had silver lace and button on their hats. They wore a red collarless coat; the coat had silver buttons, grouped in twos on each side of the coat, and four on the cuffs, also grouped in twos. The coat had horizontal pockets, each with three buttons and had dark blue cuffs and linings and turn backs. The halberdiers wore white cravats. Their waistcoats were blue with silver buttons and their breeches were also blue. They all wore white stockings inside and possibly white gaiters outside.

Arms and Equipment

They wore standard infantry buff leather belt and a brass hilted sword. The type of halberd they used was similar to the model used by the *Guardie svizzere*, but with a rounded axe head and a straight bladed point and a red fringe below the axe head.

Great and Royal Livery Laces (detail) Right; The Great Livery lace, a rather complex lace only used on the livery coats of the *Guardie svizzere*, taken from a sample conserved in the Royal Library (*Biblioteca Reale*) in Turin. Left; The Royal Livery lace, called '*Biscia*' (snake) as used by trumpeters and drummers. Blue azur lace edged with white or silver lace depending on the regiment. Probably made of wool for the ordinary drummers and trumpeters and velvet for the guard and those with NCO status. (Author's Illustration)

5

The Infantry: Organisation, Uniforms, Arms and Colours

Between 1738 and 1741 the establishment of the Piedmontese army consisted of 30,524 men in 39 battalions of infantry and 32 squadrons of cavalry and dragoons.

By 1747, under Charles Emmanuel III, the infantry (called *pista pauta* – mud pests – by the local population) consisted of 32 regiments, with a total of 55 battalions. Eighteen of these were the Piedmontese regiments, composed of 25 battalions divided into the eight provincial and 10 national regiments referred to as the '*fanteria grigia*', from the coat's grey main colour. The *Guardie* regiment was included with them, even though they wore blue coats, and there were 30 battalions of foreign infantry divided into 14 regiments.

The uniforms of the Piedmontese army had been regulated by a number of decrees following the end of the War of the Polish Succession in 1735. The first of these 'clothing contracts', as they were called, dates to 1736 which laid down the uniforms for all of the regiments, including infantry, cavalry, dragoons and the artillery. A supplementary 'Regolamento' to this contract was published 17 September 1741 which gave more details for the musicians' and NCOs' dress, but not for the Swiss or German regiments. All of these details were confirmed in new Regolamento in 1742.

These were the uniforms worn during the War of the Austrian Succession and new dress regulations only came into force in 1750 and 1751, when there was a complete change and they adopted blue uniforms in a more Prussian style, but this lies outside the scope of this book.

The organisation and composition of the units were very different between national, provincial and foreign infantry regiments, and within each group there were exceptions, but this work notes as much as possible.

The national regiments consisted of two battalions, except for *La Regina* which had only one battalion and *La Marina*, whose second battalion had only five companies who were exclusively marine troops. Each battalion was made up of nine fusilier companies and a grenadier company, with a total strength of 700–800 men.

The national regiments' first battalions had 10 companies; a *colonnello*'s company, a *maggiore*'s company, a grenadier company and seven fusilier companies numbered 4, 5, 6, 7, 8, 9 and 10. The second battalion had a *luogotenente colonnello*'s company, a grenadier company and eight fusilier companies, numbered 3, 4, 5, 6, 7, 8, 9 and 10. The composition of each company varied.

Here is a typical infantry *colonnello*, attired for mounted service. Note that senior officers wore their sash around their waist, sometimes under their coat and occasionally over it. He is wearing the uniform of the *Reggimento di Fucilieri*. (Author's Illustration)

The Regimental staff consisted of the *colonnello*, a *luogotenente colonnello*, a regimental *aiutante maggiore*, and a senior *furieri*, a *cappellano*, a *chirurgo*, a *tamburo maggiore*, four *falegname*, two *armaioli*, a *preposto*, an *arciera* and six junior *furieri*.

The grenadier company of the first battalion was commanded by a *luogotenente colonnello* theoretically and was composed of a *capitano*, a *luogotenente*, an *alfiere* in the sense of a junior officer, not necessarily a standard bearer, four *furieri*, two *sergenti*, four *caporali*, four *nominatos* (similar to a lance corporal or private first class), a *tamburo* and 32 *granatieri*.

The grenadier company of the second battalion had the same composition, except that it was commanded by a *maggiore*. This gave a total of 51 officers and men.

The *colonnello*'s company was composed of the *colonnello*, a *capitano*, an *alfiere* in the sense of a junior officer, not necessarily a standard bearer, three *furieri*, two *sergenti*, four *caporali*, two *tamburi* and 43 *fucilieri*. This gave a total of 57 officers (including the *colonnello*) and men. Not mentioned in most records is the *frater* – a medical orderly – as he was a trained and uniformed soldier he was probably listed among the NCOs. There was one in every company in all of the infantry regiments.

The company of the *luogotenente colonnello* was composed of the *luogotenente colonnello*, a *luogotenente*, an *alfiere*, five *furieri*, two *sergenti*, four *caporali*, two *tamburi* and 40 *fucilieri*. This gave a total of 56 officers (including the *luogotenente colonnello*) and men.

The *maggiore*'s company was composed of the *maggiore*, an *alfiere*, four *furieri*, two *sergenti*, four *caporale*, a *tamburo* and 42 *fucilieri*. This gave a total of 55 officers (including the *maggiore*) and men.

The ordinary fusilier companies of both battalions were composed of a *capitano*, a *luogotenente*, an *alfiere*, four *furieri*, two *sergenti*, four *caporali*, a *tamburo* and 44 *fucilieri*. Again, there were some variations; the ninth and tenth companies were commanded by the *alfiere*. This gave the company a total of 58 officers and men (including the *capitano*).

The grenadier companies were permanent in the national regiments, but only a temporary wartime organisation in the provincial regiments. Where they were commanded by a *capitano*, the rest of the company was made up of a *luogotenente*, an *alfiere* drawn from the regimental staff and considered as supernumeraries, two *sergenti*, five *caporali*, four *nominatos*, a *tamburo* and 47 *granatieri*.

The provincial regiments had a different composition; they were composed of one battalion of eight companies. They did not have a regular grenadier company; a number of the fusiliers were converted to grenadiers and equipped as such when the regiment went on to a wartime footing; at the end of the war the grenadiers returned to fusiliers. Originally composed of 600 men their establishments rose to 700 men from 5 May1742, and then rose again to 800 men from 1747, except for *Chiablese* and *Tarantasia* regiments who remained at 700 men. Their battalions were made up of a *compagnia colonnella*, a *compagnia luogotenente colonnella*, a *compagnia maggiore*, a grenadier company, four fusilier companies and a reserve company.

The regimental staff consisted of the *colonnello*, a regimental *aiutante maggiore*, and a senior *furieri*, six *furieri*, a *cappellano*, a *chirurgo*, a *tamburo maggiore*, six *zappatori* and *armaioli*, a *preposto* and an *arciera* – a military policeman. The *colonnello*'s company was composed of the *colonnello*, a *capitano*, a *luogotenente*, an *alfiere*, four *sergenti*, six *caporali*, two *tamburi* and 76 *fucilieri*. The *luogotenente colonnello*'s Company was composed of the *luogotenente colonnello*, a *luogotenente*, an *alfiere*, four *sergenti*, six *caporali*, two *tamburi* and 77 *fucilieri*. The *maggiore*'s company was composed of the *maggiore*, a *luogotenente*, an *alfiere*, three *sergenti*, seven *caporali*, two *tamburi* and 77 *fucilieri*. The fusilier companies were composed of a *capitano*, a *luogotenente*, an *alfiere*, four *furieri*, three *sergenti*, seven *caporali*, a *tamburo* and 76 *fucilieri*. The eighth or reserve company was composed of a *capitano*, a *luogotenente*, an *alfiere*, four *furieri*, three *sergenti*, six *caporali*, a *tamburo* and 77 *fucilieri*.

From 1735, the reserve company was created in each provincial regiment, which served as a depot and as a reserve of recruits to keep the battalion up to strength. In reality the term 'company' masked a second battalion, although reduced in numbers, and was generally employed as a garrison in the various fortresses. The composition of these companies, again according to the Royal Viglietto of 5 May 1742, was a *capitano*, two *luogotenenti*, two *alfieri*, six *arcieri*, eight *sergenti*, 14 *caporali*, four *tamburi*, 40 *fucilieri*, 200 new recruits; giving a total of 271 men.

The real number of men in these reserve companies could vary greatly. In 1747 recorded composition for the following regiments was; *Chiablese* 230 men, *Tarantasia* 230 men, *Aosta* 700 men, *Torino* 900 men, *Nizza* 300 men, *Mondovi* 750 men, *Vercelli* 900 men, *Asti* 800 men, *Pinerolo* 800 men, *Casale* 800 men.[1]

The assembly of the reserve companies took place in the following locations: in Susa for the *Chiablese* and *Tarantasia* regiments; In Ivrea for the *Aosta*; in Cuneo for the *Nizza*, in Torino for the *Torino*; in Vercelli for the *Vercelli*; in Asti for the *Asti*; in Mondovi for the *Mondovi*; in Pinerolo for the *Pinerolo*; and in Casale for the *Casale*.

The organisation of the foreign regiments was different. The Swiss and German regiments organised their battalions in four to six large companies with varying

1 Minutoli Atlante, vol. 2; *Stato Generale delle Truppe di S.M. esistenti in Terraferma, ed in Sardegna, e della loro rispettiva Forza, 1747*, Archivio di Stato Torino.

Piedmontese infantry officers. Note that the officers of the *Provinciali* regiments have been given less intricate lace to reflect the different status, but in reality, it probably only depended on the depth of each officers' pockets. They have been given powdered periwigs, but when on active service they were ordered not to powder their hair. Steel or silvered sword hilts appear to have been popular, this may be related to their button colour. Concerning their sashes, as stated in the main text, before 1750 there do not appear to be any rules, so some may have had all blue or all gold sashes. 1. *Capitano, Reggimento Nazionale di Piemonte*. 2. Senior *Capitano, Reggimento Nazionale di Savoia*. 3. *Capitano, Reggimento Nazionale La Regina*. 4. *Luogotenente, Reggimento Provinciali di Torino*. 5. *Capitano, Reggimento Provinciali di Aoste*. 6. *Luogotenente, Reggimento Provinciali di Nizza*. (Author's Illustration)

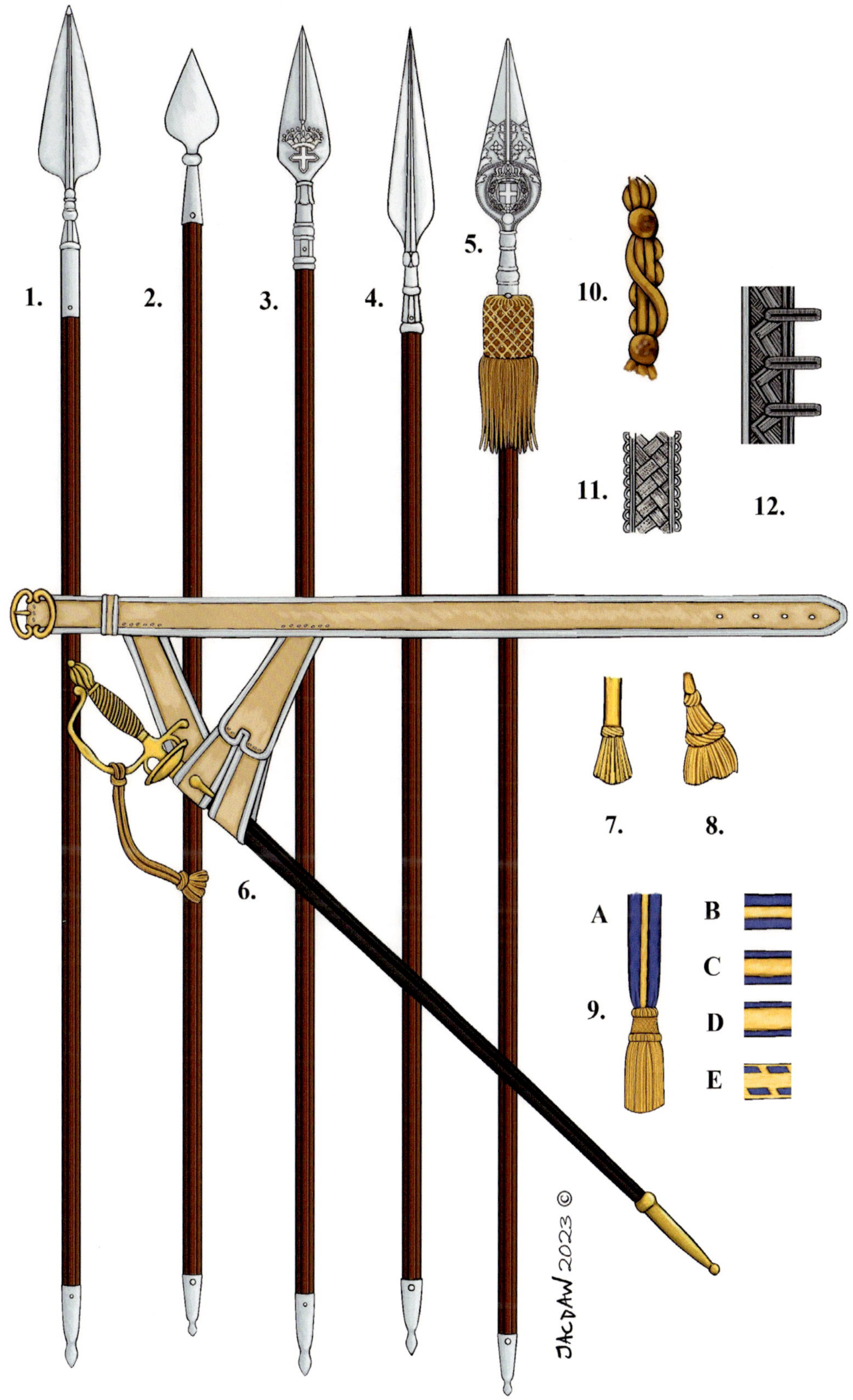

Infantry officers' weapons. 1., 3. & 4. Officer's mezza pica (half pike). Collection America Reale di Torino. 2. Officers Mezza Pica (half pike). After Embser. 5. Senior officer's mezza pica. Collection America Reale di Torino. 6. Officer's sword, sheath and belt. Before 1751 there was not an official model for officers' swords, before this, their swords were made privately, so there were a number of different models. The hilt was frequently silvered. 7. & 8. Contemporary sword knots, they were only regulated in 1750. 9. Officer's sashes were only regulated in 1750. This was to avoid the disputes of the previous decades about the amount of gold silk used by junior officers. A. *Luogotenente*, *sottoluogotenente*, *alfiere* & *cornetta*. B. *Capitano* & *capitano-luogotenente*. C. *Maggiore*. D. *Tenenza Colonnella*. E. *Colonnello*. 10., 11. & 12. Samples of officer's lace from contemporary paintings. (Author's Illustration)

numbers of effectives. Each company was organised as a small independent unit, each with its own colour and its own unit of grenadiers who, according to the archives, were only formed into a specific grenadier company when the country was at war. The German regiments each had two battalions, each of five to seven companies of around a 100 officers and men.

The *Monfort* foreign regiment, which was composed of mixed nationalities, had two battalions, each of 10 companies, and this was the only foreign regiment whose grenadier companies were permanent and not disbanded when a conflict ended.

The regimental staffs consisted of the *colonnello*, a regimental *aiutante maggiore*, and a senior *furieri*, an *uditore*, a catholic *cappellano*, a protestant *cappellano*, a *chirurgo*, a *tamburo maggiore*, four *zappatori* two *armaioli*, a *preposto* and an *arciera*.

The regiments' first battalions had a *compagnia colonnella*, a *compagnia maggiore*, a *compagnia di granatieri* and seven *compagnie di fucilieri*, which could vary, depending on the number of companies in each battalion, depending on the nationality.

The *compagnia colonnella* was composed of the *colonnello*, a *capitano*, a *luogotenente*, two *alfieri*, two *sergenti*, four *caporali*, a *tamburo* and 60 *fucilieri*. The *compagnia maggiore* was composed of the *maggiore*, a *capitano*, a *luogotenente*, two *alfieri* two *sergenti*, four *caporali*, a *tamburo* and 58 *fucilieri*. The *compagnia di granatieri* of the first battalion was composed of a *capitano*, a *luogotenente*, two *alfieri*, two *sergenti*, four *caporali*, a *tamburo* and 50 *granatieri*. The grenadier company of the second battalion was the same.

The *compagnie di fucilieri* of both battalions were composed of a *capitano*, a *luogotenente*, two *alfieri*, two *sergenti*, *caporali*, a *tamburo* and 59 *fucilieri*. The second battalion had a *compagnia tenenza colonnella*, a *compagnia di granatieri* and seven *compagnie di fucilieri*. Depending on the nationality, the number of companies could vary in each battalion and the composition of each company could also vary. The *compagnia luogotenente colonnella*, was composed of the *tenenza colonnella*, a *capitano*, a *luogotenente*, two *alfieri*, two *sergenti*, four *caporali*, a *tamburo* and 59 *fucilieri*.

Uniforms

The uniforms followed fairly closely the French cut and style for this period, which again were very similar to prevailing civilian fashions. The most elegant and comfortable style of the period was chosen, with the presence of real turnbacks and finer facings. White gaiters were also adopted.

Clothing Terms

The equipment of the infantry was divided into four categories, the clothing itself, the clothing accessories called the *equipaggio*, the small, and the 'grand' armament.

The clothing consisted of:

A woollen cloth coat (*giustacorpo*) every three years.
A waistcoat (*veste*) made of woollen cloth or ratteen[2] every three years.
A pair of breeches, known as *calze*, distributed every year.
A pair of woollen gaiters (*uose* or *ghette*) every two years.
A felt tricorn every two years.
For the Grenadiers, a fur cap, called a *bonetto*, and a pair of special gaiters called *bottine alla grenadiera* which were to last six years.

The accessories, presumably issued every year included:

A canvas knapsack (*zaino di tela*).
A pair of shoes (*scarpe*).
A pair of socks (*calzette*).
Two shirts (*camicie*).
Two neck stocks (*cravatte*).

The small armament (*piccolo armamento*) was in fact their leather equipment – belt, bayonet frog, cartridge box and bandoleer. The grand armament (*grande armamento*) referred to their fusil, bayonet, and sword or sabre.

Headwear

Like most other European armies, the Piedmontese wore a black felt tricorn (*tricorno*) of a regimental model, it appears to have been slightly lower than the French model, with the horns not angled up as much. It had a border of a yellow or white woollen tape (*bordo di gallone*) and was garnished with a Savoy blue silk cockade (*coccarda*), held in place with a loop made of white or yellow goat's hair and a button (*ganza e bottone*) for *caporali* and *soldati*. It was sewn under the boarding galloon, coming down V-shaped and buttoned in the angle of the V. The cockade was under the V, most probably sewn on as well so as not to lose it. The loop, *ganza*, was made of metallic galloon for NCOs and officers, in either gold or silver. In camp the soldiers also had a bonnet for fatigues made up from old coats; this was probably a grey-white bag and turned up in the facing colour for the national and provincial regiments and blue for the Swiss and Germans. The tricorn of the men of the German *Schulemburg* regiment of had a white/silver tassel hanging down from the corner of the left-hand side.

2 Ratteen/Ratine was a thick napped twilled woollen material which was produced in France, Italy and Holland.

Non-commissioned officers. 1. *Sergente, Reggimento Nazionale di Savoia.* 2. *Sergente, Reggimento Nazionale di Fucilieri.* Note, this partisan is specific to this regiment. 3. *Sergente, Reggimento Nazionale della La Marina.* 4. *Caporale, Reggimento Nazionale di Piemonte.* Note, the hatchet carried behind the cartridge pouch. 5. *Sergente, Reggimento Provinciali di Asti.* 6. *Sergente, Reggimento Provinciali di Nizza.* (Author's Illustration)

The soldier wore his hair pulled back and dressed in a queue, or simply tied back with a black ribbon. The ribbon sometimes went around their necks to secure the tail.

All the men were to be supposed to be clean-shaven, including the officers and musicians, but in reality they probably only shaved once a week for Sunday service. The only exceptions were the grenadiers, the dragoons and most of the line cavalry, who wore moustaches, but they were never worn by their officers or the musicians. Moustaches appear in some illustrations of Swiss and German soldiers.

Coats

Piedmontese infantry wore a generously cut grey-white woollen coat or *giustacorpo*, which, when the soldier was kneeling down on the ground, reached to an inch above the knee. The coat was split at the back and had a couple of false pleats sewn in on each side, topped with a button. The coat was double breasted and had buttons and button holes down both sides. Sometimes the coat could be turned back to give the impression of lapels, something that had been done since the War of the Spanish Succession. The button holes were stitched with either a very fine silk thread made from the fibres the silkworms shed around them before beginning their cocoon called *bave*, or cotton thread in the colour of the coat. The coat was generally, but not always, lined in the facing colour. The buttons were generally flat and made of brass, pewter or tin and in two or three different sizes on the coat.

The regimental coats usually had bucket cuffs (*paramani*) in the regimental facing colour, with three buttons on each. Collars (*colletto*) were just putting in their first appearances at the end of the period, mainly in newly raised regiments. For the few that had them, they were in either the facing colour or grey-white.

The grey-white colour could be in a variety of shades with a tendency to an off white/very light cream warm grey for the majority, to a very light grey, but rarely darker than this for this period. Even a buff colour has been recorded. The coat could be pipe-clayed white. On the left shoulder there was a shoulder strap closed with a button by the collar in the colour of the coat, often it was placed to the back of the shoulder.

The 1741 *Regolamento* stated that the pocket flaps (*patellette delle tasche*) should have four buttons, but both manufacturing contracts and contemporary illustrations always show only three buttons.

The coat was worn unbuttoned, allowing the sword belt to pass under it, and the coat skirts were worn turned back (*risvolti*) and secured with a button and loop. Another distinctive part of the coat was the pockets, cut in different regimental forms like the French, but with only two basic models.

Waistcoats, Shirts and Breeches

The sleeved woollen waistcoat (*veste*) had 12 buttons and split cuffs with three buttons. It was worn under the coat, but could be worn on its own in hot weather. It usually had two pockets with three buttons, frequently false for the men. It was made in the regimental facing colour. Contemporary illustrations tend to show the waistcoat worn partially unbuttoned. The belt was worn over the waistcoat in all regiments.

The waistcoat is frequently shown un-buttoned to the waist. All wore long shirts (*camicia*) of bleached white linen, sometimes of wool, tied with tapes at the throat and wrists. The shirt was long as it also served as underpants, as these did not yet exist! As the shirt tended to bunch up at back it led to the French expression '*cul de poulet*' or a chicken's bum. The breeches (*calze*) had a fly front and a split at the back of the waist and were tied with tapes for adjustment. On each leg, the breeches were closed with three buttons and, theoretically, a small buckle just below the knee.

Neck Stocks

A cloth cravat (*Cravatta*) was worn wound around the neck over the shirt in the regimental colour. Initially, they were red for all the Piedmontese regiments, but from 1747 the national regiments appear to have switched to black cravats. The foreign regiments in general wore black cravats; but the few variations are noted under the individual regimental descriptions.

Gaiters and Shoes

By 1741 at the latest, the men generally wore white canvas gaiters for field service, closed with brass or pewter buttons depending on the regimental button colour, and a gusset which passed under the instep of the shoe. The gaiters were adjusted just below the knee with a narrow black leather garter. Sometimes they may have been made of grey cloth or ticken.

The shoes were of blackened bovine leather, made with the rough side out. They were square toed, the sign of a military shoe, and closed with a brass or steel buckle, usually square or slightly rectangular. Although hidden by the gaiters the stockings are frequently mentioned as being white, made of bleached or unbleached wool and, in some cases, made in the facing colours, particularly in the foreign units.

NCOs Uniforms and Distinctions

The *sergenti* wore the same uniform as the men but theirs were generally made of a better-quality cloth. They had a thin lace around the edge of their cuffs and a wider lace beneath the buttons in false gold or silver lace in the regimental button colour, and sometimes around their pockets as well.

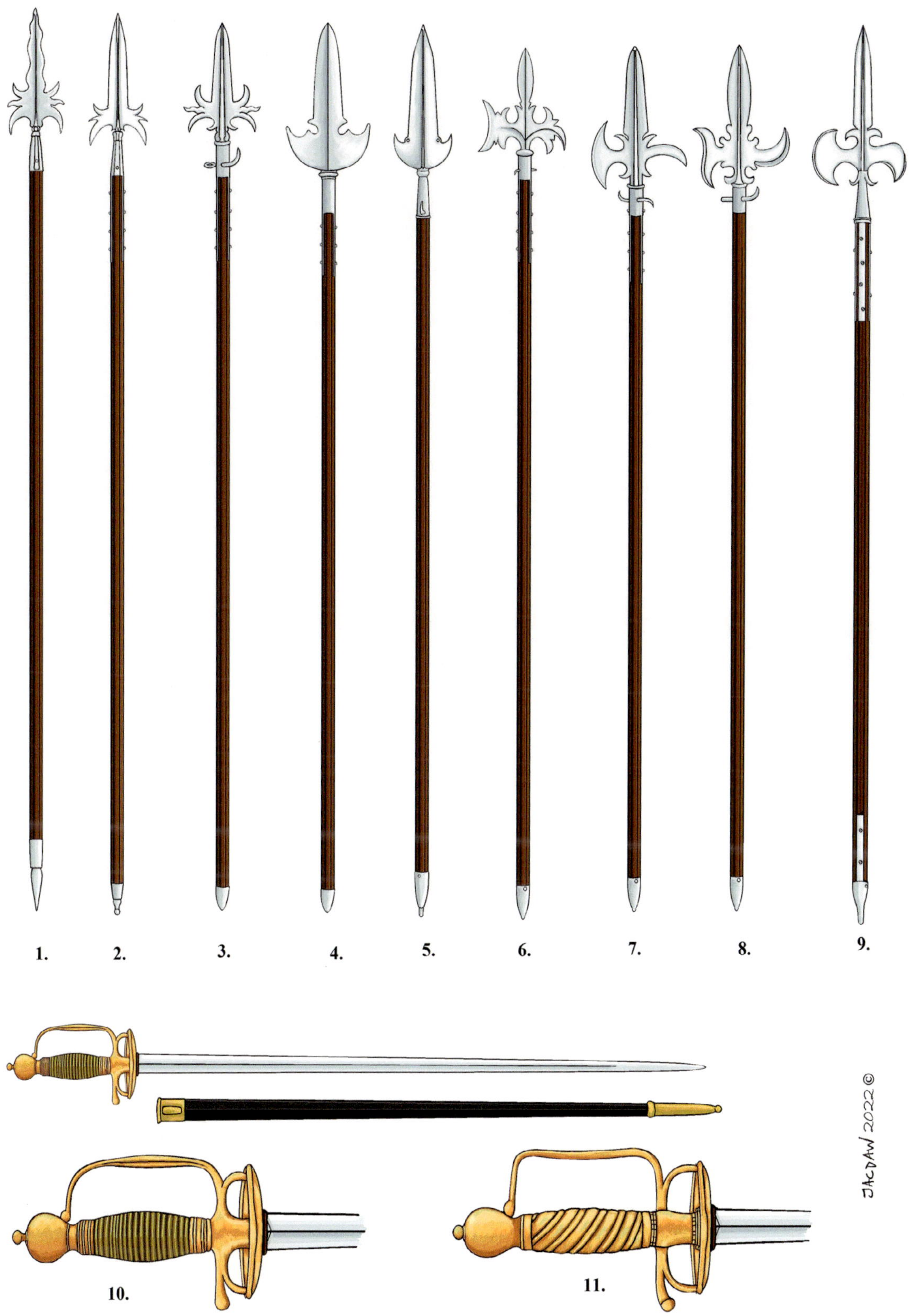

Arms of the *sergenti* including partisans (*partigianetta*), halberds (*alabardine*) and swords, 1739–1750. 1. Partisan, *Sergentina* Piedmontese regiments, variant. 2. Partisan, *Sergentina* Piedmontese regiments, variant. 3. Partisan, *Sergentina* Piedmontese regiment after Embser 4. Partisan, *Reggimento Fucilieri* after Embser 5. Partisan, *Reggimento Fucilieri*, variant. 6. Halberd, Swiss regiments, after Embser. 7. Halberd, German regiments, after Embser. 8. Halberd, German regiments, after Embser, variant. 9. Halberd, German Regiment, c.1720. These were all around 2.27m long including the blade which varied between 20–25cm long and the ferrule was 7–9cm long. Obviously there would have been some variations. The diameter of the staff was around 30mm. 10. *Sergenti* sword, *Spada* M 1734/1742. The overall length of the sword including the hilt was 94cm. 11. *Caporali* sword, *Spada* M 1734. In 1734, when the sword was abolished in general for the infantrymen, only the corporal retained his sword. (Author's Illustration)

Infantrymen (*Fucilieri*) 1739–1750. 1. *Reggimento Nazionale La Regina*. 2. *Reggimento Nazionale di Saluzzo*. 3. *Reggimento Nazionale di Monferrato*. 4. *Reggimento Provinciali di Torino*. 5. *Reggimento Provinciali di Aosta*. 6. *Reggimento Provinciali di Casale*. (Author's Illustration)

The tress of the lace is described as '*à la Mousquetaire*', but as no samples have survived its form is unknown. The fusilier *caporali* wore the same uniform as the men. They had the same lacing as the *sergenti*, but in white or yellow wool. The *appuntati*, or appointees, only had one thin woollen galloon around the edge of their cuffs. The *caporali* also carried the same arms and equipment as the rest of their company, but they also carried a sword or sabre as a mark of their rank. It is not clear if this included the *appuntati* as well.

The *Guardie* regiment had their own system which was slightly different, described in the regimental section.

Grenadier Uniforms

The grenadiers wore a fur bonnet of imported black bearskin, with a hanging cloth bag or bonnet in the shape of a sugar loaf in the regimental colour piped in white or yellow according to button colour with a matching tassel. The bonnets were all supplied from a centralised depot and were purchased from one furrier called Antonio Guinet. They were supposed to last for 10 years. The contract specified the size and shape of them. The piping and tassels on the officers and *sergenti*'s bonnets were in metallic thread. E. Ricchardi suggests in his 1980 article in *Armi Antiche* a more intricate form of lacing, but this probably came later.[3] The grenadiers still carried a brass match case on the front their bandoleer, a traditional accessory of which they were rather proud. The shoulder belt had a traverse on the back with a sheath for their hatchet.

The grenadiers and their *caporali* carried a larger black leather cartridge case (*gibassiera*). The flap of the cartridge box had a thin red leather border stitched around the edge. The NCOs of the *Reggimento Guardie* had a yellow gold lace border and a flaming grenade on their cartridge case. The grenade was embossed with the arms of Savoy decorated in gold leaf and embroidered flames, the other ranks had the same but with a red leather border. The cartridge case was suspended on a buff leather shoulder belt which had a brass buckle. Inside the cartridge case there was a block of wood drilled out for cartridges and a space for some small spherical grenades filled with powder which they still used on occasion.

The grenadiers wore thick black cloth gaiters closed with brass buttons and 12 buckles, with a reinforced knee. The grenadiers carried a short sabre with a brass single branched hilt and a heart shaped guard. The curved blade had a groove and a length of 73cm for an overall length of 88.5cm. It was carried in a black leather scabbard with a brass locket and chape.

Sappers and Carpenters

Each battalion had four regimental *falegnami* (carpenters). They were distinguished by their leather apron and an axe with an ash wood haft. From the beginning they appear to have worn bonnets and sported a beard or a moustache, but as they were only regulated in 1750 there would probably have been some variations. They definitely had bearskins by 1750, but it was probably much earlier, possibly around 1747.

They were armed with a musket and sabre carried on a waist belt, and wore a cartridge box on a shoulder belt. By 1750 they appear to have lost their musket and cartridge box, which had been replaced by a pistol, carried on a shoulder belt, although there were some regimental variations. They marched on the right of the grenadier companies when the unit was in battle order, usually at the disposal of regimental or brigade commander. They could be placed in a mixed company for assaults on fortifications.

Grenadier NCOs

Grenadier *caporali* carried the same arms and equipment as the rest of their company. They had either white or yellow thin woollen lace stitched around edge of their cuffs, corresponding with the regimental button colour, or laced and stitched buttonholes, as their sign of rank. They also carried a brass hilted NCO model sword or sabre on a waist belt in a black leather scabbard, with a length of 102.7cm. The *sergenti* had metallic lace on their cuffs in the button colour, usually around the cuffs but sometimes around the button holes as well, again depending on the wishes and pocket of the *colonnello*.

Grenadier *sergenti* carried cartridge boxes which had a metallic lace around the flap and the bandoleer was edged with metallic lace as well, there is some suggestion that there was some form of decoration on the flap, a grenade or the arms of Savoy would be a possibility.

Officers Uniforms

The officers wore the regimental uniforms but they were made from in better quality cloth and were fairly heavily laced with lace on all seams, around the pockets, and on all leading edges with galloons of rank around the cuffs. The width and form of the lace denoted the rank of the officer. The button holes were laced as well. They wore a black tricorn with a metallic lace border corresponding to the regimental button colour and most of the senior officers added a white feather around the edge and a Savoy blue silk cockade. In addition, senior officers and generals wore braided breeches.

3 This elaborate embroidery can be seen on the tail of a bonnet shown in a painting by Giovanna Michele Graneri, 'Deer hunting in Sardinia', dated to 1749, now preserved in Palazzo Madama in Turin. It shows a cross hatching of lace. Before 1750 there is no record of standardisation or variants.

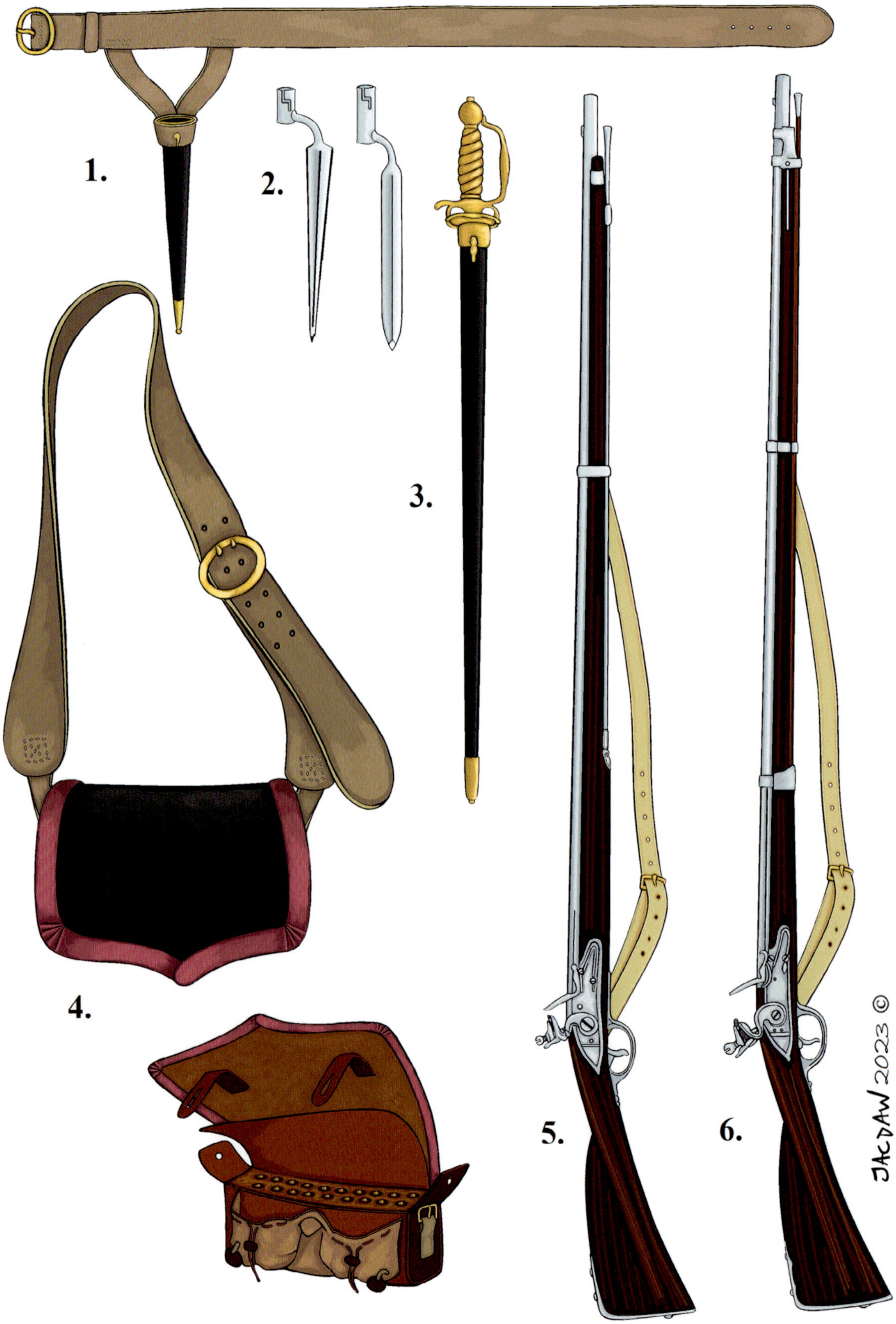

1. Belt with bayonet frog for *fucilieri*, including bayonet scabbard for the old model bayonet. 2. Bayonets, left, old model (after *Embser* and 1744 manuscript), and on the right, the new model. 3. Musket, Piedmontese model M 1730. 4. Musket French model M 1728. 5. Cartridge box and bandoleer, including open *giberna* showing wooden block drilled out for cartridges. 6. Sword for *fucilieri* of the *Reggimento Guardie*. The same model was probably carried by the German infantry *Reggimento Burgsdorff.* (Author's Illustration)

1. *Granatiere* officer, *Reggimento Nationale di Savoia*. 2. *Granatiere sergente, Reggimento Nationale di Saluzzo*. Note that after 1743, they probably replaced the *sergentina* with a musket. 3. *Falegnami, Reggimento Provinciale di Tarantasia*. 4. *Granatiere, Reggimento Provinciale di Vercelli*. 5. *Granatiere, Reggimento Provinciale di Mondovi*. 6. *Granatiere, Reggimento Nationale Della Marina*. (Author's Illustration)

The officers usually cut their hair short and wore a powdered wig, the style of which varied. There were often one or two rolls on each side of the head with the tail tied back with a bow of large black ribbon or enclosed in a black silk bag called a '*crapaud*' (toad) and tied in place with a black silk bow. If contemporary paintings are to be believed the officers tended to affectatious hair styles which were a little old fashioned. In fact, they preferred the regency style periwigs, the senior officers in particular. Note that the officers only powdered their hair in peacetime. On campaign they probably just pulled their hair back and attached it with a ribbon.

Their coats, except for the *Guardie*, were not supposed to be so heavily laced, but judging from the number of letters condemning such practices it is obvious that the regulations were not respected, and elegance came first. Some of the extravagances went as far as having silk covered buttons with metallic lacing. Their waistcoats were invariably laced in the button colour and were sometimes of a different colour to the troops.

The officers did not always wear gaiters, some preferring the elegance of stockings, even on the battlefield. Some senior field officers on mounted service still occasionally wore breastplates under their coats as well as heavy riding boots. Around their neck and under or over their coats the officers invariably wore a white cravat, with or without a lace jabot.

Their rank was shown by a sash of Savoy blue and possibly with yellow or gold silk with two twisted gold hanging tassels, one on each end of the sash. The tassels of the earlier models appear to have some blue thread mixed with the gold. The widths of the gold and blue which denoted the rank were only officially regulated in 1750. Before this we do not have much information, but there is some indication that they may have been simply blue with gold fringes. The 1750 regulations ordered that the sashes for *luogotenenti*, *sottoluogotenenti*, *alfieri* and *cornetti* were blue with a thin gold stripe down the centre and two gold tassels. The sashes of the *capitani* had three stripes – blue and gold and blue – all of the same width and two gold tassels. A *maggiore*'s sash had three stripes – ¼ blue, ½ gold and ¼ blue – and two gold tassels. The *luogotenente colonnello*'s sash had three stripes – ⅛ blue, ¾ gold and ⅛ blue – and two gold tassels. The *colonnello*'s sash was gold with a thin broken stripe of blue top and bottom and two gold tassels. These sashes probably reflected earlier practices, just more carefully regulated. The junior officers usually wore the sash over their shoulders, while the more senior officers would wear them around their waists, under their coat. Officers' sword knots were blue and gold with a gold tassel, but again only regulated in 1750.

All the officers of the grenadier companies wore a bearskin cap with gold or silver lacing on the bag and they carried a fusil and either a ventral cartridge box or a cartridge box on a bandoleer, usually embossed with the crowned arms of Savoy and highlighted in gold leaf or embroidered. A manuscript showing manoeuvres dating to the 1750's shows the bandoleer worn over the right shoulder.

All officers and most NCOs wore gloves. They were usually made of fine soft chamois-type leather and were back stitched with three lengthwise bands called 'sleeves' which gave a goose foot pattern. Many officers are shown with canes, usually varnished wood with a strap, tassel, and a brass or silver knob. This was probably a sign of rank, as in the Austrian and Spanish armies. They were not carried on the battlefield, and probably reserved for ordinary service and off duty hours.

Generally, only the *colonnello*, *maggiore* and *aiutante maggiore* were mounted when in action, and as such they wore riding boots, but only when they were on mounted duty.

Saddle cloths (*gualdrappa*) appear to be of the regimental facing colour and laced in the regimental button colour; those of the *colonnello*, *luogotenente colonnello* and *maggiore* had two wide laces and a fringe. The *capitano*'s had one wide lace and a fringe. Possibly they had the King's cypher VE in the lower posterior corners. Even in the new 1751 regulations there are no specifications.

Although they had officer status, the *chirurghi* apparently did not wear regimental uniforms, just their civilian dress. When operating they probably took off their coat and wore an apron over their waistcoat, as was standard practice in France and Britain.

Tamburi and Musicians Liveries

The *tamburi*, *tamburo maggiori* and musicians of the national ordnance regiments, the regiments of provincial infantry, the artillery, and the cavalry and dragoons were subjects of the king and as such they all wore the Royal livery of the House of Savoy. The Italian regiments also observed these rules. The former regulations, in reality a '*contratto*' (clothing contract) dated to 1736, were not as detailed as the 1741 *contratto*.

The text of a clothing contract (*biglietto regio*) of September 1741 gives a detailed description of the uniform of the musicians and *tamburi* of the regiment *Savoye* only, which was to serve as a pattern for all the regiments and services of how to place the lace on the coat.

This contract specified a red coat lined and cuffed in a deep medium blue. Generally, but not always, the colour is noted as scarlet and the few contemporary images show a more crimson red; both are probably correct. The livery lace of *Savoye* was made of blue '*Lodeve*' cloth cut in an undulating snake shape with a border of thin silver/white yarn, called '*Bave*' stitched on both edges. But there are some vague references of a straight white lace with just the blue undulated, this may have possibly been an earlier or cheaper version.

The *tamburi* usually had six bands of lace on the sleeves, one around the cuffs and two around the pockets, down the front of the coat, and around the lower edge of the coat, according to the official regulations. Buttons were usually in the regimental colour. There was also some silver lace on the waistcoat, usually just down the front edge.

The *piffero*'s coat was additionally adorned with nine 'flames' of the livery lace on the front of the coat and a swallow's nest of flames. The hautboy's coats had only five flames – placed from the top, one, two and two on the front of the coat– and the swallow's nest. The coats of the *pifferi* and hautboys did not have the lacing on their sleeves. But both had a narrow silver-white lace down their coat fronts and around their collar. This lace appears to have been stitched with diamonds in thin blue thread. The *tamburi*, *pifferi* and hautboys all carried swords or sabres. The *Guardie* regiment appears to have used a slightly different application of the lace, in particular for the *pifferi*.

By 1745, each regiment now had a *tamburo maggiore*; their coats were similar to the *tamburi*, but with more lace embellishments and the rank distinctions of *sergenti*. Their cuffs were probably made of cheap velvet (*Panne*), and their coats were usually made of a better-quality scarlet cloth. The *tamburo maggiori* had a mace and carried a sword.

The regulations were quite strict and in 1739, when the *La Marina* regiment was inspected and their drummers were found to be wearing green coats faced red, the reaction was immediate from the Minister and within a couple of months they were back in the regulation king's livery.

The musicians were usually civilian domestics paid by the regiment and or the *colonnello*, but only the *tamburi*, *pifferi*, *timballieri* and *trombetti* were purely military personnel. The drummers and fifers were usually the most literate men in the company and as such frequently handled the correspondence, both official and private, and as such were used as messengers, their livery showed to all who was their master.

The military drums used in the 1740 to 1750 period were large and made of a wooden case, usually birch wood, rolled, glued and nailed, with wooden hoops used to stretch the skins. They had a diameter of around 43cm by 42cm high, including the hoops. The skins were usually of calf or goatskin. They had one or two cat gut 'timbres' stretched over the lower head and a small hole drilled out on one side for resonance. They were carried on a soft buff leather shoulder belt, usually covered with livery lace. The belt ended with two brass plates joined by a ring, which supported an 'S' hook by which the drum was suspended.

In the majority of national and provincial regiments the drum cases were usually painted red and decorated with the white cross of Savoy (although a few regiments had their own variations and where known they are noted) and the crowned royal or provincial arms, or sometimes with an anchor if they had a maritime connection.

The *tamburi* in the foreign regiments did not have to follow the same regulations and were dressed as the *colonnello* saw fit, usually in his livery, although sometimes this consisted of no more than some extra lacing on the same coats as the rest of the regiment. Unfortunately, the details of many of these private liveries are now lost. Their drum cases were also decorated at the *colonnello*'s whim, with the crowned arms of the owner of the regiment, framed by trophies, or with flames in the cantonal colours, but there is a contemporary print of a foreign regiment with a drum painted as that of a Piedmontese regiment. They will be described separately.

On the back the drums would probably have had the name of the company's *capitano*. The rims could be red, blue which appears to correspond to their uniform facing colour (but this cannot be known for certain) or plain wood. There are two contemporary (French) drums with unpainted hoops, so they may have become worn easily. The *tamburo*'s leather drum carrying bandoleers were usually covered in red or blue cloth and the regimental livery lace. The drums of the German and Swiss regiments, as well as some of the Piedmontese regiments, had the drum cases painted with flames. They may also have had the *colonnello*'s arms painted on them, or in the case of the Swiss regiments, their cantonal arms.

Pifferi, present in most regiments, carried their fifes in cases made up of two or three wooden tubes which had brass stoppers top and bottom. They were carried on a shoulder cord, generally in the livery colours. This would probably only concern the German and Swiss regiments, although one painting shows what appears to be a simple rounded wooden case painted blue. By 1750 the tubular fife cases were made of brass for all regiments.

There are some references to regimental bands in the 1750's and judging by the text it appears they were already around during period in question, there are even some references to dragoon bands. The *regimento del Guardie* had had a band from the beginning of this period and the *Piemonte* infantry regiment was authorised to raise one in 1737.

The most common woodwind instruments in use by the regimental musicians, after the fife were the hautboys (a form of oboe). The regiments of *Piemonte*, *Saluzzo*, *Monferrato* and *Fucilieri* each had four *oboista* using hautboys, as well as four *cornisti* as well. These brass horns appear to have been a smaller version of the French hunting horn.

Infantry *tamburi* and *pifferi*. This is the basic lacing for the *tamburo maggiori*, *tamburi*, *pifferi* and Hautboy. As the 1741 regulations only describe the *Reggimento di Savoia*, other possible regimental variations have been shown, accounting for button colour and pocket shape. These are interpretations based on the adaptions of the French royal lace of which we have a little more information. The *Guardie* regiment is shown in another plate as the pocket lace is somewhat different. 1. *Tamburo, Reggimento Provinciale di Asti*. 2. *Piffero, Reggimento Nationale di Piemonte*. 3. *Tamburo, Reggimento Provinciale di Torino*. 4. *Oboista, Reggimento Nationale di Monferrato*. 5. *Tamburo maggiore, Reggimento Nationale di Saluzzo*. 6. *Tamburo, Reggimento Nationale di Savoia*. (Author's Illustration)

Arms and Equipment

The official distribution of arms was as follows: *Fucilieri* – fusil and bayonet only, bu the fusiliers of the regiments *Guardie* and *Bourgsdorff* carried a sword as well as the fusil and bayonet; *Caporali di fuciliere* – fusil, bayonet and sword, and in some regiments a hatchet as well; *Sergenti di fuciliere* – partisan and sword; *Granatieri* and *caporali di granatiere* – fusil, bayonet, sabre and hatchet; *Sergenti di granatiere* – fusil, bayonet and sabre (hatchet not specified) – some grenadier *sergenti* carried a partisan and sabre, rather than a musket, but this may only have concerned certain regiments, for example the *Guardie*; *Tamburi* and musicians – a sabre; *Ufficiale di Fuciliere* (fuslier officers) – sword and spontoon.

The Sardinian tactical doctrine was based upon firepower, so from October 1743, all NCOs and junior officers up to *capitani* were to be armed with muskets. After the war the NCOs again carried their partisans.

The principal firearm during the war was the Piedmontese made model M 1730 fusil, this was the principal weapon of the army – some 67,000 were made – it was somewhat inferior to the French fusil, which was considered by all as vastly superior weapon. The M 1730 fusil had a calibre of 13.5mm, barrel length 120cm and overall length 160cm and weighed 4.6kg.

To supplement the lack of quality firearms, the Piedmontese acquired a quantity of the French model M 1728 fusil (calibre 17.5 mm), of which some 10,000 were bought in 1736 together with another 7,000 which were acquired indirectly.

This resulted in the Piedmontese redesigning their fusil which was issued as the model M 1730/1745, but only some 12,000 had been produced by the end of the war. There was another model in circulation, and this was known as the 1727 'German' model. They also acquired some Spanish and Austrian fusils as well as a number of other muskets which were captured from Modena.

With all these different weapons in circulation, supplying the regiments with the correct ammunition became a nightmare, so much so that some regiments had to be rearmed so that at least all the regiment had muskets of the same calibre. This happened to the regiments of *Schulemburg*, *Rietmann* and *Guibert* in 1742. The cartridges weighed 15.37g. The muskets recoil was extremely violent, and the soldiers, being more worried about the excessive kickback of the weapon, placed less emphasis on actually aiming it.

After the adoption of *Lugotenente Generale* Seyssel d'Aix's new firing drill in 1744, taken from his drill book written in the previous year, a new cartridge with a charge reduced to 11.5g was tested. The experiences on the battlefield confirmed the increased accuracy of the new ammunition. This amendment was officially authorised on 2 February 1746. After experimenting in the 1730's, metal ramrods were finally issued from 1742, firstly to the *Fucilieri* regiment, but the changeover had not been completed before the end of the war, so some regiments continued to use wooden ramrods for the duration of the conflict. Other regiments known to have received the new steel ramrods were *Guardie*, *Savoye* and *Monferrato*. The provincial regiments probably received them last.

The bayonet was of the usual triangular form, carried in a leather sheath – early illustrations show them as brown-buff, later illustrations show them as black. The metallic chapes were brass, later replaced with steel. They were suspended from a frog stitched to the waist belt.

Cartridges were carried in a black leather cartridge case called '*gibassiera*' suspended on a buff leather shoulder belt which had an oval brass buckle with two prongs. The flap of the cartridge box had a thin crimson red leather border stitched around the edge. Inside was a block of wood, drilled out for 24 cartridges. The bandoleer of the grenadiers' *gibassiera* still had a brass match case attached to it.

Sabres, carried by NCOs, musicians and grenadiers, were suspended on a buff leather waist belt which had an oval brass buckle with one prong. The fusilier and grenadier *corporale*'s belt had separate frogs for their bayonet and sabre on the same belt.

The fusiliers' swords had been officially withdrawn in 1741, but many regiments were slow to comply with the order and a couple of regiments were authorised to carry them throughout the war. They are not usually shown with sword knots – *dragona* – but they probably did have them. The *Bourgsdorff* regiment had a yellow wool sword knot in 1744.

The haversack (*abersacco*) was made of a heavy fabric like ticken, probably striped vertically blue and white, and served as a backpack. According to a contemporary painting by Jan Peter Verdussen they resembled the French model. They used a dried hollowed out gourd as a canteen and carried it on a cord or a thin leather strap.

For siege work, both for defence and attack, the infantry used military forks and some scythes, amongst other tools. They were probably carried in the baggage and doled out as and when needed.

Officers' Arms

Officers carried swords of better quality in the *mousquetaire* style, with brass hilts bound in gold, or brass-wired leather grips. These were frequently privately made and had an early model sword knot, in their regiment's button colour. The chiselled blades were frequently marked 'VIVE LE ROY DE SARDAIGNE'. Their length was 102.7cm. The swords were carried in a black leather scabbard with a brass locket and chape, which were sometimes gilded, suspended from buff leather waist belt, sometimes whitened, the borders of which were stitched with white thread (very much '*à la mode*') and which had a brass or gilded buckle. Some senior officers' swords were carried with suspension rings. Officers of regiments which had silver buttons sometimes had their sword hilts silvered. The officer's sword knots were to correspond with their sashes, but they are generally absent from contemporary iconography and again only regulated in 1750, but these regulations probably officialised current practice.

The spontoon (*mezza picca*) was carried by all field officers, even the senior officers, at least on official parades, as a sign of his rank. 'The spontoon was to be seven feet long; it will have a blade eight inches long, four inches of socket, a shaft five feet and nine inches long, made from ash wood, and three inches of ferrule, of one-inch diameter. They had two strips of steel, sufficiently thick and of six lines width, starting at the socket spreading over the wood to the length of eighteen inches, and will be pierced by six nails, the heads flattened and riveted, and weighed three pounds.'[4]

Those of the senior officers were mounted with a fringed tassel of silk and metallic lace and the blades could be finely engraved with the crowned eagle or regimental motifs. Those of the *Guardie* could possibly have had the king's monogram.

Although these spontoons were all of the same basic design as they were not yet regulated so there were a number of variants. The blade of the junior officers spontoons appear to be a little stubbier and more angular than those of *capitani* and above, theirs being more elongated and more rounded at the base and having a gold tassel around the neck of the blade in the Austrian style. All appear to have been engraved, usually with variations of the cross of Savoy, sometimes with a crown above it. Some blades appear to have been gilded.

From 1743, the junior grenadier officers carried a fusil and a ventral cartridge box, usually embossed with the crowned arms of Savoy and highlighted in gold leaf or embroidered.

NCOs' Arms

Officially the NCOs had had their halberds (*alabardine*) and partisans (*partigianetta*, generally called a *sergentina*), withdrawn in 1743 and they were to be replaced with fusils, but most illustrations, in particular those of the Swiss regiments, show them still in use. Possibly the halberds and partisans were carried in peace time, during training and parades, but fusils were taken on campaign, or quite simply the order was just not strictly obeyed. They are still shown in use after the Seven Years War. The fusilier *sergenti* usually carried their partisan on their right shoulder

Generally, these staff weapons were mounted on ash wood shafts of around 198cm long with a diameter of 27mm. The shafts were usually varnished, or oiled and polished. It is possible those of *Guardie* were painted. There were several different models in use with either national or regimental particularities. The Piedmontese regiments used a model based on the French *sergente*'s partisan, except the *Fucilieri* regiment who had their own specific model.

There were specific models for the Swiss regiments and a couple of models for the German regiments, one of which had a circular blade and a rounded hook – these were all closer to stylised halberds. According to regulations grenadier *sergenti* carried a halberd or partisan in peacetime, but on campaign they carried a musket and bayonet.

The *sergenti*'s swords (*spada*) had a single branched brass hilt carried in a black leather scabbard which had a brass chape, neck and stud, but there are indications that on occasion their sword was replaced with a grenadier's sabre.

According to a document dated 1741, the *caporali* of the fusilier companies are said to have carried an axe like the grenadiers with a sheath on the rear of their bandoleer. The grenadier *sergenti* carried a large cartridge box on a bandoleer, similar to the grenadiers. It was edged with regimental coloured metallic lace, as was the bandoleer. In the centre there was a large brass grenade bearing the crowned arms of Savoy. This model continued to be used until 1751.

The fusilier *sergenti* of the *Guardie* regiment also appear to have carried a large cartridge box on a bandoleer, similar to the grenadiers' grenade satchel, with extra cartridges for the company. It was edged with company coloured metallic lace as was the bandoleer. The other regiments appeared to have done the same The *sergenti* of the *Guardie* regiment had both their bandoleers and waist belts edged with gold lace. The fusilier *sergenti* of *Guardie* carried cartridge boxes stamped with the crowned arms of Savoy, decorated in gold leaf with extra cartridges for the troop alongside their partisan.

Infantry Colours

Each regiment was to carry a *colonnello*'s colour and a company or ordnance colour in the first battalion, the subsequent battalions of the regiment had only one company or ordnance colour. The number of company or ordnance colours appears to variable in the foreign units, in fact the same situation as in France. They also had a colonels colour.

4 E. Ricchiardi, *Il Costume Militare Sabaudo, Carlo Emanuele III 1730-1773* (Torino, Ed. Lucchetti, 2000), vol.1, p.63.

Regimmento delle Guardie. 1. *Capitano.*2. *Sergente di Fuciliere.* 3. *Fuciliere.* 4. *Sergente di Granatiere.* 5. *Granatiere.* 6. *Tamburo di Fuciliere.* (Author's Illustration)

We are very fortunate that the Sabaudian's kept a careful record of their colours and standards. The collection of Gaetano Ozelletti, who made several albums: one dated to 1740, dedicated to the Baron Rehbinder (cavalry and dragoons) is conserved in the Biblioteca Reale de Turin; an album dated 1744 (cavalry and dragoons) is conserved in the State Archives of Turin; an album dedicated to S.M. Charles Emanuel in 1745 (cavalry and dragoons) is also conserved in the Biblioteca Reale de Turin; and a second album was made in 1745 and was dedicated to the Roy de Sardaigne. An anonymous album dated 1747 (infantry, cavalry and dragoons) also shows all the uniforms, if somewhat crudely. An album dated to 1734/1736 (infantry colours) made by the tapestry maker Nicolas Lauro gives us an insight to the previous patterns, many of which would still have been in use at the start of the war.

A few original colours have also been conserved, which is quite helpful as this gives some idea how the patterns were actually applied. Chronologically, the regiments received a stand of colours in 1736, this stand was replaced around 1744 with new designs. Another new stand was issued about three years later with a few modifications, mainly the colour of the sleeve and stave. In 1750, another new stand of colours was issued, in which only those of the provincial and some foreign regiments show any changes.

It is interesting to note that although the *colonnelli* received official patterns for their colours; it was they who then contracted them out to local manufacturers. It was these craftsmen and painters who then interpreted the official model; the result was that, although they respected the general patterns, their interpretations could vary somewhat.

Another detail is that some regiments, particularly in the provincial regiments continued to carry ancient colours dating back to the previous 1736 patterns, because they had not received the new model, or simply to preserve their new ones.

The official dimensions of the flags were around 2.2m by 2.2m, with all the usual variations of the period. The fabric to be used was either silk or '*Samit*'. To try to stop the flags tearing and fraying, a band of white or coloured tape or binding (*bindello*) was stitched around the edges of the flag to protect it. The interior of the sleeve was then reinforced with canvas and around the sheath was a reinforcing band of coloured velvet cloth. The various pieces of cloth were stitched together using a method generally called '*couture à l'anglaise*' (English stitch) which is our equivalent of a lapped or tucked seam.

Generally, an ordinary colour was composed of seven pieces of fabric (for a provincial or national regiment) – one piece of dyed fabric for each quarter and three pieces for the cross (one traverse and two vertical pieces) – but there could be more pieces depending on the complexity of flags using more than one colour for the quarters. All other details were painted on with oil paint.

Although the contemporary albums of colours show variations of the patterns flames etcetera in each quarter, in reality they would have been fairly symmetrical as the artisans generally only cut one set of master cutting patterns which were then used for each quarter.

The cloth was nailed to the stave, which was made of ash or lime wood with up to 500 small gilt nails, or rather tacks, applied in vertical rising spiral lines, after an old tradition. They were still using this method at the end of the Napoleonic wars, although some other sources show the nails placed in straight lines.

The staves appear to have been painted but judging from the contracts they were supposed to have been covered with velvet until 1773. According to some contracts they were supposed to be blue for all of the *colonnello*'s colours and for the ordnance colours of the regiments of the *Guardie*, of *Montferrat*, of artillery and *Kalbermatten*, and red for all other ordnance colours. But the 1744 and 1747 manuscripts show different colours.

The finial (*freccia*) and the ferrule (*calciolo*) were made of steel and were originally shown as such but would have been varnished or silvered to avoid rusting. But by 1744 they appear to have been gilded. The finial had the form of an elongated laurel leaf, and some may have been engraved or stamped with the armorials of the regiment or a simple cross of Savoy. But as they were not regulated before 1773 there were probably a number of variants. There are a couple of references of finials pierced with either the king's monogram or another design, but these were probably for cavalry standards.

A silk cord and tassels were looped around the finial. Generally, they were made of woven gold silk thread, but again, there were a number of variants.

In line of battle, the colours were carried in the centre of the first battalion in front of the fifth company of fusiliers; the *colonnello*'s colour was carried by the *alfiere* of the first company and the ordnance colour by the *alfiere* of the second company. The second, third and fourth battalions if they had them, carried two ordnance colours.

The colours were only unfurled for parades or before the enemy, at other times they were rolled and preserved in blue and white striped ticken cloth bags which in turn were inserted into a black varnished and oiled waterproof canvas cover. On the march the rolled colours were carried by the senior NCOs.

Between 1730s and 1744 when new colours began to be issued there were some minor and some major changes made to them. It is highly probable that both versions could be found side-by-side as the new ones arrived and the older ones were not yet retired at the beginning of the war. Again in 1747, when colours appear to have been replaced, presumably to replace those lost or damaged, there appear to have been yet more minor changes.

Another particularity was that the *colonnello*'s colour was to be the same for all the infantry regiments except for the *Guardie* regiment, who had their own special model. On the obverse, a dark blue field with a black eagle with beak and claws, or displayed looking left, with an oval shield with a gold border bearing the arms of Savoy, gules, a cross argent under a large gold crown with white pearls and a red cap. The reverse is the same except that the eagle is looking right. The standard had a thin white border all around, including the stave edge. The eagle takes up most of the surface of the colour.

Two of these models have been conserved; one in the Armeria Reale di Torino and one in the National Museum of Switzerland.[5] There was a third one in the Zeughaus in Berlin before the Second World War, which is now believed to have been lost.

Despite what the official pattern books prescribed, it is quite possible that older colours continued to be carried for some time. Apart from the albums there are only two existing fragments of the previous model one in the museum of Neuchatel – the eagle of the regiment *Dupasquier*, circa 1734 – and a one belonging to the *Regimento di Saluzzo*, dating to around the same time. The principal difference of this model was that the eagle was placed on a scroll or shield with a baroque border or frame. Obviously with different artists at different times there would probably have been a number of variations.

The sleeve was blue, and the stave was red, studded with brass nails in a spiral design. The spear shaped finial was gilded as was the cone shaped butt which was secured with a ring. The cords and tassels were gold or blue and gold. Obviously, as all the colours were not all decorated by the same artisans there were variations in the form of the eagle as well as the form of the baroque shield bearing the arms of Savoy.

The price of these colours was quite varied, from 112 Piedmontese *livres* up to 170 *livres*.

5 This colour is very interesting, as on each point of the cross there are what appears to be a church or cathedral incrusted into the frame. If these churches could be identified it could give a clue as to which regiment, it originally belonged to. The church at the top and bottom of the cross is different to the one on either side of the cross. The church on the sides could be that of Lucerne.

6

The National Ordnance Foot Regiments

The regiments are listed in order of precedence.

Reggimento Nazionale delle Guardie

This regiment was first raised in 1659. In 1740 the regiment was two battalions strong, consisting of 1,200 officers and men, by 1743 the number of officers and men had risen to 1,400, and by 1747 the numbers had risen again to 1,690. The regiment was reduced in 1748. Although this regiment was called 'Guard' they were not part of the Household troops, but they were an elite line foot regiment and they were classed as a National Ordnance Infantry Regiment. They also had an official band of six musicians who played Hautboys (Oboes).

This regiment was nominally commanded by the King. The *colonnello luogotenente* of the *Guardie* under Charles Emmanuel III were, from 1731 Chevalier Carlo Giuseppe Ignazio Asinari di Mombercelli, who was succeeded by Giuseppe Ottavio Cacherano Osasco, Conte della Rocca Marchese di Lanzo, in 1744.

Service

In 1742, the *Guardie* regiment was in north-east Italy in the Plains of the Po, at the Siege of Modena, and the Siege of Mirandola.[1] In September the regiment marched to the Alps; they camped at La Thule in Aosta Valley. The regiment fought in Savoy during the counter-offensive against the invading Spanish army.

In January 1743 the *Guardie* returned to Piedmont and regiment waited for the main Franco -Spanish invasion of Piedmont beneath the shadows of the Monviso in the Varaita valley. The regiment fought a bitter combat against an enemy column in the mountains around Casteldelfino on 8 October.

Guardie, colonello's colour. This is the author's reconstruction. It is important to note that certain armouries have been altered and now display the correct blazons. The corrections are based on a contemporary official document and the near contemporary illustration in the *Encyclopaedia* by Diderot and Alembert. The craftsmen may not have rectified these errors when the colour was actually made, but it is hard to imagine that the *colonnello*, the King, and his officials would have let this pass as it is on the verge of an act of '*lèse-majesté*'. (Author's Illustration)

The following year *Guardie* fought at the redoubt of Mount Cavallo (19 July 1744). During the Battle of Pietralunga, one of the toughest encounters of the war, the lucky second battalion lost only 36 men. The regiment was present at Madonna dell'Olmo (30 September 1744). The two battalions were placed on the right wing, in the front line.

In 1745, the Piedmontese had no chance of stopping de Maillebois' offensive. At the Battle of Bassignana (27 September) *Guardie* was in the right wing of Sardinian line. The following year they were at the front of Leutrum's

1 The Siege of Mirandola in 1742 was a siege that took place during the War of the Austrian Succession between the Spanish army (occupiers of the city since 1735) who were besieged by the Piedmontese army of the Kingdom of Sardinia led by Charles Emmanuel III of Savoy, together with the Austrian troops of Count Otto Ferdinand von Traun. Mario Longhena, Encylopedia Italiana Mirandola (Roma:Treccani,1938).

counter offensive and the regiment fought beneath the walls of the city of Valenza (17 April–3 May 1746).

Then the two battalions marched to the south-west – the Mediterranean theatre. The first battalion fought during the offensive in Provence. The second battalion was employed at the siege of the fortress of Priamar in Savona (1 December–18 December 1746) and at the Siege of Genoa, where on 21 May 1747, with the *Piemonte* regiment, they fought off an enemy attack at Madonna della Misericordia. They then left the siege to defend the southern frontiers of Piedmont.

The first battalion, after their adventure into Provence, were recalled to Piedmont and marched up to the Alps to confront a French army which was crossing the border at Montgenèvre into Suze valley. This battalion held the centre of the Austro-Piedmontese front alone at the Assietta ridge (19 July 1747) where at the head of the Assietta, they stood firm and repulsed all of the French assaults.

Uniforms

The colour of their lace was originally silver/white, but was changed to gold around 1739 and reverted to silver in 1750. The fusilier companies wore a black tricorn with a Savoy blue cockade on the left brim with a black loop and a brass button and yellow lace border.

They wore a dark blue coat with button holes stitched with yellow *bave*; the coat had seven brass buttons on each side of the coat, three on the cuffs. The coat had horizontal pockets, each with three buttons and the button holes stitched with yellow *bave*, the cuffs were red with the button holes stitched with yellow *bave*, red linings and turn backs. The men wore red neck stocks, but are shown with black neck stocks in 1747. Their waistcoat was red with the button holes stitched with yellow *bave* down both sides of the front of the coat on the pockets. Their breeches were red.

In a contemporary illustration dating to 1744, the red of the cuffs, waistcoat and breeches is shown in a bright scarlet-orange colour and the linings and turn backs are shown in a deeper crimson red hue. This contemporary illustration also shows 10 buttons on the coat.

When they were not on campaign, they all wore white stockings. Exceptionally, all the fusiliers of this regiment continued to carry swords, while the grenadiers carried sabres.

Grenadiers

In the grenadier company, all the ranks wore the bearskin cap, including the officers and the musicians. The bearskin cap had a red bag with yellow lacing and a yellow hanging tassel.

NCOs

The NCOs are shown with imitation gold lace on their tricorn and on the edges of their belts and around the border of their cartridge box which had a plate embossed with the arms of Savoy in brass, possibly gilded. Their button holes were stitched with gold thread. Their rank galloon was gold. The grenadier NCOs bearskin cap had a red bag with gold lacing and a gold hanging tassel.

Officers

The officers had gold lace and gilt buttons on their hats. The officers' coats had gold lace and gilt buttons. Their bearskin cap worn in the grenadier company had a scarlet red bag with gold lacing and a gold hanging tassel. The grenadier *capitano* carried a sword, not a sabre.

Tamburi and Pifferi

The *tamburi* and *pifferi* wore the Royal Livery coat and a red waistcoat with yellow stitched button holes down the front and on the pockets, and the breeches were red for the *tamburi*.

The lace on the *tamburi*, *pifferi* and musicians' coats was different to the other regiments. The colour of the coats worn by the all the various musicians was different to those of the men and it was called '*Scarlatta d'Ormea*'. The grenadier *tamburi* and *pifferi* wore bearskins as well.

Colonnello's Colour

The *colonnello*'s colour of around 1744 had the crowned arms of Charles Emmanuel III King of Sardinia, Duke of Savoy, Duke of Chablais and Prince of Piedmont, on a dark blue field. The standard had a thin white border all around, including the stave edge. Both the obverse and reverse were identical. The sleeve was blue, and the stave was covered in red velvet with brass headed studs nailed in a spiral design. In 1747 the sleeve is shown as red. The gilded finial was shaped like a pike head. The brass or gilded steel ferrule was round in shape and with a ball on the tip. The cords and tassels were gold, or gold and blue mixed.

Company Colours

In 1744 the colours were crimson red with a large central white cross. They had a large blue border. This border was decorated with an undulating white ribbon, rounded at all four corners. The outer edge was blue and the internal edge, probably wrongly, was shown as white. In 1736 the quarters were, one and four blue, two and three crimson. The border was red and the frieze was blue, red and white. Each of the four quarters were charged diagonally with the crowned monogram of Charles Emmanuel III. The obverse and reverse were identical. The standard had a thin white border all around, including the stave edge. The sleeve was blue and the staff was painted red and studded with brass nails in a spiral design. In 1747 the sleeve is shown as red. The spear shaped finial was gilded as was the cone shaped ferrule which was secured with a ring. The cords and tassels were gold.

Company colour, *Reggimento delle Guardie*. This colour has been redrawn and corrected and the inside blue band has been added. In the original album it has been drawn, but not coloured. Also, the symmetry has been corrected. (Author's Illustration)

The standard version of the *colonnello*'s colour as used by all foot regiments, but there were probably some variations between different manufacturers. (Author's Illustration)

Reggimento Nazionale di Savoia

The *Reggimento Nazionale di Savoia* was first raised in 1664 from existing units. In 1740 the regiment consisted of 1,200 officers and men in two battalions. Their strength rose to 1,400 officers and men in 1743. This was a French speaking regiment, and even after Savoy had been overrun, they still recruited French speaking men.

The *colonnelli* of the regiment under Charles Emmanuel III were Charles Philibert, Baron de Verger 1734, who was killed in action at the Battle of Pietralunga (19 July 1744). He was succeeded Charles Ludovic, Baron of Chabeau (Chabaud) 1744, who in turn was succeeded by Janus, Count of Eutremon (Entremont) in 1748.

Service

The *Savoia* began the war in the spring of 1742 by marching along the Via Emilia, in order to occupy Parma and Piacenza, driving off a Spanish army. In 1743 the regiment won honour at the Battle of Camposanto (8 February) when, in coordination with *Piemont* and *Rhebinder*, it attacked the Spanish line, breaking the right wing. A Spanish battalion, the first battalion of the *Guadalaxara* regiment, with its line of retreat cut off, took up a position in a farm near Camposanto. *Savoia*, led by *Luogotenente Colonnello* Baron de Chabeau and supported by the artillery, overran the Spanish unit taking three colours (one of which is still preserved at the Armeria Reale in Turin) and 410 prisoners.

During the combined '*Gallispan*' offensive in the Alpine theatre at Pontechianale in the Varaita valley on 8 October 1743, *Savoia* confronted Anjou's brigade. In 1744 the regiment had one of its toughest days, again in the Alps, and again in Varaita valley, during the Battle of Pietralunga, in a vicious struggle around the redoubt of Mount Cavallo (19 July). The first battalion lost 154 men and its *colonnello*, Charles Filibert du Verger. At the Battle of Madonna dell'Olmo (30 September) both battalions were reunited and they formed up on the left wing. The following year, de Maillebois' offensive crushed Charles Emmanuel III's strategic defence plan.

At the Battle of Bassignana, the regiment was on the right wing, but they were compelled to retreat with the rest of the Piedmontese army.

In 1746 *Savoia* played an important role during Baron Leutrum's counter offensive, especially at the second Siege of Valenza (17 April–May 3). During the same year they fought at the Siege of Priamar, a fortress in Savona (1–18 December). The second battalion eventually took position in Ligurian theatre until the end of the war, while the first battalion was in the Alps in 1747 and were in reserve on the ridge of the Assietta during the battle (19 July).

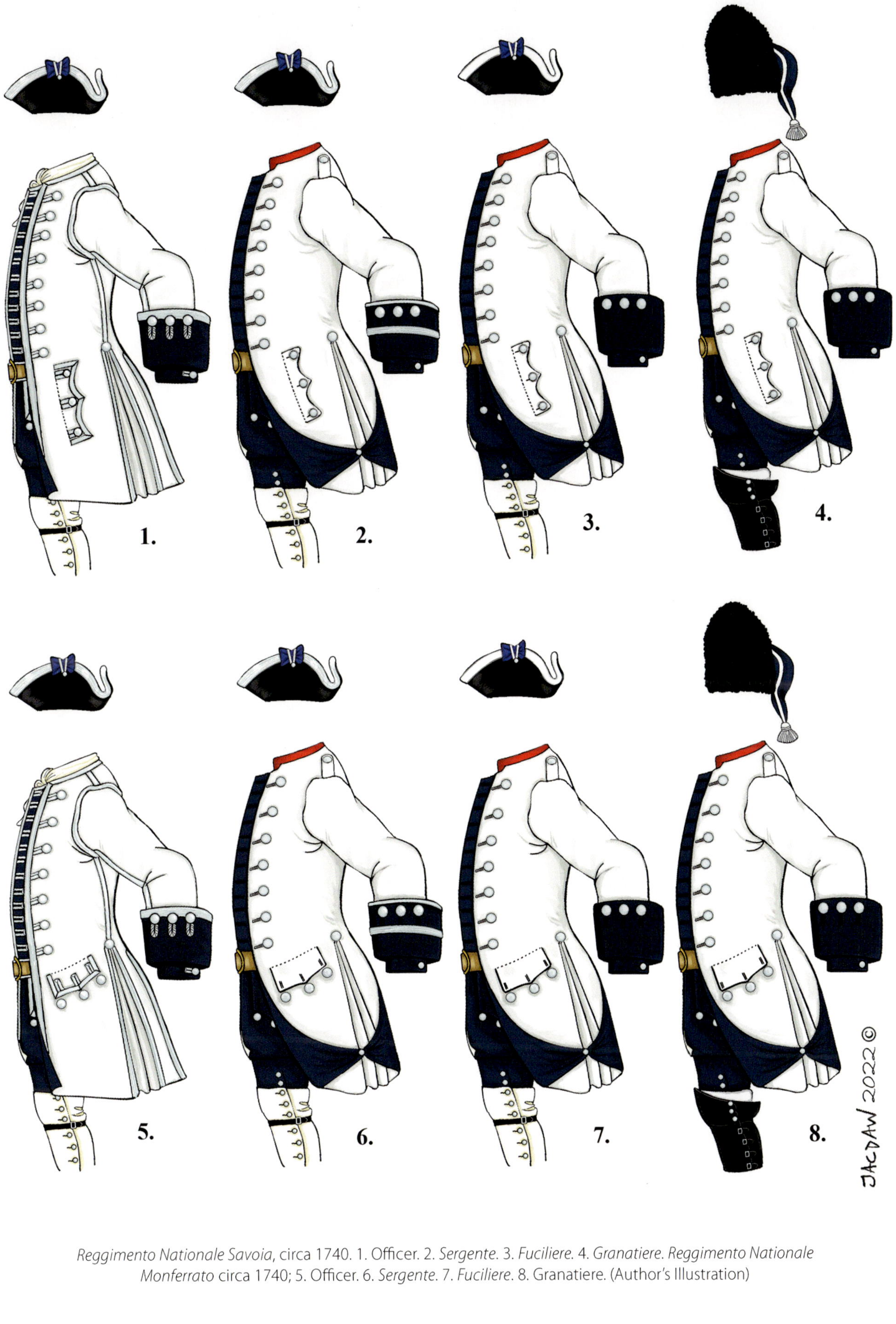

Reggimento Nationale Savoia, circa 1740. 1. Officer. 2. *Sergente*. 3. *Fuciliere*. 4. *Granatiere*. *Reggimento Nationale Monferrato* circa 1740; 5. Officer. 6. *Sergente*. 7. *Fuciliere*. 8. Granatiere. (Author's Illustration)

Uniforms

The fusilier companies wore a black tricorn with a Savoy blue cockade on the left brim with a black loop and a pewter button and white lace border. They wore red cravats and a greyish-white collarless coat. The coat had eight evenly spaced pewter buttons on each side of the coat, with three on the cuffs. The coat had vertical pockets, each with three buttons. The cuffs, linings and turn backs were blue. Their waistcoats were blue lined with white and their breeches were blue. When they were not on campaign, they all wore white stockings.

Grenadiers

The Grenadiers had a bearskin cap had a blue bag with white lacing and a white hanging tassel.

NCOs

The NCOs button holes were stitched with white *bave* and their galloons were imitation silver as was their hat lace. In the grenadier company the NCOs wore the bearskin cap; it had a blue bag with imitation silver lacing and an imitation silver hanging tassel.

Officers

The officers' tricorn had silver lace border and loop a Savoy blue cockade and silver button on their hats. The officers' coats and waistcoats had silver lacing. The officers' bearskin cap had a blue bag with silver lacing and a silver hanging tassel.

Tamburi and Pifferi

The *tamburi, pifferi* and musicians wore the Royal Livery with blue waistcoats and breeches. The grenadier *tamburi* and *pifferi* wore bearskins as well.

Colonnello's Colour

On the obverse, a dark blue field with a black eagle with beak and claws or displayed looking left with an oval shield with a gold border bearing the arms of Savoy, gules, a cross argent on his breast under a large gold crown with white pearls and a red cap. The reverse was the same except that the eagle was looking right. The standard had a thin white border all around the standard, including the stave edge. The sleeve was blue and the stave was painted red and studded with brass nails in a spiral design. The spear shaped finial was gilded as was the cone shaped ferrule which was secured with a ring. The cords and tassels were gold.

Unless otherwise stated, the *Colonello's* colour of the rest of the foot regiments followed this pattern.

Company Colours

Obverse, on a red field there was a white cross. In each quarter, emanating from the angle of the cross were four flames in different combinations of blue, white and red. In the first quarter positioned on the central white flame a gold crowned shield bearing the quartered arms of Savoy and a double headed eagle. The obverse and reverse were identical in mirror image.

The reverse was the same except that the eagle was looking right. The standard had a thin white border all around, including the stave edge. The sleeve was blue, and the stave was painted red and studded with brass nails in a spiral design. The spear shaped finial was gilded as was the cone shaped ferrule which was secured with a ring. The cords and tassels were gold.

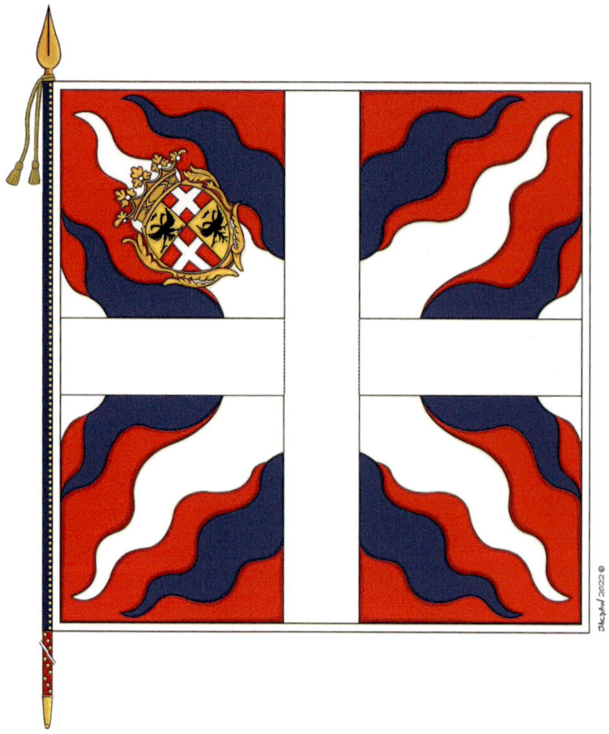

Company colour, *Nationale Infantry Regiment Savoia.* (Author's Illustration)

Reggimento Nazionale di Monferrato

The *Reggimento Nazionale di Monferrato* was first raised in 1619 as *Cheynez*, this was changed to *di Livorno* in 1649 and they were again renamed to *Monferrato* in 1664. The regiment's establishment was 1,200 officers and men, in two battalions, in 1740. This rose to 1,400 officers and men in 1743, and by 1747 it had risen again to 1,600.

The *colonnelli* of the regiment under Charles Emmanuel III, were, from 1739 Giovanni Amedeo Capris di Ciglié who was succeeded by Giovanni Francesco Pallavicino di St Etienne in 1744, who in turn was succeeded by Giuseppe Alciati in 1746. Carlo Maurizio Maria Costa d'Ariagnano became *colonnello* in 1748.

Service

The regiment started the war by marching in the direction of Parma and Piacenza. In 1742 *Monferrato* was transferred to the Alps. On 16 September the regiment was in camp at la Thuile and a few days later it was from here that the Piedmontese launched their counter offensive against Spanish forces invading Savoy. The struggle went on for 100 days.

In 1744 the regiment was again in the Alps, at Casteldelfino in the Varaita valley, to stop the Franco-Spanish offensive (24 September–10 October 1743).

The follow year the combined Franco-Spanish army broke through the Alpine front in the Stura valley. The second battalion fought in the defence of the city of Cuneo (9 September–22 October 1744). The first battalion was present in the relieving army and fought at the Battle of Madonna dell'Olmo (30 September 1744). The battalion was in the centre of the front line.

In 1745 at the Battle of Bassignana (27 September), where the Piedmontese were severely beaten, the regiment was probably on the right of Sardinian line, attached to Schulenburg's brigade. After this heavy defeat, the second battalion held the defences of Alessandria (6–11 October) and after the surrender of the city it defended the strong new fortress of the Citadel of Alessandria during de Maillebois's blockade (12 October 1745–11 March 1746). In 1746 the first battalion fought on the western front, during the offensive in Provence in November and the following year, around the port of Oneglia in the Ligurian theatre.

Uniforms

The fusilier companies wore a black tricorn with a Savoy blue cockade on the left brim with a black loop and a pewter button and white lace border. They wore a greyish-white coat without a collar. The coat had seven evenly spaced pewter buttons on each side of the coat and three on the cuffs. The coat had horizontal pockets, each with three buttons, and they had blue cuffs, linings and turn backs. The officers' coats had silver lace and buttons. The regiment wore red cravats. Their waistcoats were blue lined with white, as were their breeches. When they were not on campaign, they all wore white stockings.

Grenadiers

The grenadiers' bearskin caps had blue bags with white lacing and a white hanging tassel.

NCOs

In the grenadier company the NCOs wore the bearskin cap, it had a blue bag with imitation silver lacing and an imitation silver hanging tassel.

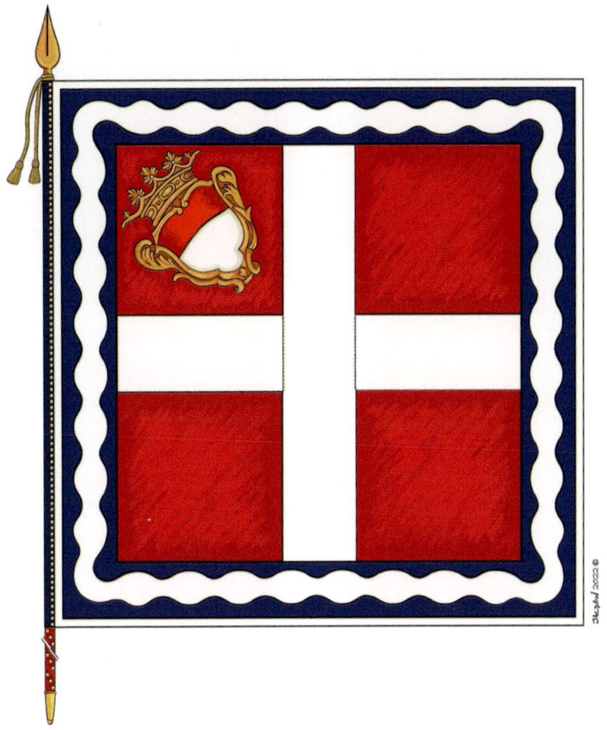

Company colour, *Reggimento Nazionale di Monferrato*. (Author's Illustration)

Officers

The officers' tricorns had silver lace border with a loop a Savoy blue cockade and silver button. The officers' coats and waistcoats had silver lacing. The officers' bearskin caps had blue bags with silver lacing and a silver hanging tassel.

Tamburi and Pifferi

The *tamburi*, *pifferi* and musicians wore the Royal Livery with blue waistcoats and breeches. The grenadier *tamburi* and *pifferi* wore bearskins.

Company Colours

Obverse, on a red field there was a white cross, with a large deep blue border all around. This border was charged with, in the centre a wavy white 'ribbon' all round, with rounded corners. In the first quarter there were the arms of Monferrato surrounded by a gold shield and topped with a gold Baroque ducal crown painted diagonally. The standard had a thin white border all around, including the stave edge. The reverse was identical in mirror image.

The sleeve was blue and the stave was painted red with brass headed studs nailed in a spiral design. The gilded finial is shaped like a pike. The brass ferrule is round in shape and with a ball at the tip. The cords and tassels were gold.

Reggimento Nazionale di Piemonte

The *Reggimento Nazionale di Piemonte* was first raised in 1636 as *Catalano Alfieri*, then renamed *Piedmontese di S.A.R.* in 1641, and then *Piemonte* in 1664. In 1740 the regiment consisted of 1,200 officers and men in two battalions. This rose to 1,400 officers and men in 1743, and by 1747 this had risen to 1,600 officers and men.

The *colonnelli* of the regiment under Charles Emmanuel III were, from 27 January 1734 Giacinto Antonio, Canale di Cumiana who was succeeded by Giovanni Battista Settimo, Chevalier and conte di Numaglio on 1 November 1745. He was in turn succeeded by G. Francesco Bonaventura Sesto on 4 May 1746 followed by Francesco Tana (Tommaso), Conte Palatino on 25 March 1747.

Service

The regiment had already been divided at the start of the war, the first battalion was in garrison in Modena and the second was soon in action on the Alps in Savoy. On 8 February 1743, the first battalion fought at the Battle of Camposanto. They were placed in the second line, alongside *Savoia* and *Rhebinder*. The first battalion broke through the Spanish front line on the right wing.

Both battalions of the regiment were present at Battle of Madonna dell'Olmo (30 September 1744). The two battalions were situated on the right wing, second line. During the struggle *Piemonte* retook a battery which had been captured by the enemy, after a tough combat with Lyonnais' and Stainville's brigades of the French army.

In 1745 they were at the Battle of Bassignana (27 September). The regiment was in the centre of the Sardinian line but due to a wrong movement on the left, the *Guibert* regiment became separated, and they were left on their own against the approaching Count de Dumontal's column and were badly mauled. After this sad affaire, *Piemonte* was sent to defend the walls of Valenza (20–30 October).

In 1746 the two battalions were again divided. The first battalion fought in the west, in the invasion of Provence and around the port of Oneglia. The second battalion was employed at the Siege of Genoa, where the on 21 May 1747 it helped fight off an enemy attack at Madonna della Misericordia.

Uniforms

The fusilier companies wore a black tricorn with a Savoy blue cockade on the left brim with a black loop and a pewter button, and white lace border. The regiment wore red cravats, but are shown with black in 1747.

The regiment wore a greyish-white coat without a collar; the coat had seven pewter buttons on each side of the coat, three on the cuffs. The coat had horizontal pockets, each with three buttons and had red cuffs, linings and turn backs. Their waistcoats were red as were their

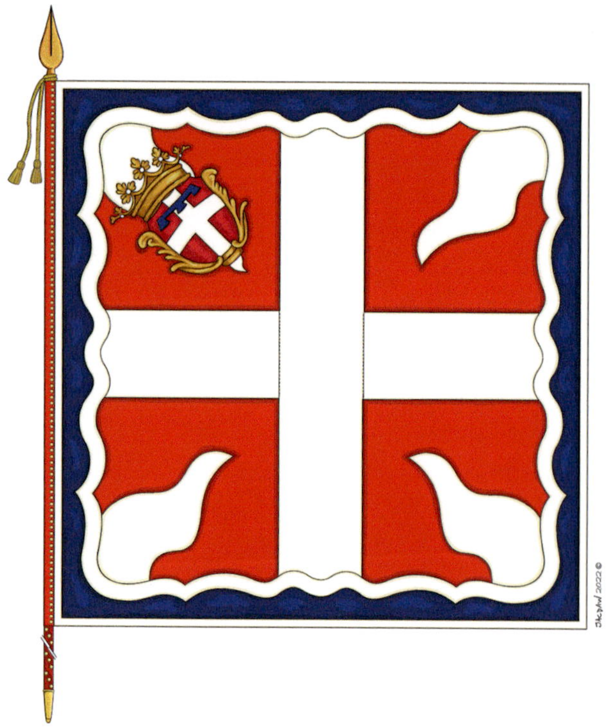

Company colour, *Reggimento Nazionale di Piemonte*. (Author's Illustration)

breeches. When they were not on campaign, they all wore white stockings.

Grenadiers

The grenadiers wore the bearskin cap which had a red bag with white lacing and a white hanging tassel.

NCOs

The NCOs tricorns had imitation silver hat lace and galloon. In the grenadier company, they wore the bearskin cap which had a red bag with imitation silver lacing and an imitation silver hanging tassel.

Officers

His tricorn had silver lace, loop and button with a blue cockade. The Officer's coats had silver lace and buttons. The Officer's in the Grenadier Company wore the bearskin cap which had a red bag with silver lacing and a silver hanging tassel.

Tamburi and Pifferi

The *tamburi, pifferi* and musicians wore the Royal Livery with red waistcoats and breeches. The grenadier *tamburi* and *pifferi* wore bearskins as well.

Company Colours

The company colour had a red field, with a white cross, with a large deep blue border all around. This border is charged with a wavy white 'ribbon' all round, with rounded corners. In the first quarter there were the arms of

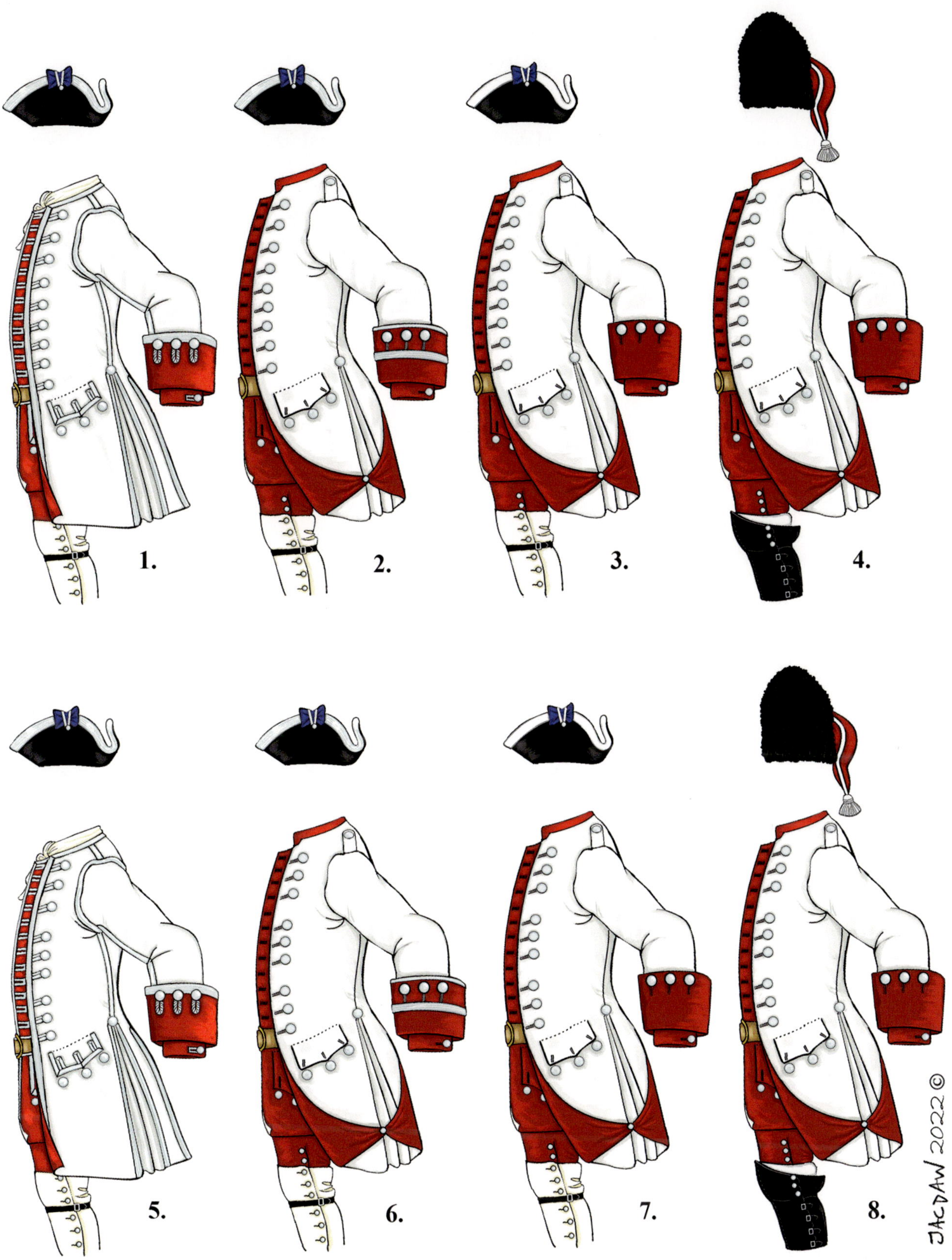

Reggimento Nazionale di Piemonte, circa 1740; 1. Officer. 2. *Sergente*. 3. *Fuciliere*. 4. *Granatiere*. *Reggimento Nazionale* Saluzzo circa 1740; 5. Officer. 6. *Sergente*. 7. *Fuciliere*. 8. *Granatiere*. (Author's Illustration)

Piemonte surrounded by a gold shield and topped with a gold Baroque ducal crown painted diagonally. In 1744 they were modified with the addition of a white flame on the red quarters pointing towards the centre. The standard had a thin white border all around, including the stave edge. The reverse was identical in mirror image. The sleeve was blue and the stave was painted red with brass headed studs nailed in a spiral design. The gilded finial was shaped like a pike. The brass ferrule is round in shape with a ball at the tip. The cords and tassels were gold.

Reggimento Nazionale di Saluzzo

The *Reggimento Nazionale di Saluzzo* were first raised in 1672 as *Lullino*, they were renamed *Bagnasco* in 1676, then *Masino* in 1678 and *Saluzzo* in 1680. In 1740 the regiment consisted of 1,200 officers and men in two battalions. This rose to 1,400 officers and men in 1743, and by 1747 this had risen to 1,600.

The *colonnelli* of the regiment under Charles Emmanuel III were Giuseppe Faletto di Castagnole, 1735–1744, who was wounded in action on 17 July 1744 and died shortly afterwards of his wounds. He was succeeded by Carlo Amedeo Isola from 13 August 1744 until 1747, when he was succeeded by Vincenzo Alessandro Ferrero, marchese d'Ormea.

Service

In 1742 *Saluzzo* was campaigning in the plains of the Po and in August they were in garrison in the Citadel of Parma. In 1743, in the mountains around Casteldelfino in the Varaita valley, the regiment fought to stop the Franco-Spanish offensive (7–10 October). The following year the regiment defended the port of Villefranche-sur-Mer. On 20 April 1744, the regiment's grenadiers fought hard during the bloody defence of the entrenched camp. The regiment defended Villefranche until 22 April 1744. The regiment fought at the redoubt of Mount Cavallo (19 July 1744). During this bloody combat, *Saluzzo* had only one battalion present, probably the first, who lost 98 men.

The regiment was present at the battle of Madonna dell'Olmo (30 September 1744). The two battalions were reunited and were placed in the centre of the second line. In 1745, Maillebois' offensive was no match for the Piedmontese army. At the battle of Bassignana (27 September) the regiment defended the village of Rivarone in vain. The following year they took part in the Leutrum's counter offensive. The two battalions fought together in the south-west, in the Mediterranean theatre. The second battalion was engaged during the offensive in Provence. The first battalion was present at the siege of fort Priamar in Savona (1–18 December 1746). The regiment was then reunited in 1747 to defend the southern frontiers of Piedmont.

Uniforms

The fusilier companies wore a black tricorn with a Savoy blue cockade on the left brim with a black loop and a pewter button and white lace border. The regiment wore red neck stocks, but are shown with black in 1747. The regiment wore a greyish-white coat without a collar; the coat had nine pewter buttons, grouped in threes, on each side of the coat, and six in two groups of three on the cuffs. The coat had horizontal pockets, each with three buttons and had red cuffs, linings and turn backs. Their waistcoats were red as were their breeches, the buttons were also grouped in threes. When they were not on campaign, they all wore white stockings.

Grenadiers

The grenadiers' bearskin cap had a red bag with white lacing and a white hanging tassel.

NCOs

In the grenadier company the NCOs wore the bearskin cap, it had a red bag with imitation silver lacing and an imitation silver hanging tassel.

Officers

The officers' tricorns had a silver lace border and loop, a Savoy blue cockade, and silver button. The officers had silver lacing on their coats and waistcoats. The officers' bearskin caps had a red bag with silver lacing and a silver hanging tassel.

Tamburi and Pifferi

The *tamburi*, *pifferi* and musicians wore the Royal Livery with red waistcoats and breeches. The grenadier *tamburi* and *pifferi* wore bearskins as well.

Company Colours

The company colours had a red field, a white cross, with a large red border all around. This border was charged in the centre with a wavy white 'ribbon' all round, with rounded corners. From 1747 the border became medium/light blue. In the first quarter there were the arms of the Marquis of Saluzzo surrounded by a gold shield and topped with a gold Baroque ducal crown painted diagonally. The standard had a thin white border all around, including the stave edge. The reverse was identical in mirror image. The sleeve was red and the shaft was painted red as well and it was studded with brass headed tacks nailed in a spiral design. The gilded finial was shaped like a pike. The brass ferrule is round in shape with a ball at the tip. The cords and tassels were gold.

Reggimento Nazionale Fucilieri

The *Reggimento Nazionale Fucilieri* were first raised in 1690. The regiment had originally been raised to escort and to support the artillery train and gunners on the battlefield (hence their fusiliers title), but it always acted as an elite infantry unit. In 1740 the regiment consisted of 1,200 officers and men in two battalions. This rose to 1,400 officers and men in 1743, and by 1747 this had risen to 1,600.

The *colonnelli* of the regiment under Charles Emmanuel III were Giovanni Giacomo de Rossi from 1743 to 1746, who was succeeded by Giovanni Andrea de Martini in 1746 and followed by Giovanni Secondo Canale di Cumiana in 1748.

Company colour, *Reggimento Nazionale di Saluzzo*, 1737–1744. (Author's Illustration)

Service

In 1742, the regiment was campaigning in north-east Italy, in the plain of the Po, and was present March to April in the cities of Parma and Piacenza. In September the regiment marched to the Alps from the camp at the pass of Mont Cenis in the Susa valley. The Regiment fought in Savoy during the counter-offensive against an invading Spanish army.

In January 1743, *Fucilieri* returned to Piedmont. After the debacle in Savoy, the operational theatre for the regiment was to be the Varaita valley, where the Franco-Spanish army had chosen to invade Piedmont. The first battalion fought at the Battle of Casteldelfino (8 October 1743).

Company colour, *Reggimento Nazionale di Saluzzo*, from 1747. (Author's Illustration)

The following year, both battalions of the regiment were engaged in the hard-fought defence of the entrenched camp of Villefranche-sur-Mer (20-21 April 1744) on the Mediterranean front. During the defence of the Col of Villefranche, the regiment was surrounded with other units and was compelled to surrender with two batteries of cannons. During the summer, the they fought again in the Alps. The first battalion defended the walls of Cuneo during the Franco-Spanish siege (12 September–22 October 1744). The second battalion was present at the Battle of Madonna dell'Olmo (30 September 1744), and was situated on the right wing, in the first line. In 1745 the objective of de Maillebois' offensive was to eliminate or capture as many of the Piedmontese fortresses as possible.

The following year the regiment was one of the units employed in Baron Leutrum's counter offensive and the regiment fought an action under the walls of the city of Valenza (17 April–3 May 1746). Then the two battalions fought in the south-west, in the Mediterranean theatre. The second battalion fought at the siege of the Fort of St Paul in Vintemille (5–23 October 1745). The first battalion took part in the winter offensive on Provence (30 November 1745–3 February 1746). The regiment continued to fight in the Mediterranean theatre until the end of the war.

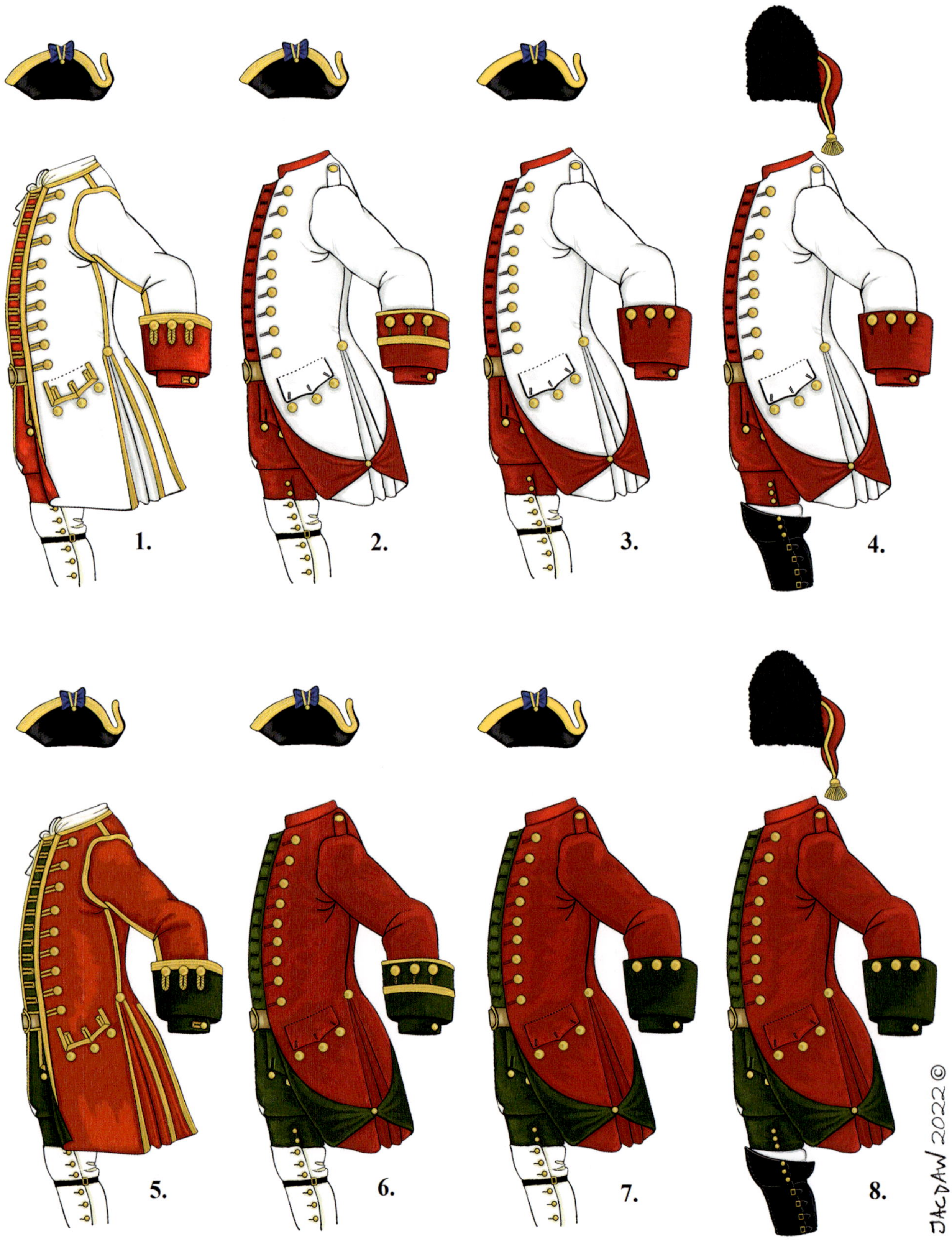

Reggimento Nazionale Fucilieri, circa 1740; 1. *Officer*. 2. *Sergente*. 3. *Fuciliere*. 4. *Granatiere*. *Reggimento Nazionale della Marina* circa 1740; 5. *Officer*. 6. *Sergente*. 7. *Fuciliere*. 8. *Granatiere*. (Author's Illustration)

Uniforms

The fusilier companies wore a black tricorn with a Savoy blue cockade on the left brim with a black loop, a brass button and yellow lace border. The regiment wore red neck stocks, but are shown with black neck stocks in 1747. They wore a greyish-white coat without a collar. The coat had seven brass buttons on each side of the coat, and three on the cuffs. The coat had horizontal pockets, each with three buttons, and had red cuffs, linings and turn backs. Their waistcoats were red, as were their breeches. When they were not on campaign, they all wore white stockings.

Grenadiers

The grenadiers wore the bearskin cap with a red bag with yellow lacing, and a yellow hanging tassel.

NCOs

The NCOs' tricorns had imitation gold hat lace and galloon. The NCOs carried a partisan of a model which was specific to this regiment; it had the form of a medieval pole arm. The grenadier NCOs wore the bearskin cap which had a red bag with imitation gold lacing and an imitation gold hanging tassel.

Officers

The officers' tricorn had gold lace, loop and button with a blue cockade. Their coats and waistcoats had gold lace and gilt buttons. The grenadier officers wore the bearskin cap which had a red bag with gold lacing and a gold hanging tassel.

Tamburi and Pifferi

The *tamburi*, *pifferi* and Musicians wore the Royal Livery with red waistcoats and breeches. The grenadier *tamburi* and *pifferi* wore bearskins as well.

Company Colours

The company colours had a white field, a white cross, with a large red border. This border is charged, in the centre with a wavy white 'ribbon' all round, with rounded corners. In each quarter are three red flames emanating from the inner angles of the cross. The colours were modified around 1744 by the addition of the arms of Saxe. The standard had a thin white border all around, including the stave edge. The reverse was identical in mirror image. The sleeve was red, and the stave was covered with crimson velvet and had brass headed studs nailed in a spiral design. The cords and tassels were gold. The gilded finial was shaped like a pike. The brass ferrule was round in shape and had a ball on the tip.

Company colour, *Reggimento Nazionale Fucilieri*. (Author's Illustration)

Reggimento Nazionale della Marina

The *Reggimento Nazionale della Marina* was first raised in 1701 as *Nizza II*, but became *della Marina* in 1714. In 1740 the regiment consisted of 600 officers and men in one battalion, but the number of effectives varied all though the war. This number of effectives was raised to 1,400 officers and men in two battalions in 1743. The first battalion had 10 companies, but the second had only five companies. By 1747 the total establishment had risen to 1,500. The regiment was closely associated with the town of Nice and the port of Villefranche-sur-Mer (Villafranca).

The *colonnelli* of the regiment under Charles Emmanuel III were Giovanni Giacomo de Rossi, from 1742 to 1743. He was succeeded by Giovanni Andrea Martini in 1743 and in 1746 by Chevalier Antonio Falletti, Conte della Morra until 1759.

Service

In 1742 the regiment was stationed in the plain of the river Po. In October they moved up to the Alps to face the Spanish offensive against the Savoy. They participated in the counter attacks, without success until early December and in January they withdrew into Piedmont. The regiment was quartered in the valley of Varaita. On 8 October, all the regiment was engaged at the Battle of Casteldelfino which stopped the Franco-Spanish (the *Gallispans* in local terms) offensive.

In 1744 the regiment found themselves in the region of Nice. In April they were attacked by the *Gallispans*, fighting around Villefranche-sur-Mer, on Mont Alban, and protecting the retreat of the garrison from the citadel Saint Elme. Following the fighting in July, the redoubt of Pietralonga was taken by the *Gallispans* and the Varaita valley was lost during a series of violent clashes. Legend has it that the streams ran red with blood. In September the French laid siege to Cuneo, the Sabaudian troops made a series of manoeuvres to lift the siege, and the regiment was part of that army. At the Battle of Madonna dell'Olmo, both battalions were placed in the centre of the front line and were again at the Battle of Bassignana, in the region of Montferrat. In 1745 the regiment returned to the south, actually crossing the frontier into Provence. The second battalion was sent to Corsica, landing at Bastia.

Uniforms

The fusilier companies wore a black tricorn with a Savoy blue cockade on the left brim with a black loop, a brass button and yellow lace border. The regiment wore a red coat without a collar. The coat had seven evenly spaced brass buttons on each side of the coat, with three on the cuffs. The coat had horizontal pockets, each with three buttons and had green cuffs, linings and turn backs. The green is shown as olive green in most contemporary illustrations. The men wore red neck stocks, but are shown with black neck stocks in 1747. Their waistcoats were olive green, as were their breeches. When they were not on campaign, they all wore white stockings.

Grenadiers

The grenadiers' Bearskin cap had a red bag with yellow lacing and a white hanging tassel

NCOs

In the grenadier company the NCOs wore the bearskin cap which had a red bag with imitation gold lacing and an imitation gold hanging tassel.

Officers

The officers' tricorns had gold lace border and loop, a Savoy blue cockade, and a gilt button. The officers' coats had gold lacing on their scarlet coats and green waistcoats. The officers' bearskin caps had a red bag with gold lacing and a gold hanging tassel.

Tamburi and Pifferi

The *tamburi*, *pifferi* and musicians wore the Royal Livery after 1739 with olive green waistcoats and breeches. Before 1739 they had worn green coats with red cuffs and lining with the Royal livery lace. The grenadier *tamburi* and *pifferi* wore bearskins as well.

Company colour, *Reggimento Nazionale della Marina*. (Author's Illustration)

Company Colours

The company colour bore a white cross on a red field, in each quarter, emanating from the angles of the cross were three sea green flames. In the first quarter there was a four-pronged anchor with two rings in natural colours with a sea green ribbon interlaced in the rings positioned diagonally. The reverse was identical in mirror image. The standard had a thin white border all around, including the stave edge and a sea green sleeve and a red painted stave which was studded with brass nails in a spiral design. The spear shaped finial was gilded as was the cone shaped ferrule which was secured with a ring. The cords and tassels were red.

Reggimento Nazionale La Regina

The *Reggimento Nazionale La Regina* was raised in 1734, and was financed by the Comte di Bricherasio in honour of Queen Polisea d'Assia, the wife of Carlo Emanuele III. There had been an earlier Swiss regiment of *La Regina* which had been financed by the British government and the British queen's own purse during the War of the Spanish Succession. In 1740 the regiment had 600 officers and men in one battalion. This rose to 1,400 officers and men divided into two battalions in 1743, but by 1747 this had fallen to one battalion of 800. A substantial number of recruits were of Huguenot or Waldesian origin.

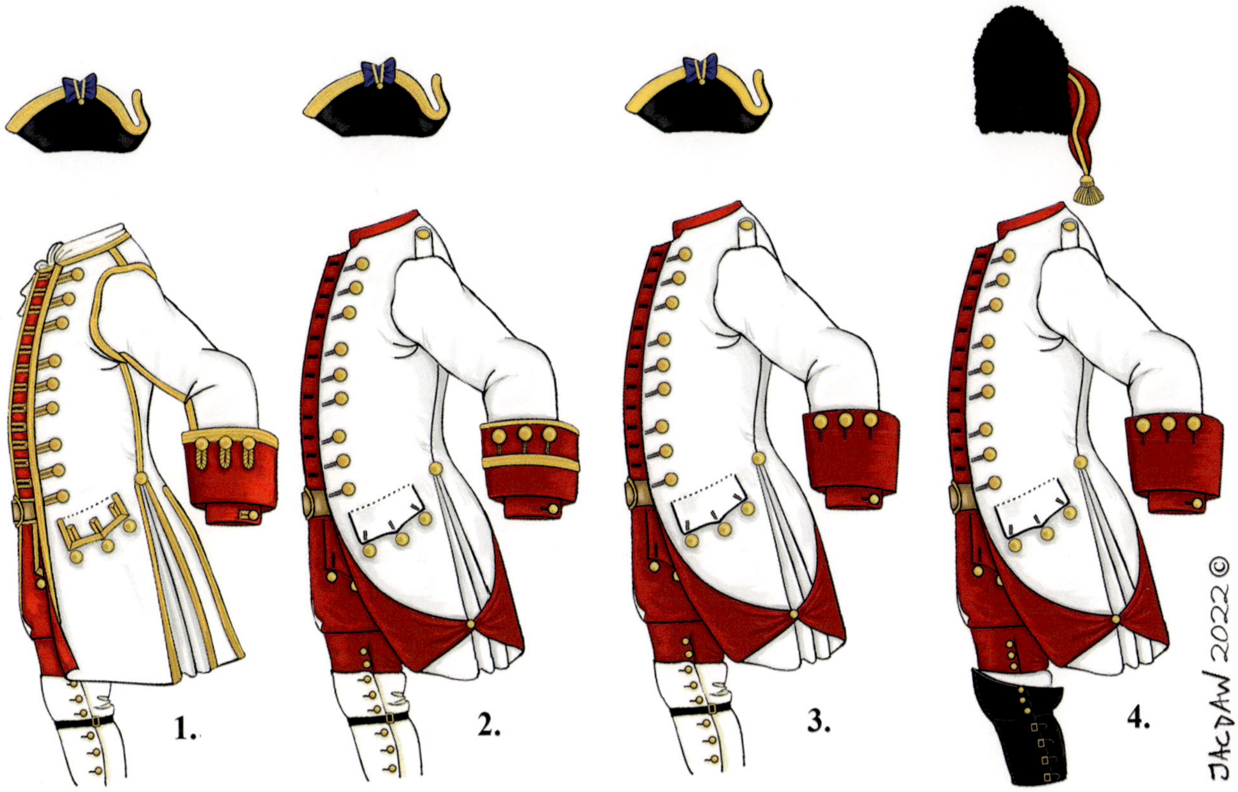

Reggimento Nazionale La Regina, circa 1740; 1. Officer. 2. *Sergente*. 3. *Fuciliere*. 4. *Granatiere*. (Author's Illustration)

The *colonnello* of the regiment under Charles Emmanuel III was Giovanni Battista Cacherano Comte du Bricherasio, from 1734 to 1750.

Service

At the outbreak of the war, *La Regina* was in north-east of Italy in the plains of the Po, and based on the town of Cortemaggiore. In September the first battalion was sent to the Alps, specifically to the camp at La Thuile, near the pass of the Petit St Bernard in the Aosta valley. The regiment fought in Savoy during the counter-offensive against the invading Spanish army.

In January 1743 *La Regina* returned to Piedmont. After the defeat in the Savoyard theatre, it was stationed in the Varaita valley, where the main *Gallispan* army was on the offensive. The first battalion fought at the Battle of Casteldelfino (8 October 1743) during the attempt to stop this offensive.

The following year the whole regiment was present at the battle and siege around the entrenched camp of Villafranche-sur-Mer (20–21 April 1744) on the Mediterranean front. During the defence of the summit above Villefranche, the regiment was surrounded with some other units and was forced to surrender with two batteries of cannons. During the summer they fought in the Alps. The *Gallispan* offensive broke the defensive line. Both battalions were at the Battle of Madonna dell'Olmo (30 September 1744), situated in the centre of the second line. The regiment suffered heavily during the battle and lost one of its colours. In 1745, *La Regina* defended the southwestern sector of Piedmont, supported by the fortresses. In the following years, *La Regina*, now much reduced, was assigned to garrison duties and they were later transferred to the Mediterranean theatre.

Uniforms

The fusilier companies wore a black tricorn with a Savoy blue cockade on the left brim with a black loop, a brass button and yellow lace border.[2] The regiment wore red cravats, but are shown with black neck stocks in 1747. They wore a greyish-white coat without a collar. The coat had nine brass buttons, grouped in threes, on each side of the coat, and six in two groups of three on the cuffs. The coat had horizontal pockets, each with three buttons, and had red cuffs, linings and turn backs. Their waistcoats were red as were their breeches, the buttons were also grouped in threes. When they were not on campaign, they all wore white stockings.

Grenadiers

The grenadiers' bearskin caps had a red bag with yellow lacing and a yellow hanging tassel

2 Note that in 1741 the regimental button and lace colour was changed from silver/white to yellow/gold.

NCOs

In the grenadier company the NCOs wore the bearskin cap which had a red bag with imitation gold lacing and an imitation gold hanging tassel.

Officers

The officers' tricorn had gold lace border and loop, a Savoy blue cockade and gold button. The officers' had gold lacing on their coats and waistcoats. The officers' bearskin cap had a red bag with gold lacing and a gold hanging tassel.

Tamburi and Pifferi

The *tamburi*, *pifferi* and musicians wore the Royal Livery with red waistcoats and breeches. The grenadier *tamburi* and *pifferi* wore bearskins as well.

Company Colours

In 1744 the company colour had on the obverse a white cross on a red field. Each quarter was charged with a blue 'L' in each angle, and with three white flames billowing from the blue ribbon placed at the outer corner. On the first quarter were the arms of the Queen, consisting of the great arms of Lorraine, placed diagonally over the flames, surrounded by a golden baroque frame under a Royal crown, lined red and adorned with red ribbons. The reverse was identical in mirror image. By 1747 the colours had been changed and now only the lesser Arms of Lorraine were displayed.

The sleeve was red. The standard had a thin white border all around, including the stave edge and a red sleeve. The cords and tassels were red. The stave was painted red and decorated with brass studs placed in a spiral design. The finial was a gilded iron spear head. The ferrule plate is brass in the shape of an inverted cone.

La Regina, company colour. This is the probably the original company colour presented in 1737 as shown in the Ozelletti album of 1744. This colour bears the greater arms of Elisabeth-Therese of Lorraine, Queen of Sardinia. (Author's Illustration)

La Regina, company colour. This is the second model of company colour, as shown in the 1747 album now bearing only the lesser arms of Elisabeth-Therese of Lorraine, Queen of Sardinia. (Author's Illustration)

7

The Provincial Foot Regiments

These regiments had a semi-regular organisation; in practice the senior officers were on permanent service, but the men, aged between 18 to 40 years old, were only assembled twice a year to drill and train together during times of peace, but they became assimilated as regular troops in time of war. Effectively this meant that they were on active service for most this period. As previously noted, their grenadier companies were only formed in wartime.

Reggimento Provinciali di Chablais

This regiment was first raised in 1714. In 1740 the regiment consisted of 600 officers and men in one battalion. This rose to 700 officers and men in 1743, and remained unchanged in 1747. As their homeland was occupied by the Spanish, they had difficulty in recruiting. It was a French speaking regiment.

The *colonnelli* of the regiment under Charles Emmanuel III were Giuseppe de Sales, comte de la Thuile until 1743. He was succeeded by Giuseppe Francesco Sallier, comte de la Tour, in 1744.

Service

The *Reggimento Provinciali di Chablais* was essentially a garrison regiment, but by necessity they went on campaign. They were present at the defence of Cuneo from 13 August to 23 October 1744, and they participated in the invasion of Provence in 1746–1747. They were present at the Battle of l'Assietta on 19 July 1747, but were not engaged.

Uniforms

The fusilier companies wore a black tricorn with a Savoy blue cockade on the left brim with a black loop and a pewter button, and white lace border. The regiment wore red cravats. They wore a greyish-white coat without a collar. The coat had eight evenly spaced pewter buttons on each side, and three on the cuffs. The coat had vertical pockets, each with three buttons and had red cuffs, linings and turn backs. They had red waistcoats and breeches. When they were not on campaign, they all wore white stockings. In 1743, it was noted that their uniforms, equipment and colours were in a very poor condition.

Grenadiers

The grenadiers' bearskin caps had a red bag with white lacing and a white hanging tassel

NCOs

In the grenadier company the NCOs wore the bearskin cap which had a red bag with imitation silver lacing and an imitation silver hanging tassel.

Officers

The officers' tricorns had silver lace border and loop a Savoy blue cockade and silver button. The officers' coats and waistcoats had silver lacing. The officers' bearskin cap had a red bag with silver lacing and a silver hanging tassel.

Tamburi and Pifferi

The *tamburi*, *pifferi* and musicians wore the Royal Livery with red waistcoats and breeches. The grenadier *tamburi* and *pifferi* wore bearskins as well.

Company Colours

Obverse, they had a white cross on a red field. In the first quarter, a shield surrounded by a baroque frame and surmounted by a ducal crown, both coloured gold. From the top of the frame parts protruded two elongated palm leaves. On the shield are the arms of the Duchy of Chablais. The reverse was identical in mirror image. The exact date of the fabrication of this model is unclear, but it was in service in 1744. The previous model was similar, but the quarters two and threee were medium blue, according to the Album of Lauro circa 1734–1736. The standard had a thin white border all around, including the stave edge. The sleeve and the staves were painted red and studded with brass nails in a spiral design like the *colonnello*'s colour. In 1747, the sleeve and stave are shown as a medium or light blue. The spear shaped finial was gilded as was the cone shaped ferrule which was secured with a ring. The cords and tassels could be red or gold.

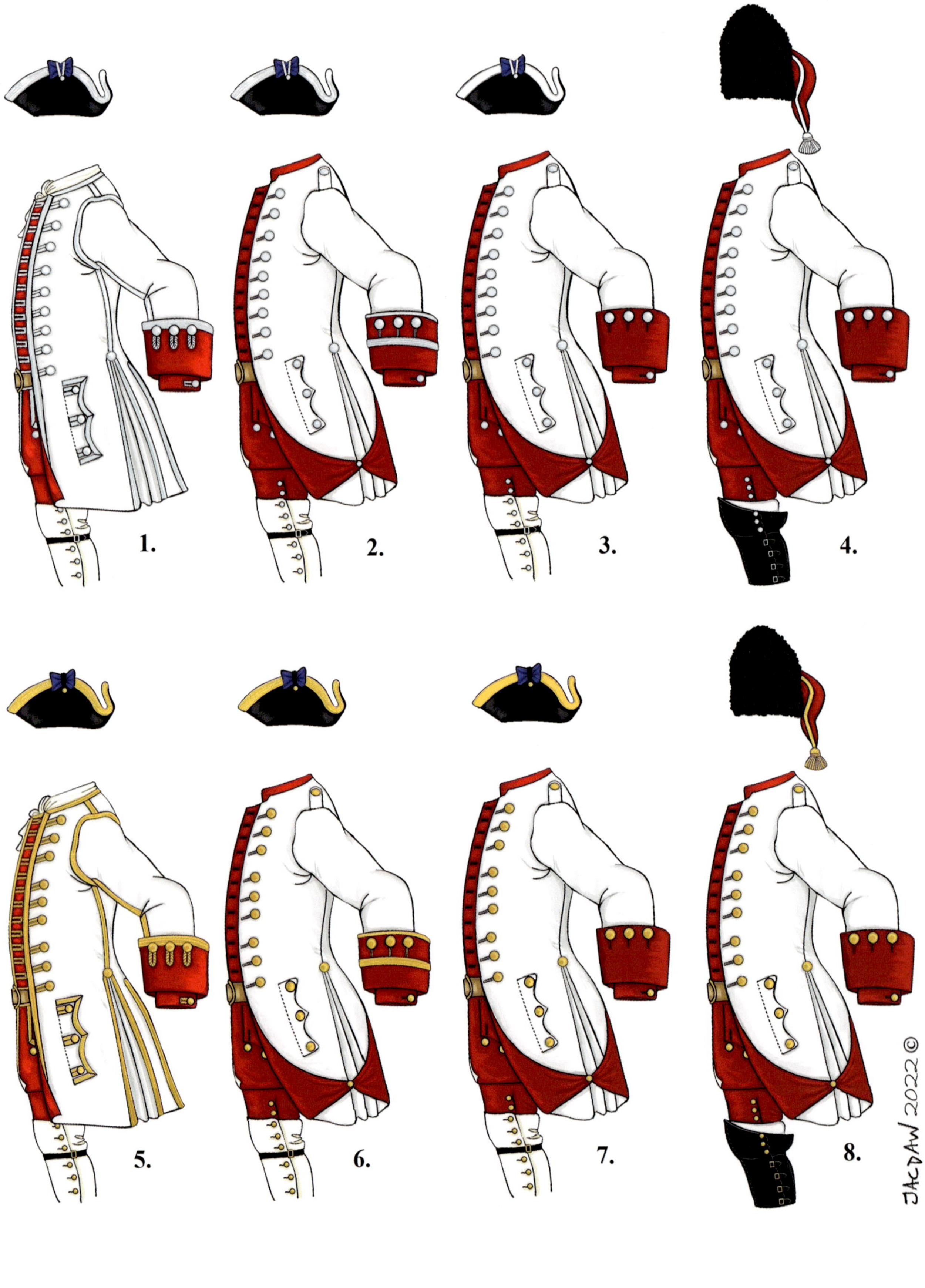

Reggimento Provinciali Chiablese circa 1740; 1. Officer. 2. *Sergente*. 3. *Fuciliere*. 4. *Granatiere*. *Reggimento Provinciali Tarantasia* circa 1740; 5. Officer. 6. *Sergente*. 7. *Fuciliere*. 8. *Granatiere*. (Author's Illustration)

Company colour, *Reggimento Provinciali Chiablese.* (Author's Illustration)

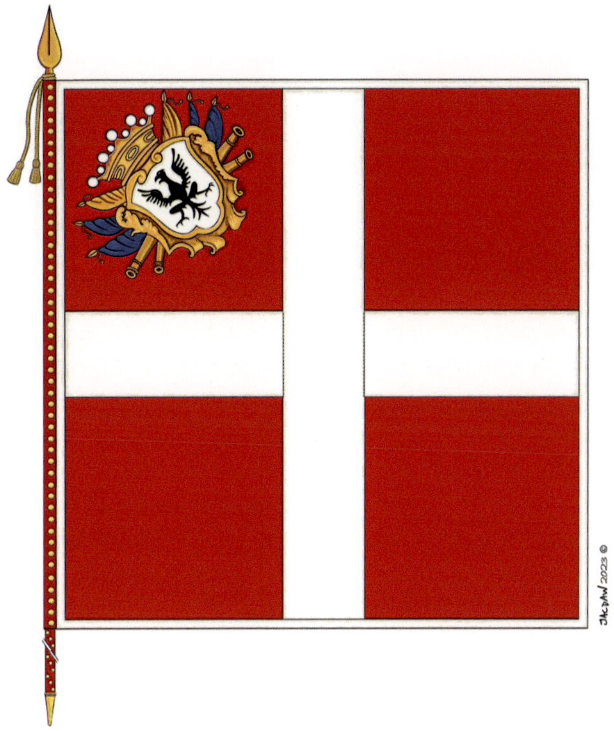

Company colour, *Reggimento Provinciali di Tarantasia.* (Author's Illustration)

Reggimento Provinciali di Tarantasia

This regiment was first raised in 1714. In 1740 the regiment consisted of 600 officers and men in one battalion. This rose to 700 officers and men in 1743, and they remained unchanged in 1747 for the same reasons mentioned above. The *colonnello* of the Regiment under Charles Emmanuel III was Giano Bellegarde, comte d'Entremont, from 1743 to 1748.

Service

The regiment fought at the Battle of Villefranche in 1744.

Uniforms

The fusilier companies wore a black tricorn with a dark blue cockade on the left brim with a black loop and a brass button, and yellow lace border. The regiment wore red neck stocks.

They wore a greyish-white coat without a collar. The coat had nine brass buttons, grouped in threes, on each side of the coat, and six on the cuffs, grouped in threes. The coat had vertical pockets, each with three buttons and had red cuffs and linings and turn backs. Their waistcoats were red and had nine brass buttons, grouped in threes, their breeches were also red. When they were not on campaign, they all wore white stockings.

Grenadiers

The grenadiers' bearskin caps had a red bag with yellow lacing and a yellow hanging tassel.

NCOs

In the grenadier company the NCOs wore bearskin caps which had a red bag with imitation gold lacing and an imitation gold hanging tassel.

Officers

The officers' tricorns had gold lace border and loop a Savoy blue cockade and gold button. The officers' coats and waistcoats had gold lacing. The officers' bearskin caps had a red bag with gold lacing and a gold hanging tassel.

Tamburi and Pifferi

The *tamburi*, *pifferi* and musicians wore the Royal Livery with red waistcoats and breeches. The grenadier *tamburi* and *pifferi* wore bearskins as well.

Company Colours

On the obverse there was a white cross on a red field. In the first quarter was the coat of arms of the county of Tarantaise. The reverse was the same with the arms in the top quarter by the stave. The standard had a thin white border all around, including the stave edge. The exact date of the fabrication of this model is unclear, but it was in service in 1744. The previous model was similar, but the quarters one and four were medium blue. The sleeve and the staves were painted red and studded with brass nails in a spiral design. In 1747, the sleeve and stave are now shown as medium/light blue. The spear shaped finial was gilded as was the cone shaped ferrule which was secured with a ring. The cords and tassels could be red or gold.

Reggimento Provinciali di Aosta

The *Reggimento Provinciali di Aosta* was first raised in 1714. In 1740 the regiment consisted of 600 officers and men in one battalion. This rose to 700 officers and men in 1743, and was raised to 800 officers and men in 1747.

The *colonnelli* of the regiment under Charles Emmanuel III were Paul Syessel, Baron de la Serre, from 15 April 1739 until he was succeeded by Giovanni Francesco Bonaventura Sesto on 22 January 1742, who in turn was succeeded by Giuseppe Massetti, Conte di Frinco on 5 April 1747.

Service

At the beginning of the war *Aosta* had a total strength of nine companies ready to take the field and one company in reserve. In 1742 the regiment was transferred to the plains of the Po. In May they were in Plaisance (Piacenza), in August they were in garrison in the city of Pavia. They continued in garrison duty in 1743. The following year the combined Franco-Spanish offensive was mounting in the west. The *Aosta* were one of the 14 battalions who defended the entrenched camp in the citadel and port of Villefranche. On 26 April 1744 the regiment was compelled to surrender on the Col de Villefranche. A year later the regiment had been rebuilt and they were again operational.

During the first half of 1745 the regiment was in the south of Piedmont, especially in the country of Bene Vagienna. In early part of September, they were sent to the fortress of Alessandria, then to the little fortress of Valenza overlooking the river Po. In September 1745, the *maréchal* de Maillebois defeated the Piedmontese army at the Battle of Bassignana.

After this sad defeat *Aosta* again defended the walls of the fortress (14–30 October 1745). The defence was quite active, and the governor, Marquise de Balbiano made a great number of sorties. On 30 October, under a heavy fog, Balbiano and his men managed to evacuate the city.

In 1746, the battalion was again in eastern part of Piedmont, in Alessandria. From there they climbed the hills of Acqui Terme, in the Heights of Montferrat. They then marched and fought in the west. On 5 October they were present at the liberation of Nice and on 23 October it was one of their units that forced Fort San Paolo to surrender. In November they fought in the offensive in Provence.

The *Aosta* was one of the battalions available immediately to defend the Ligurian front during the summer offensive of the *Gallispans* in 1747. The regiment was still in the entrenched line of the Roya valley at the end of the war.

Uniforms

The fusilier companies wore a black tricorn with a dark blue cockade on the left brim with a black loop and a pewter button, and white lace border. The regiment wore red cravats. They wore a greyish-white coat without a collar. The coat had eight pewter buttons, grouped in twos on each side of the coat, and four on the cuffs, also grouped in twos. The coat had vertical pockets, each with three buttons and had red cuffs, linings and turn backs.

Their waistcoats were red with pewter buttons also grouped in twos and their breeches were red. When they were not on campaign, they all wore white stockings.

Grenadiers

The grenadiers' bearskin caps had a red bag with white lacing and a white hanging tassel.

NCOs

In the grenadier company the NCOs wore the bearskin cap which had a red bag with imitation silver lacing and an imitation silver hanging tassel.

Officers

The officers' tricorns had silver lace border and loop a Savoy blue cockade and silver button. The officers' coats and waistcoats had silver lacing. The officers' bearskin cap had a red bag with silver lacing and a silver hanging tassel.

Tamburi and Pifferi

The *tamburi*, *pifferi* and musicians wore the Royal Livery with red waistcoats and breeches. The grenadier *tamburi* and *pifferi* wore bearskins as well.

Company Colours

Obverse, there was a white cross on a red field. In the first quarter were the arms of the Duchy of Aosta. The reverse was identical in mirror image. The exact date of the fabrication of this model is unclear, but was in service in 1744. The previous model was similar, but the quarters two and three were medium blue. The standard had a thin white border all around, including the stave edge. The sleeves and the staves were painted red and studded with brass nails in a spiral design. In 1747, the sleeve and stave are now shown as medium/light blue. The spear shaped finial was gilded as was the cone shaped ferrule which was secured with a ring. The cords and tassels could be red or gold.

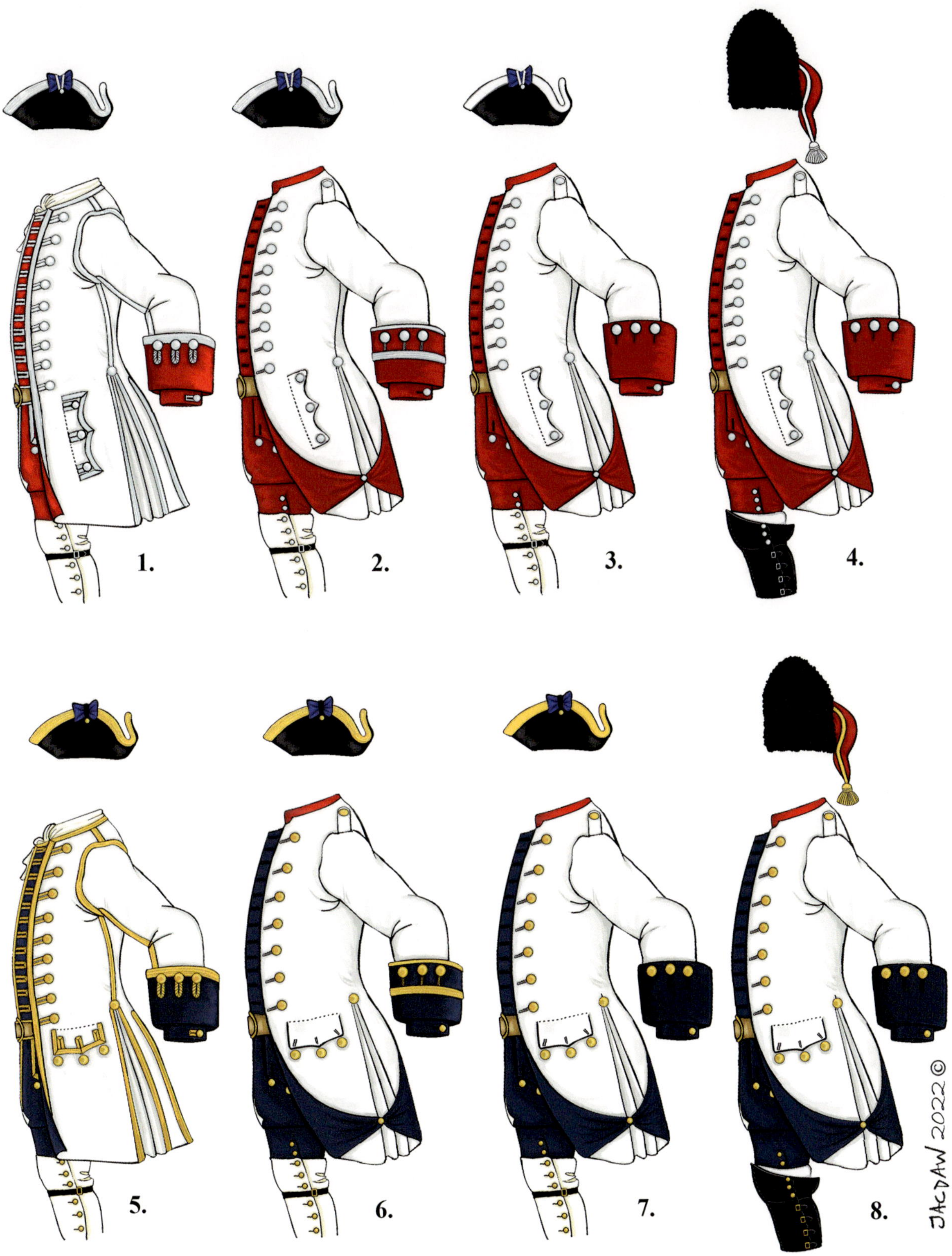

Reggimento Provinciali Aosta circa 1740; 1. Officer. 2. *Sergente*. 3. *Fuciliere*. 4. *Granatiere*. *Reggimento Provinciali Torino* circa 1740; 5. Officer. 6. *Sergente*. 7. *Fuciliere*. 8. *Granatiere*. (Author's Illustration)

Company colour, *Reggimento Provinciali Aosta*. (Author's Illustration)

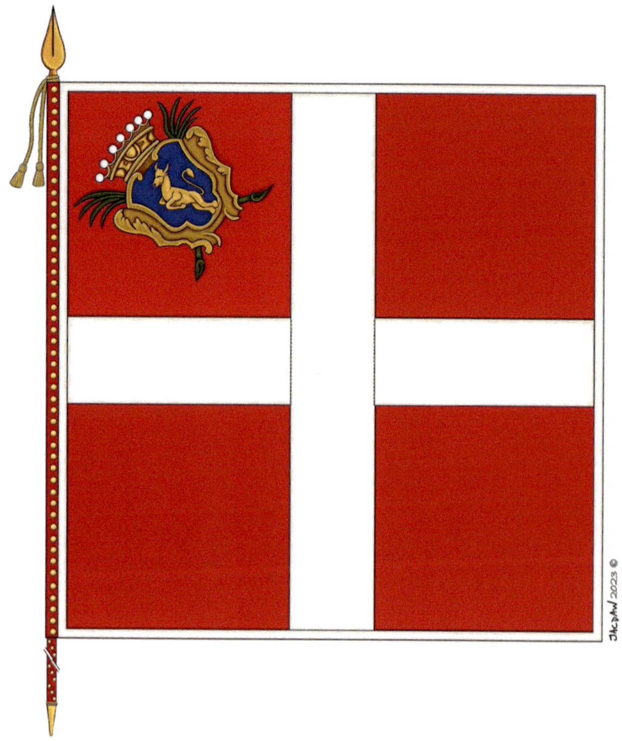

Company colour, *Reggimento Provinciali di Torino*. (Author's Illustration)

Reggimento Provinciali di Torino

The *Reggimento Provinciali di Torino* was first raised in 1714. In 1740 the regiment consisted of 600 officers and men in one battalion. This rose to 700 officers and men in 1743, and was raised to 800 in 1747. The *colonnelli* of the regiment under Charles Emmanuel III were Lorenzo Amedeo Taparello di Genola from January 1742, and he was succeeded by Claudio Ferdinando di Menthon di Soliéres in March 1744. Alessandro D'Oria, Marchese di Cirié was the *luogotenente colonnello* in 1745. He only became *colonnello* in July 1755.

Service

The regiment was at Casteldelfino in 1743 and the Battle of Camposanto in 1744.

Uniforms

The fusilier companies wore a black tricorn with a dark blue cockade on the left brim with a black loop and a brass button, and a yellow lace border. The regiment wore red cravats. They wore a greyish-white coat without a collar. The coat had eight evenly spaced brass buttons on each side of the coat and three buttons on the cuffs. The coat had vertical pockets, each with three buttons and they had blue cuffs, linings and turn backs. Their waistcoats were blue as were their breeches, both had brass buttons. When they were not on campaign, they all wore white stockings.

Grenadiers

Unusually, the grenadiers' bearskin caps had a red bonnet, not blue, with yellow lacing and a white hanging tassel.

NCOs

In the grenadier company the NCOs wore the bearskin cap which had a scarlet bag with imitation gold lacing and an imitation gold hanging tassel.

Officers

The officers' tricorn had gold lace border and loop, a Savoy blue cockade, and gold button on. The officers' coats and waistcoats had gold lacing. The officers' bearskin caps had a scarlet bag with gold lacing and a gold hanging tassel.

Tamburi and Pifferi

The *tamburi*, *pifferi* and musicians wore the Royal Livery with blue waistcoats and breeches. The grenadier *tamburi* and *pifferi* wore bearskins as well.

Company Colours

Obverse, there was a white cross on a red field. In the first quarter were the coat of arms of the city of Turin. The reverse was identical in mirror image. The exact date of the fabrication of this model is unclear, but was in service in 1744. The previous model was similar, but the quarters one and four were medium blue. The standard had a thin white border all around, including the staff edge. The sleeves and the staves were painted red and studded with brass nails in a spiral design. In 1747, the sleeve and stave were shown as medium/light blue. The spear shaped finial was gilded as was the cone shaped ferrule, which was secured with a ring. The cords and tassels were red.

Reggimento Provinciali di Mondovì

The *Reggimento Provinciali di Mondovì* was first raised in 1714. In 1740 the regiment consisted of 600 officers and men in one battalion. This rose to 700 officers and men in 1743, and was raised to 800 in 1747. The *colonnelli* of the regiment under Charles Emmanuel III were, from 1734, Giuseppe Cacherano d'Osasco Conte della Rocca, then Francesco Tana, Conte Palatino in 1744. He was succeeded by Giovanni Battista Pellegrino Alfieri di Cortemilia in 1747.

Service
In 1742 the regiment was at the siege of Mirandola. In 1743 they fought at Casteldelfino. In 1744 they defended Montecavallo. In 1745 they took part in the assault and capture of Borgo San Dalmazzo. In 1746 they took part in the assault and capture of the bridge of Sant'Ilario in Modena at the point of the bayonet, and in the 1747 campaign to liberate Nice.

Uniforms
The fusilier companies wore a black tricorn with a dark blue cockade on the left brim with a black loop and a pewter button, and white lace border. They wore a greyish-white collarless coat. The coat had six pewter buttons on each side of the coat, grouped as one, two and three, and three on the cuffs. The coat had horizontal pockets, each with three buttons and had blue cuffs, linings, and turn backs. The regiment wore red cravats. Their waistcoats were blue with pewter buttons and their breeches were also blue. When they were not on campaign, they all wore white stockings.

Grenadiers
The grenadiers' bearskin caps had a blue bag with white lacing and a white hanging tassel.

NCOs
In the grenadier company the NCOs wore the bearskin cap which had a blue bag with imitation silver lacing and an imitation silver hanging tassel.

Officers
The officers' tricorns had silver lace border and loop a Savoy blue cockade and silver button. The officers' coats and waistcoats had silver lacing. The officers' bearskin cap had a blue bag with silver lacing and a silver hanging tassel.

Company colour, *Reggimento Provinciali di Mondovì*. (Author's Illustration)

Tamburi and Pifferi
The *tamburi*, *pifferi* and musicians wore the Royal Livery with blue waistcoats and breeches. The grenadier *tamburi* and *pifferi* wore bearskins as well.

Company Colours
Obverse, there was a white cross on a red field. In the first quarter was the coat of arms of the Duchy of Mondovi. The reverse was identical in mirror image. The exact date of the fabrication of this model is unclear, but was in service in 1744. The previous model was similar, but the quarters one and four were medium blue. The standard had a thin white border all around, including the staff edge. The sleeves and the staves were painted red and studded with brass nails in a spiral pattern. In 1747, the sleeve and stave are now shown as medium/light blue. The spear shaped finial was gilded as was the cone shaped ferrule, which was secured with a ring. The cords and tassels could be red or gold.

Reggimento Provinciali di Vercelli

The *Reggimento Provinciali di Vercelli* was first raised in 1714. In 1740 the regiment consisted of 600 officers and men in one battalion. This rose to 700 officers and men in 1743, and was raised to 800 in 1747. The *colonnelli* of the regiment under Charles Emmanuel III were Lorenzo Amedeo Tapparello di Genola from April 1739 to January 1742 when he left to take command of the *Reggimento di*

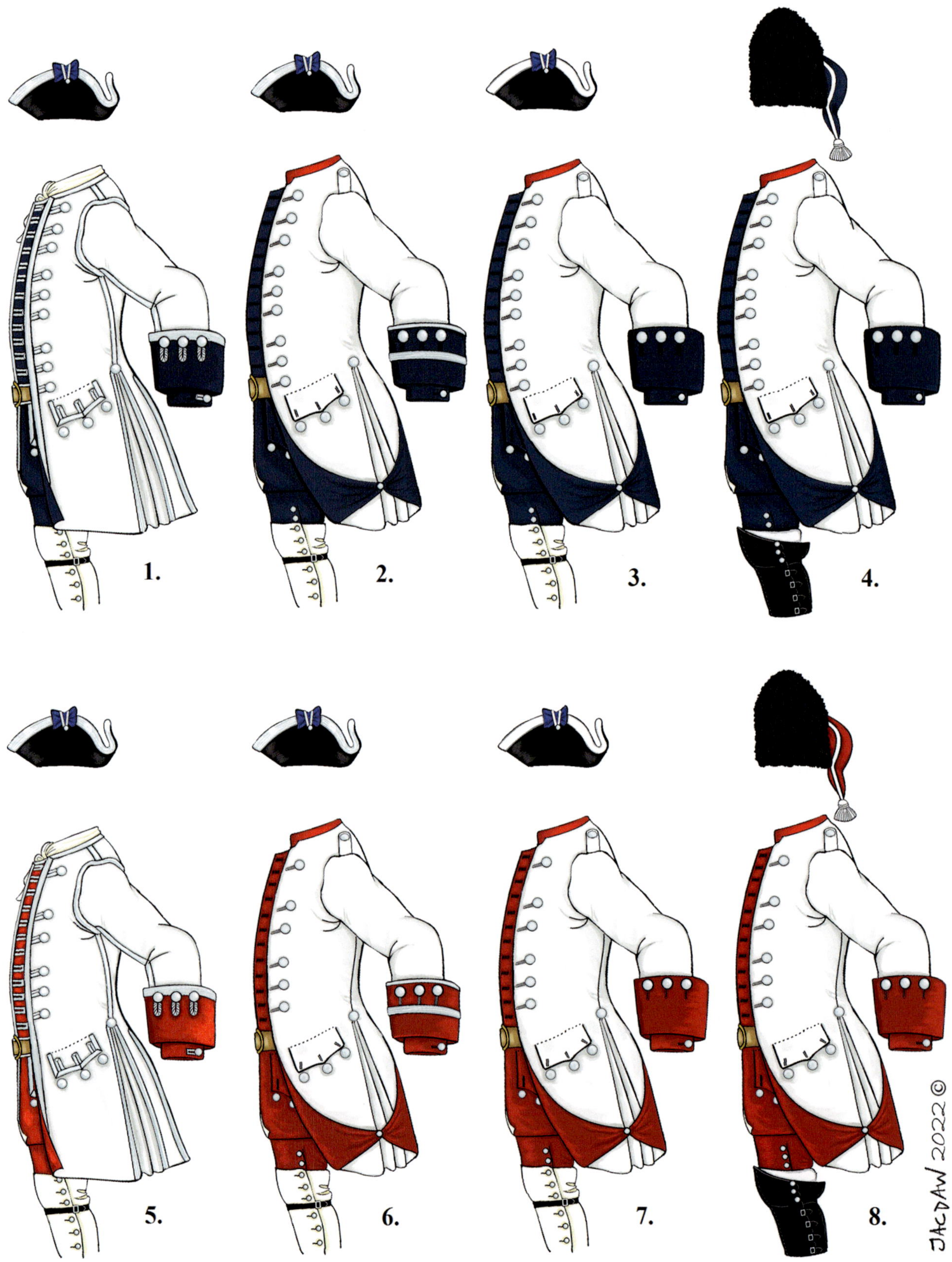

Reggimento Provinciali di Mondovì circa 1740; 1. Officer. 2. *Sergente*. 3. *Fuciliere*. 4. *Granatiere*. *Reggimento Provinciali Vercelli* circa 1740; 5. Officer. 6. *Sergente*. 7. *Fuciliere*. 8. *Granatiere*. (Author's Illustration)

Torino. He was succeeded by Francesco Alciati from 1742 to 1745, and he was succeeded by the Conte Clemente Antonio Cordero di Pamparato in February 1745.

Service

In 1742 the regiment participated in the campaign of Savoy. In 1743 they fought at Aigue Blanche and in the defence of Pierre Longue. They defended the city of Cuneo from 13 August to 23 October 1744. In 1746 they took Asti, liberated Alessandria, and on 3 October attacked the lines at Ventimiglia. In 1747 they participated in the attack on Barcelonnette.

Uniforms

The fusilier companies wore a black tricorn with a dark blue cockade on the left brim with a black loop and a silver button, and white lace border. The men wore red neck stocks. They wore a greyish-white collarless coat; the coat had six pewter buttons on each side of the coat, grouped as one, two and three, with three on the cuffs. The coat had vertical pockets, each with three buttons, and they had red cuffs, linings and turn backs. Their waistcoats and breeches were red. When they were not on campaign, they all wore white stockings.

Grenadiers

The grenadiers' bearskin caps had a red bag with white lacing and a white hanging tassel

NCOs

In the grenadier company the NCOs wore the bearskin cap which had a red bag with imitation silver lacing and an imitation silver hanging tassel.

Officers

The officers' tricorns had silver lace border and loop a Savoy blue cockade and silver button. The officers had silver lacing on their coats and waistcoats. The officers' bearskin caps had a red bag with silver lacing and a silver hanging tassel.

Tamburi and Pifferi

The *tamburi*, *pifferi* and musicians wore the Royal Livery with red waistcoats and breeches. The grenadier *tamburi* and *pifferi* wore bearskins as well.

Company Colours

Obverse, there was a white cross on a red field. In the first quarter, were the coat of arms of the county of Vercelli. The reverse was identical in mirror image. The exact date of the fabrication of this model is unclear, but was in service in 1744. The standard had a thin white border all around, including the staff edge. The sleeves and the staves were painted red and studded with brass nails in a spiral design.

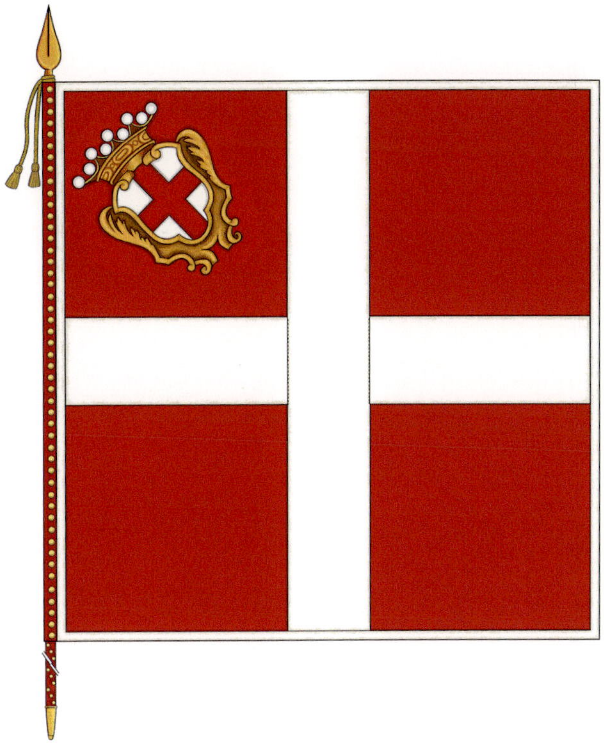

Company colour, *Reggimento Provinciali di Vercelli*. (Author's Illustration)

In 1747, the sleeve and stave are now shown as medium/light blue. The spear shaped finial was gilded as was the cone shaped ferrule, which was secured with a ring. The cords and tassels could be red or gold. The previous model was similar, but the quarters two and three were medium blue.

Reggimento Provinciali di Asti

The *Reggimento Provinciali di Asti* was first raised in 1714. In 1740 the regiment was made up of 600 officers and men in one battalion. This rose to 700 officers and men in 1743, and rose again in 1747 to 800. The *colonnelli* of the regiment under Charles Emmanuel III were Maurizio Valperga di Rivara, 1734–1743, succeeded by Guido Occa, 1743–1744, followed by Giovanni Secondo, Canale di Cumiana, 1744–1748.

Service

The regiment fought at the Battle of Madonna dell'Olmo on 30 September 1744. From April to May 1746, they were at the siege of Valenza.

Uniforms

The fusilier companies wore a black tricorn with a dark blue cockade on the left brim with a black loop and a pewter button, and white lace border. The wore had red neck stocks. They wore a greyish-white collarless coat. The coat

Company colour, *Reggimento Provinciali di Asti.* (Author's Illustration)

had six pewter buttons on each side, grouped as one, two and three, with three on the cuffs. The coat had horizontal pockets, each with three buttons and had red cuffs, linings, and turn backs. Their waistcoats and breeches were red. When they were not on campaign, they all wore white stockings.

Grenadiers
The grenadiers' bearskin caps had a red bag with white lacing and a white hanging tassel.

NCOs
In the grenadier company the NCOs wore the bearskin cap which had a red bag with imitation silver lacing and an imitation silver hanging tassel.

Officers
The officers' tricorns had silver lace border and loop, a Savoy blue cockade and silver button. The officers' coats and waistcoats had silver lacing. The officers' bearskin caps had a red bag with silver lacing and a silver hanging tassel.

Tamburi and Pifferi
The *tamburi*, *pifferi* and musicians wore the Royal Livery with red waistcoats and breeches. The grenadier *tamburi* and *pifferi* wore bearskins as well.

Company Colours
On the obverse, there was a white cross on a red field. In the first quarter was the coat of arms of the county of Asti. The reverse was identical in mirror image. The exact date of the fabrication of this model is unclear, but was in service in 1744. The previous model was similar, but the quarters one and four were medium blue. The standard had a thin white border all around, including the staff edge. The sleeves and the staves were painted red and studded with brass nails in a spiral design. In 1747, the sleeve and stave are shown as medium/light blue. The spear shaped finial was gilded as was the cone shaped ferrule, which was secured with a ring. The cords and tassels could be red or gold.

Reggimento Provinciali di Casale

The *Reggimento Provinciali di Casale* was first raised in 1714. In 1740 the regiment had one battalion composed of 600 officers and men. This rose to 700 officers and men in 1743, and rose again in 1747 to 800. The *colonnelli* of the Regiment under Charles Emmanuel III were Giovanni Francesco Pallavicino di St Etienne, 1735–1744, succeeded by Vincenzo Alessandro Ferrero marchese d'Ormea, 1744–1745, followed by Domenico Cassotti conte di Casalgrasso, 1745–1762.

Service
In 1742 the regiment participated in the campaign in Savoy. In 1744 they fought at the Battle of Madonna dell'Olmo. In 1746 they chased the Spanish troops from the mountains around Sospel (Sospello). They then laid siege to Savona and participated in campaign in Provence. They were at the Battle of l'Assietta on 19 July 1747.

Uniforms
The fusilier companies wore a black tricorn with a dark blue cockade on the left brim with a black loop and a brass button, and yellow galloon border. The regiment wore red cravats. They wore a greyish-white collarless coat. The coat had six brass buttons on each side of the coat, grouped one, two and three, with three on the cuffs. The coat had vertical pockets, each had three buttons, and they had red cuffs, linings, and turn backs. Their waistcoats and breeches were red. When they were not on campaign, they all wore white stockings.

Grenadiers
The grenadiers' bearskin caps had a red bag with yellow lacing and a yellow hanging tassel

NCOs
The NCOs had their button holes stitched with yellow *bave* and they had gold lace on their hats and faux gold galloon.

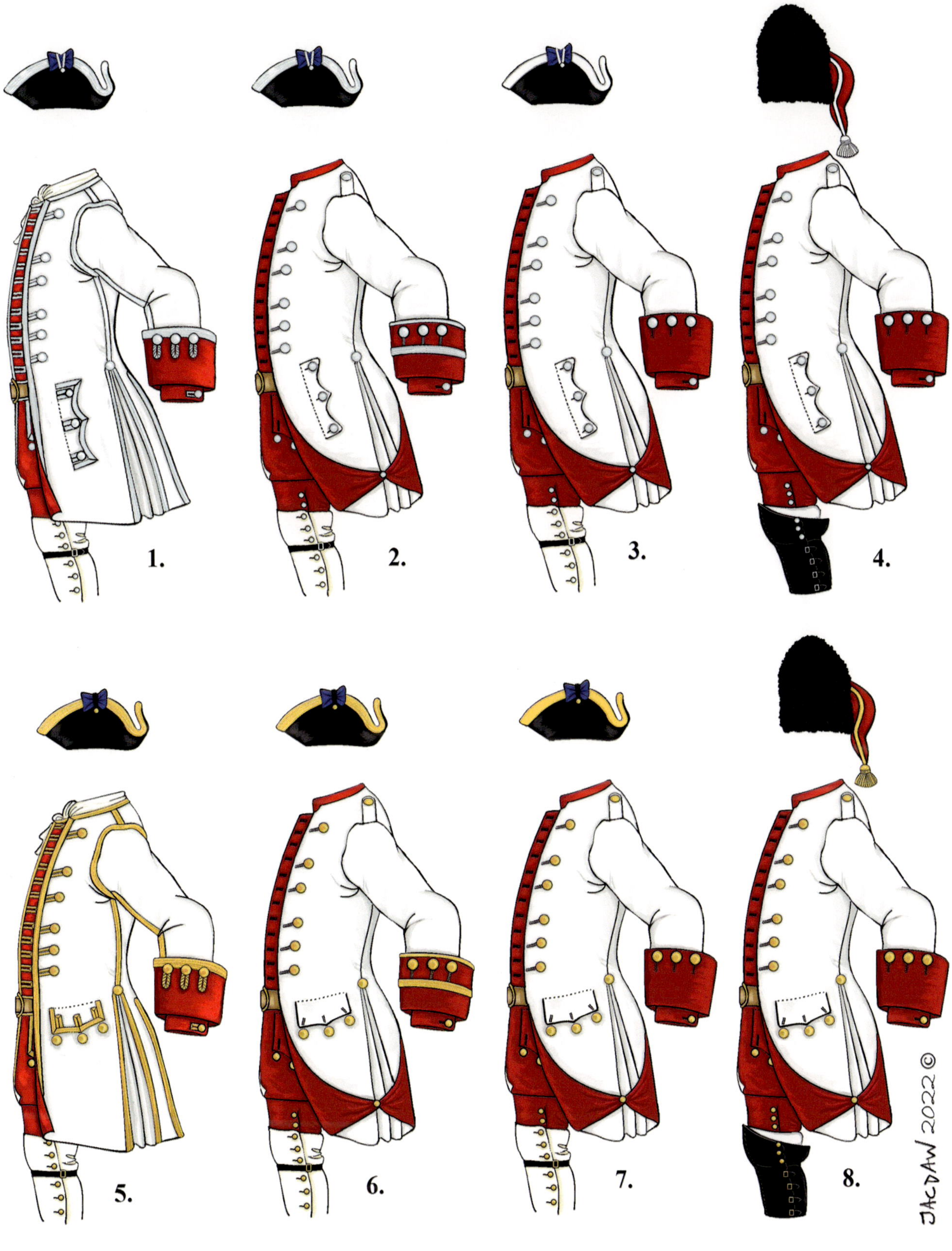

Reggimento Provinciali Asti circa 1740; 1. Officer. 2. *Sergente*. 3. *Fuciliere*. 4. *Granatiere*. *Reggimento Provinciali Casale* circa 1740; 5. Officer. 6. *Sergente*. 7. *Fuciliere*. 8. *Granatiere*. (Author's Illustration)

Company colour, *Reggimento Provinciali de Casale.* (Author's Illustration)

In the grenadier company the NCOs wore the bearskin cap which had a red bag with imitation gold lacing and an imitation gold hanging tassel.

Officers

The officers' tricorns had gold lace border and loop, a Savoy blue cockade and gold button. The officers' coats and waistcoats had gold lacing. The officers' bearskin caps had a red bag with gold lacing and a gold hanging tassel.

Tamburi and Pifferi

The *tamburi, pifferi* and musicians wore the Royal Livery with red waistcoats and breeches. The grenadier *tamburi* and *pifferi* wore bearskins as well.

Company Colours

Obverse, there was a white cross on a red field. In the first quarter was the coat of arms of the Duchy of Casale. The reverse was identical in mirror image. The standard had a thin white border all around, including the staff edge. The exact date of the fabrication of this model is unclear, but was in service in 1744. The sleeves and the staves were painted red and studded with brass nails in a spiral design. In 1747, the sleeve and stave were shown as medium/light blue. The spear shaped finial was gilded as was the cone shaped ferrule which was secured with a ring. The cords and tassels could be red or gold. The previous model was similar, but the quarters one and four were medium blue, according to the Album of Lauro (circa 1734–1736) but this illustration does not appear to have ben finished.

Reggimento Provinciali di Nizza

The *Reggimento Provinciali di Nizza* was first raised in 1714. It was initially raised as a Marine regiment. In 1740 the regiment had one battalion composed of 600 officers and men in. This rose to 700 officers and men in 1743, and was raised to 800 in 1747. The *colonnelli* of the regiment under Charles Emmanuel III were Jean Augustin Gouett from 1739, who was succeeded by Giuseppe Antonio Saluzzo Miolans Spinola, Marchese di Garessio in 1745, and who was in turn succeeded by Charles Hyacinthe De Condray in 1746

Service

In 1742, nine companies of *Nizza* were mobilized and placed in various garrisons, notably at Demonte in the valley of the Stura. As fate would have it, in 1744, this was precisely the place where the Prince of Conti, commander of the *Gallispans*, decided to attack. On 13 August the fortress della Consolata, on a hill just outside the town of Demonte, was besieged by the Marquis of Maulevrier. The fortress presented little protection and by the 16th a fire near the magazine frightened the governor, De Vialet, into negotiating with the enemy. He tried to send two officers of the regiment to speak with the besiegers, they in turn convinced De Vialet to go out himself, and as soon as he was through the gates the men promptly closed them behind him. The troops had no intention of surrendering and to finalise the situation de Vialet could not find any one to speak to. The troops then managed to evacuate the fort unseen by the French, and just a handful of men stayed behind with *Maggiore* Borello to intimidate the French when they eventually entered the place on the 19 August.

The regiment withdrew to Cuneo where they were part of the forces defending the city during the siege. In 1744 the regiment was present at the Battle of Madonna dell'Olmo, in the centre of the second line, just behind *La Marina*.

In June 1745, *Nizza*, along with the provincial regiments of *Mondovi* and *Pignerol* took part in a raid on Vintimille to slow down the *Gallispans*' advance. In September the Piedmontese army was beaten at the Battle of Bassignana after which the regiment was transferred to the Suze valley. Although they were beaten at the Joussad camp they were still able to take part in the spring offensive of 1746 and the liberation of Asti.

The regiment was then sent south towards the Mediterranean and they participated in the invasion of Provence. They were then stationed at Breil, before descending on Genova where they laid siege to the city, alongside the Austrian army. When the siege was over, the regiment returned to the Roya valley until the end of the war.

Uniforms

The fusilier companies wore a black tricorn with a dark blue cockade on the left brim with a black loop and a pewter button, and white galloon border. The regiment wore red cravats. They wore a greyish-white collarless coat lined with blue, which had six pewter buttons on each side of the coat, grouped as one, two and three, on each side of the coat, with three buttons on the cuffs. The coat had vertical pockets, each with three buttons and they had blue cuffs and turn backs. Their waistcoats were blue lined with white and their breeches were blue. When they were not on campaign, they all wore white stockings.

Grenadiers

The grenadiers' bearskin cap had a blue bag with white lacing and a white hanging tassel

NCOs

In the grenadier company the NCOs wore the bearskin cap which had a blue bag with imitation silver lacing and an imitation silver hanging tassel.

Officers

The officers' tricorn had a silver lace border and loop, a dark blue cockade, and silver button. The officers' coats and waistcoats had silver lacing. The officers' bearskin caps had a blue bag with silver lacing and a silver hanging tassel.

Tamburi and Pifferi

The *tamburi*, *pifferi* and musicians wore the Royal Livery with blue waistcoats and breeches. The grenadier *tamburi* and *pifferi* wore bearskins as well.

Company Colours

Obverse, the colours had a white cross on a red field. In the first quarter was the coat of arms of the County of Nice. The reverse was identical in mirror image. The exact date of the fabrication of this model is unclear, but was in service in 1744. The standard had a thin white border all around, including the stave edge. The sleeves and the staves were painted red and studded with brass nails in a spiral design. The spear shaped finial was gilded as was the cone shaped ferrule which was secured with a ring. The cords and tassels could be red or gold.

The previous model was similar, but the quarters one and four were medium blue.[1]

Company colour, *Reggimento Provinciali di Nizza.* (Author's Illustration)

Reggimento Provinciali di Pinerolo

The *Reggimento Provinciali di Pinerolo* regiment was first raised in 1714. In 1740 the regiment consisted of 600 officers and men in one battalion. This rose to 700 officers and men in 1743, and rose again to 800 in 1747. The *colonnello* of the regiment under Charles Emmanuel III from 1739 to 1747 was Giuseppe Antonio Bonaventura Rasino.

Service

The regiment was at Val Chisone in 1744 and at the Battle of Madonna dell'Olmo.

Uniforms

The fusilier companies wore a black tricorn with a dark blue cockade on the left brim with a black loop and a pewter button, and white lace border. The regiment wore red cravats. They wore a greyish-white collarless coat. The coat had six pewter buttons on each side, grouped one, two and three, with three on the cuffs. The coat had horizontal pockets, each with three buttons and had blue cuffs, linings and turn backs. Their waistcoats and breeches were blue with pewter buttons. When they were not on campaign, they all wore white stockings.

Grenadiers

The grenadiers' bearskin caps had a blue bag with white lacing and a white hanging tassel

1 *Les Triomphes du Roy Louis XV*, which records the names of colours and standards captured by the French army, depicts a *colonnello*'s and a company colour captured in Pragelato in 1745 as belonging to the *Reggimento Provinciale di Nizza*. The loss of these two colours is confirmed by a Savoyard report from 1746. These rather strange colours were, for the *colonnello*'s, a blue field with a white cross. The company colour had a red field with an oval baroque frame bearing the arms of Asti in the first quarter. The coat of arms is not that of Nice, but that of Asti, or the incomplete arms of Mondovì, this could be an error by the artist or the information he was given.

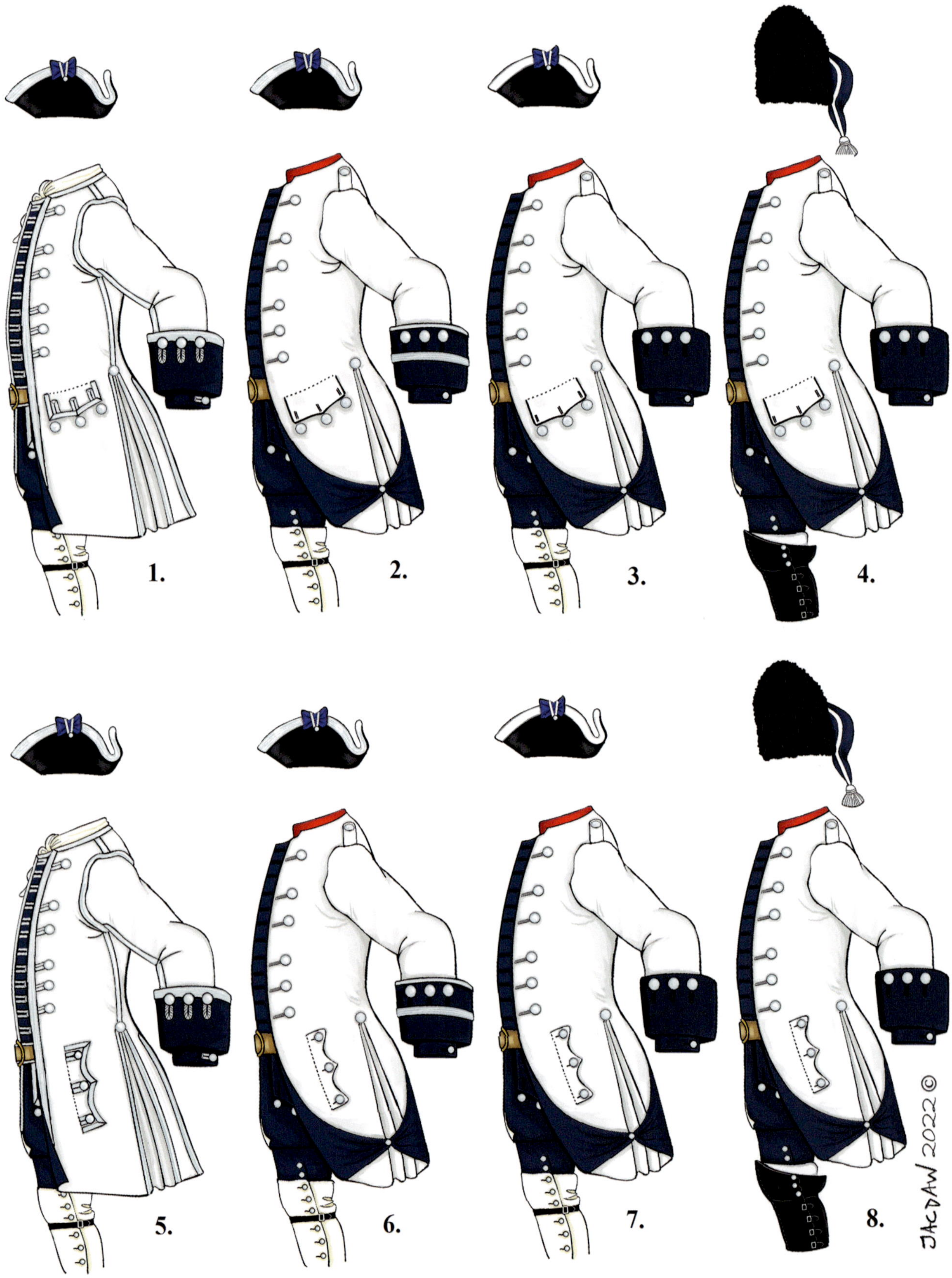

Reggimento Provinciali di Nizza, circa 1740; 1. Officer. 2. *Sergente*. 3. *Fuciliere*. 4. *Granatiere*. *Reggimento Provinciali di Pinerolo* circa 1740; 5. Officer. 6. *Sergente*. 7. *Fuciliere*. 8. *Granatiere*. (Author's Illustration)

NCOs

In the grenadier company the NCOs wore the bearskin cap which had a blue bag with imitation silver lacing and an imitation silver hanging tassel.

Officers

The officers' tricorns had silver lace border and loop, a Savoy blue cockade, and silver button. The officers' coats and waistcoats had silver lacing. The officers' bearskin caps had a blue bag with silver lacing and a silver hanging tassel.

Tamburi and Pifferi

The *tamburi*, *pifferi* and musicians wore the Royal Livery with blue waistcoats and breeches. The grenadier *tamburi* and *pifferi* wore bearskins as well.

Company Colours

Obverse, there was a white cross on a red field. In the first quarter was the coat of arms of the County of Pinerolo. The reverse was identical in mirror image. The standard had a thin white border all around, including the staff edge. The sleeves and the staves were painted red and studded with brass nails in a spiral design. The exact date of the fabrication of this model is unclear, but was in service in 1744. The spear shaped finial was gilded as was the cone shaped ferrule which was secured with a ring. The cords and tassels could be red or gold. The previous model was similar, but the quarters were medium blue with two red piles emanating from the cross in each quarter and the binding was red with a blue sleeve, according to the Album of Lauro circa 1734–1736.

Company colour, *Reggimento Provinciali di Pinerolo*. (Author's Illustration)

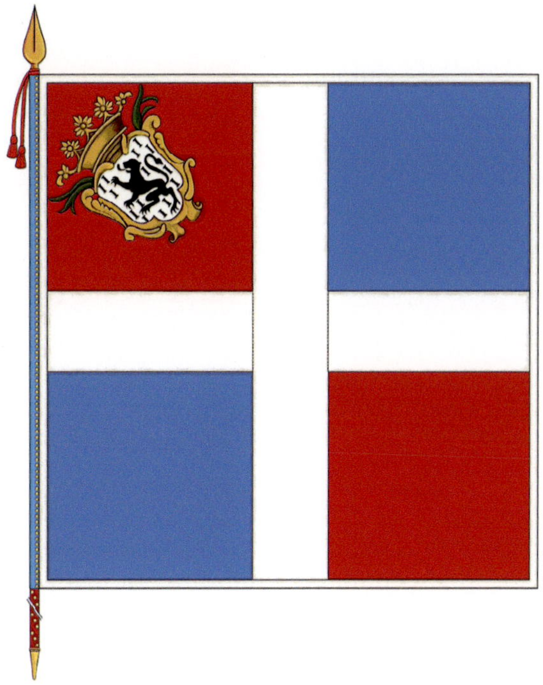

Chiablese, company colour. New colours were issued between 1734 and 1736 according to the Lauro manuscript. There were two variants. The quarters one and four were red, the quarters two and three were blue for the model A, which was issued to the *Chiablese* (illustrated), *Aosta*, *Torino* and *Vercelli* regiments. Obviously, the arms changed for each regiment. As the new colours were only recorded in 1744, these colours were probably still in service when the war commenced. (Author's Illustration)

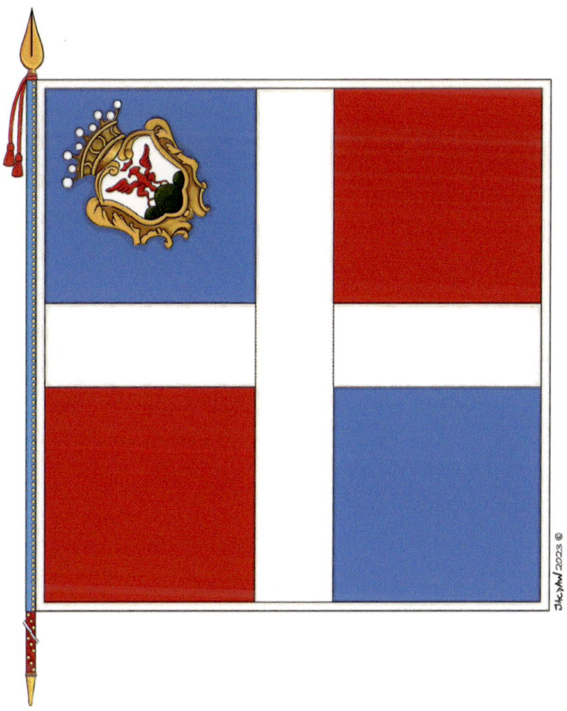

Nizza, company colour. The quarters one and four were blue, the quarters two and three were red for the model B, which was issued to the *Nizza* (illustrated), *Tarantasia*, *Mondovì* and *Asti* regiments. Obviously, the arms changed for each regiment. As the new colours were only recorded in 1744, these colours were probably still in service when the war commenced. (Author's Illustration)

8

The Foreign Foot Regiments

The *tamburi* of the foreign regiments, except the Italians, did not wear the royal livery. They wore either their *colonnello*'s livery or a regimental tenue.

The Swiss Infantry Regiments

The Swiss were the elite of the Sabaudian army. As the war dragged on the number of Swiss recruits dwindled, and although they were replaced with Germans and other nationalities, the units kept their reputation and qualities. As in the French army they were raised by a capitulation – a contract – with the different Swiss cantons.

Reggimento Svizzero di Rietmann (Kalbermatten, 1743)

This regiment was originally recruited in the cantons of Bern, Schwyz, Schaffhausen and Valais, but from 1743 they were recruited mainly in the Valais, and generally classed as a Valaisian regiment. The contract with the Catholic cantons was renewed in 1731, in 1741 for three battalions, and renewed again in 1748. For the first time this capitulation was without restrictions, the troops could now also be used offensively and on ships if needed. It was not just the largest regiment, but it was also probably the best unit of the army throughout the war.

In 1737 each of the three battalions had three companies, following the admission of three free companies from Valais, which had originally been raised in 1733 and been stationed in Sardinia until then. In 1740 the regiment's three battalions had a total strength of 1,800 officers and men. Each company consisted of around 150 officers and men. This was a German speaking regiment, and commands were given in German. In 1744 as *Kalbermatten* the regiment was raised to four battalions and now had 2,800 officers and men. Each battalion had six four companies and remained at this strength until the end of the war. By 1748 the regiment had been reduced to 2,100 officers and men in three battalions of four companies. Each company consisted of around 175 officers and men.

The *colonnelli* of the Regiment under Charles Emmanuel III were *Colonnello* Johann Rietmann, from 1732 until January 1743 when he left the regiment due to the injuries he had received in combat. He was succeeded by *Colonnello* Bruno de Kalbermatten.

Service

In 1742 *Rietman* started campaigning in north-east Italy in the plains of the Po. In September the first and second battalions marched from the camp in La Thule in Aosta valley to the Alps to campaign in against the Spanish army invading Savoy. The third battalion was placed in garrison in the fortresses of Fenestrelle, sometimes called the Great Wall of Piedmont. A second Spanish assault compelled King Charles Emmanuel III to call out several other battalions from their camps in Piedmont, so the third battalion left their barracks in Turin and by December they had re-joined the two other battalions.

In January 1743, after a cold winter campaign, Savoy was abandoned. The first and second battalions were present at the Battle of Casteldelfino, where the first battalion was heavily engaged at the village of Chateau, and they lost 86 men.

In 1744 the regiment returned to Piedmont and a new fourth battalion was raised for a grand total of 16 companies. The whole regiment marched to the Mediterranean to defend the entrenched camp built around the fort and port of Villefranche-sur-Mer (20 April 1744) where they fought a heroic defensive action.

In May the regiment received a new *colonnello*, Bruno de Kalbermatten, and the regiment became known as *Kalbermatten*. The regiment joined the army in the Varaita valley, but was only a spectator of the struggle around the redoubt of Mount Cavallo (19 July 1744). The regiment was then divided; the first and the second battalions defended the walls of Cuneo (12 September–22 October), while the third and the fourth battalions joined the main field army and were present at Madonna dell'Olmo (30 September 1744) where they lost 136 men. The two battalions were situated on the right wing of the second line.

In 1744 the regiment suffered heavy casualties together with some desertions and a number taken prisoner in the

1. Officer, *Reggimento Svizzero di Guilbert*. This junior officer has been given the lapels as worn by the men, but it is not clear as to whether the officers had them. The few small details taken from portraits of officers in their regimental uniforms do not have them, but they are senior or general officers. It is likely that the junior officers wore lapels if it was part of their regiments' uniform, but perhaps not the senior captains. 2. *Sergente, Reggimento Svizzero di Keller*. 3. Officer, *Reggimento Svizzero di Meyer*. 4. Officer, *Reggimento Italiano di Sicilia*. 5. *Sergente, Reggimento Alemanni di Baden*. 6. Officer, *Reggimento Straniera Misto di Monfort*. (Author's Illustration)

1. *Reggimento Svizzero di Kalbermatten.* This appears to be a *colonnello*'s livery. Possible variations of a lace in the cantonal colours are also shown. 2. *Reggimento Svizzero di Diesbach.* This appears to be a mix of regimental tenue and the livery of Diesbach as it was still being worn much later when they were Roy. The Diesbach lace as used by the French Diesbach regiment is also shown. 3. *Reggimento Straniera Misto di Monfort/Audibert.* This green coat appears to have been a regimental livery as it was already mentioned when they were called *Audibert*. Lace unknown, so not illustrated, some modern books have suggested the royal livery lace, but this is doubtful. 4. *Reggimento Svizzero di Salis.* This is based on the Striedbeck manuscript, circa 1761, and an anonymous 1780 manuscript, once conserved in the library of the Musée de L'Emperi, now dispersed. A variation of a different lace used by the Salis family is also shown. 5. *Reggimento Alemanni di Baden/Durlach.* This is based on a livery mentioned in a nineteenth century book, once conserved in the library of the Musée de L'Emperi, now dispersed. No secondary source has been found, so the accuracy is perhaps a little doubtful. This may only be the family's hunting livery, which was frequently, but not always, the same as a domestic livery. 6. *Reggimento Alemanni di Schulemburg.* This uniform appears to be a *colonnello*'s livery, lace unknown, but probably just silver or white. (Author's Illustration and Reconstructions)

1. *Fuciliere, Reggimento Svizzero di Diesbach.* 2. *Fuciliere, Reggimento Svizzero di Kalbermatten.* 3. *Granatiere, Reggimento Italiano di Sardegna.* 4. *Fuciliere, Reggimento Svizzero di Reydt.* 5. Granatiere, *Reggimento Alemanni di Schulemburg.* 6. *Fuciliere, Reggimento Alemanni di Burgsdorf.* Note, the *fucilieri* were still allowed to carry a sword. (Author's Illustration)

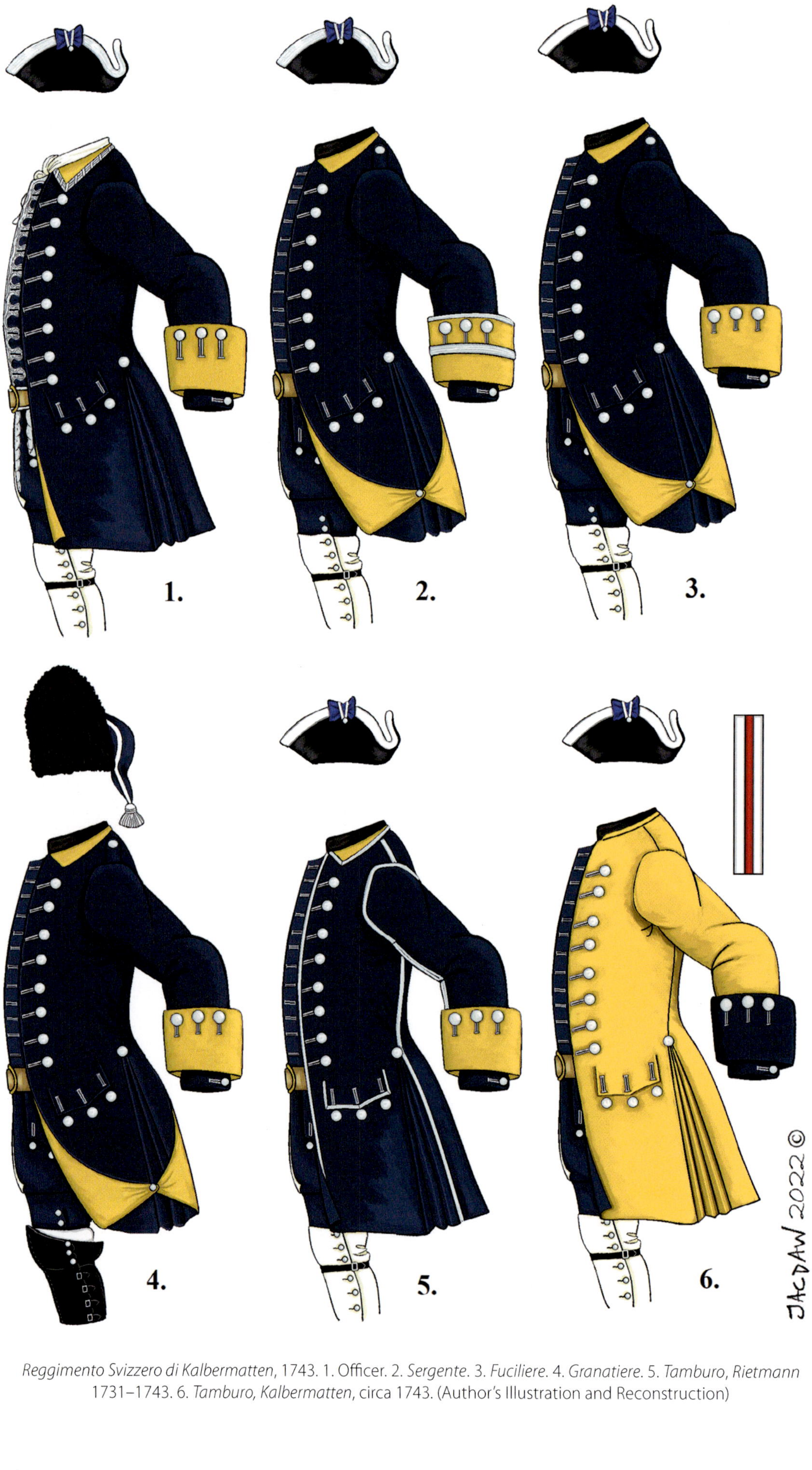

Reggimento Svizzero di Kalbermatten, 1743. 1. Officer. 2. *Sergente*. 3. *Fuciliere*. 4. *Granatiere*. 5. *Tamburo*, *Rietmann* 1731–1743. 6. *Tamburo*, *Kalbermatten*, circa 1743. (Author's Illustration and Reconstruction)

defence of the Piedmontese fortifications at Villefranche-sur-Mer and the fortress of Mont Alban, together with the regiments of *Keller* and *Roy/Roguin* among other troops.

In 1745, de Maillebois' offensive terminated with the Battle of Bassignana (27 September). *Kalbermatten* was in the centre of Sardinian line, defending from the hills a bridge over the Tanaro river. A battalion of the regiment took action to break the encirclement of *Guibert* from the rear. The following year *Kalberamatten* was part of Baron Leutrum's army, at the sieges of Asti and Tortona. The four battalions then fought in the south-west of the Mediterranean theatre. The first battalion fought during the offensive in Provence (30 November 1746–3 February 1747). During the operations on the Ligurian front, a French offensive was launched in the Susa valley. Two battalions of *Kalbermatten* immediately marched to the Alps, firstly to Breil-sur-Roya. The second and the third battalions marched through the mountains to the Assiette and were in the redoubts that defended the peak of the Gran Serin in the entrenched camp at the Assietta ridge. These battalions held their positions facing the French right column at the Battle of Assiette (19 July 1747), where they played a decisive role. They were present in the valley of Stura di Demonte. At the end of the war, *Kalbermatten* received a new capitulation for 10 years, but the 4th battalion was disbanded.

Variant version of a *colonnello*'s colour, this one is attributed to a Swiss regiment. (Author's Illustration)

Uniforms

The fusilier companies wore a black tricorn with a dark blue cockade on the left brim with a black loop and a pewter button, and a white lace border. The regiment wore black neck stocks. They wore a deep blue coat with a deep yellow collar, cuff, linings and turn backs. It had eight pewter buttons on each side of the coat, placed in pairs, and four on the cuffs. Their buttons appear to have been slightly smaller than in the national regiments. The coat had horizontal pockets, each with three buttons. All the button holes were stitched with a white *bave* thread, this included both the coat and the waistcoat. Their waistcoats and breeches were deep blue. When they were not on campaign, they all wore white stockings.

Grenadiers

The grenadiers' bearskin caps had a blue, or possibly yellow, bag with white lacing and a white hanging tassel.

NCOs

The NCOs carried a halberd of a special Swiss style, it was somewhat medieval in appearance with a rounded axe head. The NCOs had their button holes stitched with silver and had silver hat lace. In the grenadier company the NCOs wore the bearskin cap which had a blue bag with imitation silver lacing and an imitation silver hanging tassel.

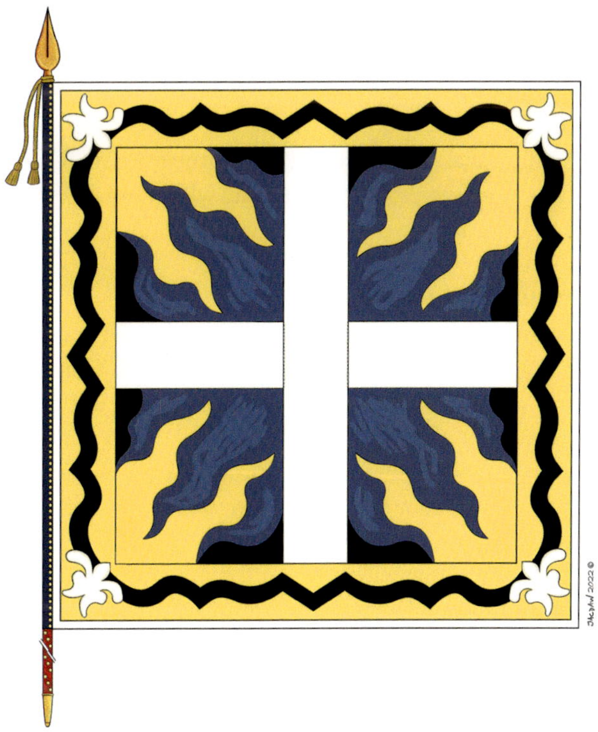

Company colour, *Reggimento Svizzero di Reitman*. (Author's Illustration)

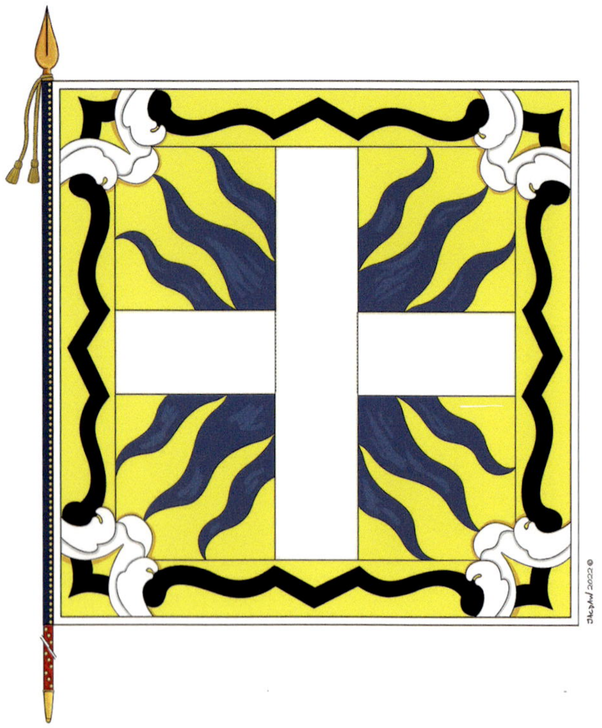

Company colour, *Reggimento Svizzero di Kalbermatten. Kalbermatten* continued to carry the old colours of *Reitmann* until 1747, if not longer. (Author's Illustration)

Officers

The officers' tricorns had silver lace border and loop, a Savoy blue cockade with a silver button. The officers' coats had silver lace with button holes stitched with silver lace and domed silver buttons. Their coats were fairly austere according to the portrait of the *colonnello*. The officers had wide floral style silver lacing on their waistcoats. The officers' bearskin caps had a red bag with silver lacing and a silver hanging tassel.

Tamburi and Pifferi

As Rietman's regiment, the *tamburi, pifferi* and musicians appear to have worn the regimental uniform. They had a deep blue coat and yellow facings, the same uniform as the rest of the men, the coat had silver lace on seams and leading edges. Their waistcoats and breeches were also deep blue. This may have been the *colonnello*'s livery, but it does not seem likely.

It appears that as *Kalbermatten* the regiment dressed their *tamburi, pifferi* and *tamburo maggiore* in reversed regimental colours – a yellow coat, with blue cuffs and lining, waistcoat and breeches. The livery lace was possibly a red line on a white galloon (the colours of Valais), as shown on the drum, but if it was used it would have been placed on seams and leading edges. The *tamburi* and *pifferi* of the grenadier company wore bearskins.

Company Colours

Obverse, there was a white cross on a yellow field, bordered by a large yellow border. This border is charged, in the centre of the yellow with a wavy black 'ribbon' all round, with a white stylised fleur de lys in the corners. In each quarter three blue flames emanating from the inner angles of the cross. There were two black counter flames at each edge. The standard had a thin white border all around, including the staff edge. The reverse was identical in mirror image. The sleeve was blue and the stave was painted red, with brass headed studs nailed in a spiral design. As *Kalbermatten* the colours did not have any black flames and the motifs in the angles appear to have changed, but this could simply be an error of the copyist. The gilded head is shaped like a pike. The brass ferrule is round in shape and with a ball at the tip. The cords and tassels appear to be gold.

Reggimento Svizzero di Guibert (Uttiger, 1746)

The regiment was first raised in 1733 and recruited in the cantons of Geneva, Solothurn, Zug, Zurich, Vaud and Neuchâtel. This was a private capitulation by Alexandre Guibert de Sissac, from Neuchâtel, with King Charles Emanuel III of Savoy. It was renewed in 1737 and in 1741, including two extra companies to raise the regiment to three battalions. In 1740 the regiment had 1,200 officers and men in two battalions each of six companies. Each company consisted of around 100 officers and men. The regiment rose to 2,100 officers and men in three battalions in 1743 and remained as such until 1747.

The *colonnelli* of the regiment under Charles Emmanuel III were Alexander Guibert de Saissac, or Seyssac. He was wounded at the Battle of Pietralunga, captured then released, but later died of his wounds in January 1746. He was succeeded by Beat Gaspard Uttiger.

Service

In 1742 the first and second battalions participated in the Po campaign, and the following year their action was decisive at Chateau Dauphin. In 1744 the third battalion fought at Villefranche-sur-Mer, and the first and second battalions at the Battle of Pietralunga, where they were heavily engaged and lost 132 men. The third battalion was present in the defence of Cuneo and the first and second battalions fought at the Battle of Madonna dell'Olmo. They returned to the south in the spring of 1744 and were part of the Piedmontese forces that halted the first onslaught of the army of the Spanish Infante Philip on the Piedmontese fortifications at Villefranche-sur-Mer and the fortress of Mont Alban.

The coats of arms of some of the *colonnelli* of the foreign regiments. These armorials could have been found painted on their drums. Top row, left to right, Kalbermatten, Uttinger, Diesbach, Roi, Swiss. Middle row, left to right, Reydt, Salis, Meyer, Keller. Bottom row, left to right, Von Schulemberg, Von Burgsdorff, Audibert de Lussan, Guillaume IV De Bude, Baron Monfort. (Author's Illustration)

In 1745 the first and second battalions were heavily engaged at the Battle of Bassignana, where they performed an excellent defensive action, but the *Colonnello* Guibert was wounded, taken prisoner, and later died of his wounds. In 1746 the third battalion was at Asti, and the Siege of Tortona, while the first battalion took part in the invasion of Provence. In 1747 they fought in the Ligurian campaign. It was a regiment with an excellent reputation mainly due to *Colonnello* Guibert, who was an exceptionally gifted tactician.

Uniforms

The fusilier companies wore a black tricorn with a dark blue cockade on the left brim, with a black loop and a pewter button, and white lace border. The men wore black neck stocks. They wore a deep blue coat, which had red lapels (*Matelotte*) from 1744 at the latest, probably before. The lapels continued down to the turnbacks. The coat had six pewter buttons on each side, and four on the cuffs. The coat had horizontal pockets, each with three buttons and all the button holes were stitched with white thread. The coat had light red cuffs, lapels and linings, and turn backs.

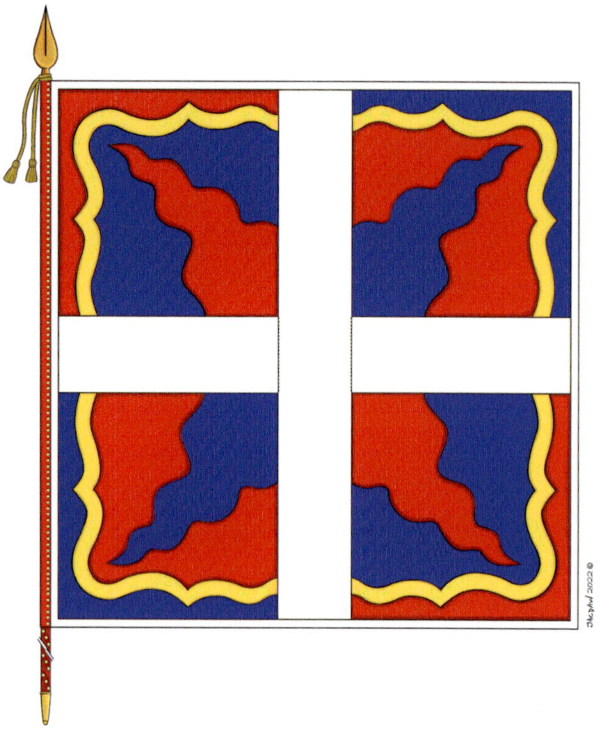

Company colour, *Reggimento Svizzero di Guibert/ Uttinger*. (Author's Illustration)

Their waistcoats and breeches were light red. When they were not on campaign, they all wore white stockings.

Grenadiers

The grenadiers' bearskin caps had a red bag with white lacing and a white hanging tassel.

NCOs

In the grenadier company the NCOs wore the bearskin cap which had a red bag with imitation silver lacing and an imitation silver hanging tassel.

Officers

The officers' tricorns had silver lace border and loop, a Savoy blue cockade and silver button. The officers' coats and waistcoats had silver lacing. The officers bearskin caps had a red bag with silver lacing and a silver hanging tassel.

Tamburi and Pifferi

The *tamburi*, *pifferi* and musicians wore the colonel's livery coat which is unknown, with light red waistcoats and breeches. The grenadier *tamburi* and *pifferi* wore bearskins.

Company Colours

Obverse, a white cross, with the quarters one and four blue with a red outer border and a single flame issuing from the angle of the cross, a thin undulating yellow border separating the outer border from the quarter. Quarters two and three were red with a blue outer border and a single flame issuing from the angle of the cross, a thin undulating yellow border separating the outer border from the quarter. The reverse was identical in mirror image. The standard had a thin white border all around, including the stave edge. The sleeves were red, and the staves were painted red with brass headed studs nailed in a spiral design. As *Uttinger* both the sleeves and the staves were blue. The gilded head is shaped like a pike. The brass ferrule was round in shape and with a ball at the tip. The cords and tassels were gold.

Reggimento Svizzero di Diesbach (Roguin, Roi, 1744)

The regiment was originally raised in 1733 in Berne as *Roguin*, but became *Diesbach* in 1737. In 1738, a capitulation for 12 years was signed by King Charles Emanuel III with Bern.

The regiment became *Roguin* again in 1744, but the new *colonnello* was killed in action just a few months later, so the regiment then became *Roi* in 1744. That same year it was decided that the capitulation should be renewed every 12 years and the royal blue uniform was introduced. The regimental language was German. In 1740 the regiment had two battalions, each of four companies with a total strength of 1,200 officers and men. Each company consisted of around 120 officers and men. The regiment was augmented to 1,800 men in three battalions in 1742. This rose to 2,100 officers and men in three battalions by 1743, and remained as such until 1747. This was another elite unit, second only to *Kalbermatten*.

The *colonnelli* of the Regiment under Charles Emmanuel III were Albert-Louis Roguin de d'Yverdon, from the Vaud, from 1733. He was succeeded by Jean Rodolfe de Diesbach until April 1744 when in turn he was succeeded by Augustin Gabriel Roguin d'Yverdon in May 1744, but as he was killed in action on 19 July, he was immediately succeeded by Pierre Antoine Louis Roi di Romainmôtier in July 1744, until he died in 1760 aged 72.

Service

In 1742 the first and second battalions fought in the Po campaign, while the third battalion took part in the Savoy campaign. The regiment participated in the successful sieges of Modena and Mirandola in the Po valley. In the early part of the year and in autumn they were engaged in counter attacks from La Salle against the Spanish invasion in the Aosta valley.

In 1743 all the battalions of the regiment were united and fought at the Battle of Camposanto where they lost 139 men and the first and second battalions were at Chateau Dauphin. In 1744, they lost about 360 men (nearly a fifth of their strength) in the Varaita valley campaign (at the Battles of Rochaz and Pierre Longue), where the *Colonnello*

Reggimento Svizzero di Guibert; 1. Officer. 2. *Sergente*. 3. *Fuciliere*. 4. *Granatiere*. *Reggimento Svizzero di Diesbach*; 5. Officer. 6. *Sergente*. 7. *Fuciliere*. 8. *Granatiere*. (Author's Illustration)

Roguin was killed in action. They fought at the Battle of Madonna dell'Olmo.

In 1745, the first battalion fought at the Battle of Bassignana, the second in the defence of Tortona, and the third in the defence of Alessandria. In 1746 the first battalion was present in Asti and the siege of Valenza. In 1747 the first and second battalions were present in the Ligurian campaign, where together with *Kalbermatten*, they and the third battalion played a decisive role in the victory at the Battle of the Assiette and in the valley of Stura di Demonte. The regiment suffered heavy losses during this conflict.

Uniforms

The fusilier companies wore a black tricorn with a dark blue cockade on the left brim, with a black loop and a pewter button, and white lace border. The troop wore black neck stocks. They wore a deep (Royal) blue coat. The coat had eight pewter buttons on each side of the coat placed in pairs (this rose to 10 in 1747), with four on the cuffs. The coat had horizontal pockets, each with three buttons. The coat had a red collar, cuffs, linings and turn backs. Their waistcoats and breeches were both deep blue. All the button holes were stitched with white thread, including both the coat and the waistcoat. When they were not on campaign, they all wore white stockings.

Grenadiers

The grenadiers' bearskin caps had a red bag with white lacing and a white hanging tassel.

NCOs

The NCOs had silver lace rank distinctions, silver hat lace, and their button holes were stitched with thin silver thread. In the grenadier company the NCOs wore the bearskin cap which had a red bag with imitation silver lacing and an imitation silver hanging tassel.

Officers

The officers' tricorns had a silver lace border and loop, a Savoy blue cockade, and silver button. The officers' coats and waistcoats had silver lacing. The officers' bearskin caps had a red bag with silver lacing and a silver hanging tassel.

Tamburi and Pifferi

As *Diesbach*, the *Tamburi* and *Pifferi* wore a canary yellow coat, lined and cuffed red, with pewter buttons, red waistcoat and breeches. The lace was probably the family model; yellow with a black serpentine. The drums had red and yellow flames with red hoops and cords. As was fairly common, the cantonal colours were shown on the drum, in this case, as a Bernese regiment, red and yellow. The grenadier *tamburi* and *pifferi* wore bearskins.

Company colour, *Reggimento Svizzero di Diesbach*. (Author's Illustration)

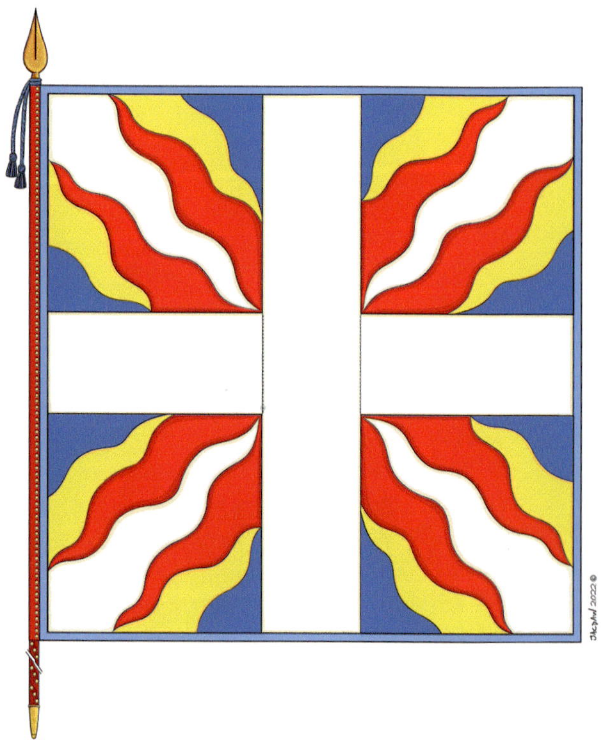

Company colour, *Reggimento Svizzero di Roi*. (Author's Illustration)

As *Roi* they still had a canary yellow coat, lined and cuffed with red. The coat had yellow swallow's nests edged with gold lace and white laced button holes. The drum was now painted with red and black flames and the hoops were striped red and white, the cords were natural. The *tamburi*, *pifferi* and musicians wore deep blue waistcoats and breeches.

Company Colours

The colour for *Diesbach* was, on the obverse, a white cross, in each quarter five flames issuing from the inner angle of the cross, red, black, red, black with four counter flames issuing from the exterior, yellow, white, white and yellow.[1] The reverse was identical in mirror image. The standard had a thin yellow border all around, including the staff edge. The sleeve was yellow and the staves were painted red and black in a spiral design. The spear shaped finial was gilded as was the cone shaped ferrule which was secured with a ring. The cords and tassels appear to be silver or possibly light blue.

When the regiment became *Roi* the colours changed. In each quarter there was a large white flame issuing from the top angle with a smaller yellow flame either side with four counter flames issuing from the lower angle, blue, red, red and blue. The standard had a thin blue border all around. The sleeves and the staves were red. The cords and tassels were blue. A colour belonging to Tscharner was conserved in Switzerland at the Chateau de Penthes, its present location is unknown.

Reggimento Svizzero di Reydt (Salis, 1746)

This regiment was raised in 1742 with a capitulation between Johannes Reydt, of Chur and Graubünden, and King Charles Emanuel III, represented by Carlo Vincenzo Ferrero di Roasio, Margrave of Orméa, who was the Foreign and Interior Minister. The regiment became Salis in 1746.

In 1743 the strength of the regiment was 2,100 officers and men divided into three battalions each of four large companies. Each company consisted of around 175 officers and men and remained as such until 1747. In 1744, the capitulation was to be renewed every 12 years, but the royal blue uniform was only adopted after 1747, or probably only after 1750.

The *colonnelli* of the regiment under Charles Emmanuel III were Jean Reydt of Coira (Chur), Grisons. He was succeeded by Thomas, Baron de Salis (Salice), Seigneur de Haldenstein in 1746, from the branch Salis-Maienfeld.

Service

In 1742 the regiment participated in the Savoy campaign. In 1743 they were at Mont Cenis, and the first battalion was at Chateau Dauphin. In 1744 the first and second battalions fought at the Battle of Madonna dell'Olmo. From September 1744 to February 1745, they were in the citadel of Alexandria where they suffered heavy losses. In 1745 the first and second battalions fought in the Defence of Alessandria, where *colonnello* Reydt fell ill and died of a disease. In 1746, under the name of *Salis* the first battalion served in the offensive on Provence, and in 1747 they fought in the Ligurian campaign.

Uniforms

The fusilier companies wore a black tricorn with a dark blue cockade on the left brim, with a black loop and a brass button, and yellow lace border. The regiment wore black neck stocks. In 1741 they had a red coat with red lining and turnbacks, with black cuffs and collar. The coat had eight brass buttons on each side, placed in pairs, and four on the cuffs. Their waistcoats and breeches were red. When they were not on campaign, they all wore white stockings.

Grenadiers

The grenadiers' bearskin caps had a red bag with yellow lacing and a yellow hanging tassel

NCOs

In the grenadier company the NCOs wore the bearskin cap which had a red bag with imitation silver lacing and an imitation silver hanging tassel.

Officers

The officers' tricorns had gold lace border and loop, a Savoy blue cockade and a gold button. The officers' coats and waistcoats had gold lacing. The officers' bearskin caps had a red bag with gold lacing and a gold hanging tassel.

Tamburi and Pifferi

The livery of *Reydt* is unknown. Logically as *Salis* the *tamburi*, *pifferi* and musicians should have worn a green coat, lined and cuffed yellow – the Salis Livery – but the lace is unknown, but red, white and green is a strong possibility with a red waistcoat and red breeches. These colours are taken from the Salis coat of arms, used by all branches in various combinations but always with a green coat faced yellow. As was fairly common, the cantonal colours were shown on the drum, in this case black and white as a Grisons regiment. The grenadier *tamburi* and *pifferi* wore bearskins. A contemporary illustration dated to 1750 shows them in red coats, probably as *Sprecher* as the men now have the new blue coats. The rest is unknown.

Company Colours

As *Reydt* they had on the obverse, a white cross, within each quarter three red flames issuing from the inner angle of the cross with four counter flames issuing from the exterior, black yellow, sky blue and black. The reverse

1 It is interesting to note the Regiment de Diesbach in the service of the France used exactly the same selection of colours as Diesbach Sabaudian which corresponded to his armouries (sable, a bend dancetté between two lions rampant or, armed and langued gules), but in a different disposition.

Reggimento Svizzero di Reydt (*Salis*, 1746); 1. Officer. 2. *Sergente*. 3. *Fuciliere*. 4. *Granatiere*. Note, the bag of the grenadier cap may have been black with yellow/gold lace. (Author's Illustration)

was identical in mirror image. The standard had a thin red border all around, including the stave edge. The sleeve was red and the stave was painted in red and black spirals in 1744. The spear shaped finial was gilded as was the cone shaped ferrule which was secured with a ring. The cords and tassels were sky blue.

Company colour, *Reggimento Svizzero di Reydt*. This colour was also used by Salis, and by his successor Schwartz. (Author's Illustration)

Reggimento Svizzero di Keller

This regiment was raised in 1742 by a 10-year capitulation with Lucerne, between Schultheiss Ludwig Schumacher and King Charles Emanuel III, represented by Carlo Vincenzo Ferrero di Roasio, Marchese di Orméa. They were recruited in the canton of Lucerne. In 1743 the regiment consisted of 1,400 officers and men divided into two battalions, each of four companies, each company consisted of around 175 officers and men and remained as such until 1747. The lack of replacements led to them accepting a number of enemy deserters. The regiment was disbanded in 1749. The *colonnello* of the regiment under Charles Emmanuel III was Johann Martin Franz Keller of Lucerne and the *luogotenente colonnello* was Anton Schumacher, the nephew of the mayor, both from Lucerne.

Reggimento Svizzero di Keller; 1. Officer. 2. *Sergente*. 3. *Fuciliere*. 4. *Granatiere*. *Reggimento Svizzero di Meyer*. 5. Officer. 6. *Sergente*. 7. *Fuciliere*. 8. *Granatiere*. (Author's Illustration)

Service

In 1742, the first battalion participated in the campaign in Savoy and the second battalion was on garrison duty in Sardinia, where this battalion suffered a high rate of desertion – nearly 50 percent of the battalion. In 1743 they were still on garrison duty. In 1744, the first battalion, which was under strength, was badly placed on the battlefield of Villefranche-sur-Mer and they were forced to surrender after a three-hour fire fight, but only after the *colonnello* received the assurance that they would not be executed. It was at this battle that Victor Amédée François Philippe de Savoie, Marquis de Suze, the king's step brother, was captured along with *Colonnello* Keller. *Luogotenente Colonnello* Schumacher left Sardinia where he had been posted and temporarily took command of the first battalion. In 1745 they were at Ceva. From 1746 to 1747 they performed more garrison service until they were disbanded. It was considered an unlucky regiment as they were nearly destroyed twice, once in Savoy and again at Villefranche-sur-Mer, and they continued to suffer heavily from desertion as well.

Company colour, *Reggimento Svizzero di Keller*. (Author's Illustration)

Uniforms

The fusilier companies wore a black tricorn with a dark blue cockade on the left brim, with a black loop and a pewter button, and white lace border. The regiment wore black neck stocks. They wore a deep blue coat that had eight pewter buttons on each side, placed in pairs, with four on the cuffs. The coat had a horizontal pocket on each side, each with three buttons. The coat had a red collar, cuffs, and linings and turn backs. All the button holes were stitched with white thread. Their waistcoats and breeches were red. When they were not on campaign, they all wore white stockings.

Grenadiers

The grenadiers' bearskin cap had a red bag with white lacing and a white hanging tassel.

NCOs

In the grenadier company the NCOs wore the bearskin cap which had a red bag with imitation silver lacing and an imitation silver hanging tassel.

Officers

The officers' tricorns had a silver lace border and loop, a Savoy blue cockade, and silver button. The officers' coats and waistcoats had silver lacing. The officers' bearskin caps had a red bag with silver lacing and a silver hanging tassel.

Tamburi and Pifferi

The *tamburi*, *pifferi* and musicians probably wore the *colonnello*'s livery coat, which is unknown, with a red waistcoat and breeches. The grenadier *tamburi* and *pifferi* wore bearskins.

Company Colours

Obverse, a white cross, each quarter was sky blue with four white flames issuing from the exterior. In the first quarter there was a cartouche within a gold frame depicting Saint Maurice on a white horse and holding a sword. The background shows a light blue sky and a terraced soldier dressed in red on the green ground. The reverse was identical in mirror image. The colour had a thin sky-blue border all around, including the stave edge. The sleeve was blue and the staves were painted red and studded with brass nails in a spiral design. The iron spear shaped finial was gilded as was the cone shaped ferrule which was secured with a ring. The cords and tassels were gold. An original colour is conserved in the Historisches Museum in Lucerne, Switzerland.

Reggimento Svizzero di Meyer

The regiment was raised in 1744. Two companies were recruited in Glarus, and two companies in Appenzell. In 1744 the regiment consisted of 700 officers and men in one battalion, and they remained as such until 1747. When they were originally raised, they were all recruited from Protestants. Each company consisted of around a 170 officers and men. Orders were given in German. The *colonnello* of the regiment under Charles Emmanuel III was Adrian Meyer of Harrisau.

Service

In 1744 they were on garrison duty. In 1745 they were present at the disaster of Joussaud were they lost 151 men, nearly a quarter of the regiment. In 1746 they were in Asti. In 1747 they fought at the Battle of the Assiette, and in the Valle Stura di Demonte. Although they were originally raised as a garrison regiment, from 1746 onwards, they were constantly employed in front line service.

Uniforms

The fusilier companies wore a black tricorn with a dark blue cockade on the left brim, with a black loop and a brass button, and yellow lace border. The regiment wore black neck stocks. They wore a deep blue collarless coat that had eight brass buttons on each side, in pairs, and four on the cuffs. The button holes were stitched with blue thread. The coat had two vertical pockets on each side, each with three buttons. The coat had red cuffs, linings, and turn backs. Their waistcoats and breeches were red. When they were not on campaign, they all wore blue stockings.

Grenadiers

The grenadiers' bearskin cap had a red bag with yellow lacing and a yellow hanging tassel.

NCOs

The NCOs' buttonholes were stitched with yellow bave, the rank distinctions and hat lace were gold. In the grenadier company the NCOs wore the bearskin cap which had a red bag with imitation gold lacing and an imitation gold hanging tassel.

Officers

The officers' tricorns had a gold lace border and loop, a Savoy blue cockade, and a gold button. The officers' coats had gold lace on all seams, and gold lace rank distinctions on their cuffs, and gilt buttons. The officers' bearskin cap had a red bag with gold lacing and a gold hanging tassel.

Tamburi and Pifferi

The *tamburi*, *pifferi* and musicians probably wore the *colonnello*'s livery, which is unknown, with a red waistcoat and red breeches. The grenadier *tamburi* and *pifferi* wore bearskins.

Company Colours

Obverse, a white cross on a red field, in each quarter there were four green flames issuing from the exterior. In the first quarter there was a diagonally placed cartouche within a gold frame depicting a brown bear. The standard had a thin white border all around, including the stave edge. The reverse was identical in mirror image. The sleeve was red, and the staves were covered with green velvet and studded with brass nails in a spiral design. The spear shaped finial was gilded as was the cone shaped ferrule which was secured with a ring. The cords and tassels were green.

Company colour, *Reggimento Svizzero di Meyer.* (Author's Illustration)

The Regiments of German Infantry

Reggimento Alemanno di Schulenburg

The regiment was originally raised in 1697. In 1740 it consisted of 1,200 officers and men divided into two battalions. This rose to 1,400 officers and men, still in two battalions, in 1743, and remained as such until 1747. The *colonnello* of the regiment under Charles Emmanuel III was Christoph Daniel von der Schulenburg, from 1729 till 1754. The *luogotenente colonnello* was Enrico Hartwig II Falkemberg, Baron di Schulenburg, from 1735 to 1745.

Service

The regiment entered the war in the spring 1742 when they marched to Parma and Piacenza. In August, while the whole army was transferred to the Alps, *Schulenburg* was in garrison at Pavia. The follow year the regiment fought at the Battle of Camposanto (8 February 1743).

They then returned to Piedmont, but saw very little action there. In 1744, when the combined *Gallispan* army broke through the Alps in the Stura valley, the two battalions

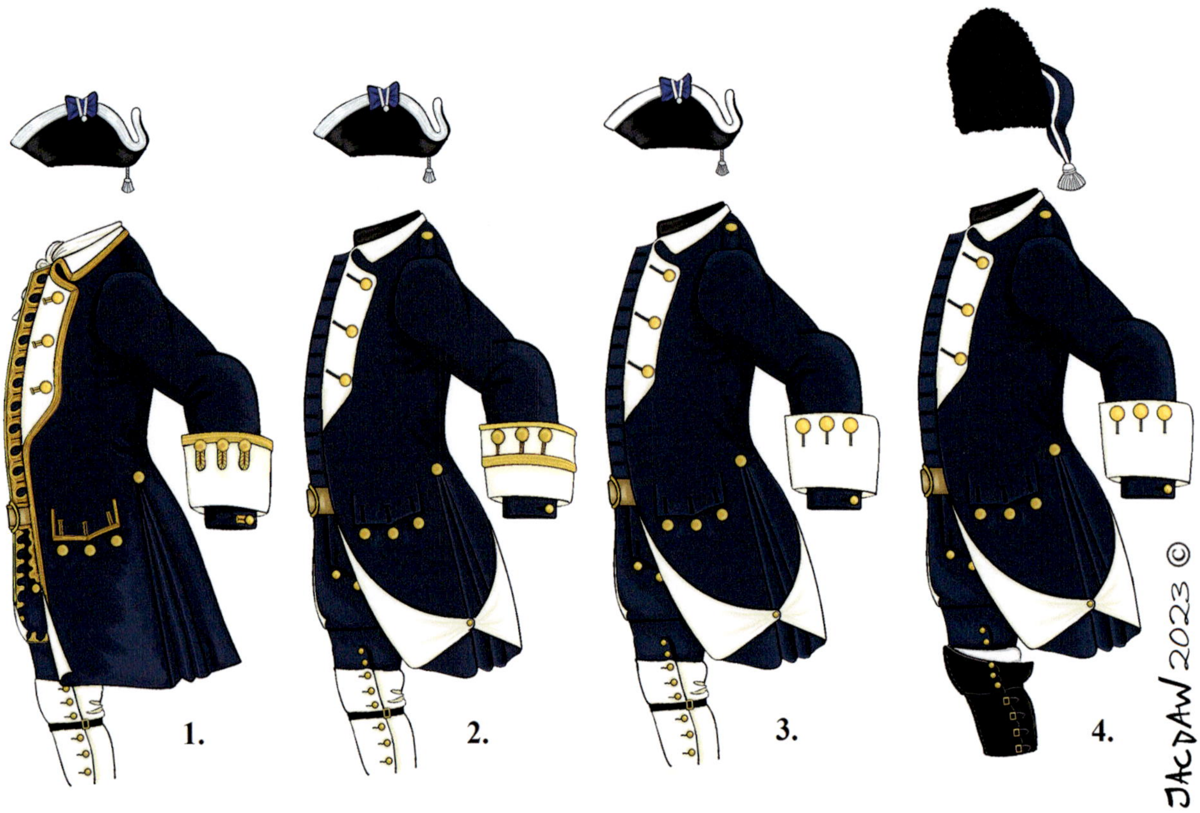

Reggimento Alemanno di Schulenburg; 1. Officer. 2. *Sergente*. 3. *Fuciliere*. 4. *Granatiere*. Note the hanging tassel on the tricorn, right side only, unique to this regiment, but it became more generally used after 1750. (Author's Illustration)

left behind their garrison life and were divided. The second battalion fought in the defence of Cuneo (9 September–22 October 1744). The first battalion was present in the relief army and it fought at the Battle of Madonna dell'Olmo (30 September 1744), where they were placed on the left wing. The battle was lost, but the siege of Cuneo was lifted.

The following year Piedmont was victim of de Maillebois' offensive. During the attempt to stop it at Bassignana on the Po and Tanaro rivers (27 September 1745) the regiment was placed on the right wing of the Sardinian line. The regiment was present during Leutrum's counter offensive in the spring of 1746. In the November of the same year, the second battalion fought in the west, in the offensive on Provence, while the first battalion besieged the fortress of Priamar, inside the port of Savona (1–18 December 1746). In 1747 both battalions were reunited in the Oneglia region, in the Ligurian theatre.

Uniforms

The fusilier companies wore a black tricorn with a dark blue cockade on the left brim, with a black loop and a pewter button, and white lace border. The tricorn had a small white tassel hanging from right corner. The men have been shown with black neck stocks in 1744, but strangely with red stocks in 1747, and then again with black neck stocks in 1750. Perhaps the red was an error of the artist.

In 1744 they wore a dark blue coat with a white collar, half lapels cuffs, linings and turn backs. The coat had three brass buttons on each lapel, with three on the cuffs. The coat had a horizontal pocket on each side, each with three buttons. Their dark blue waistcoats had small brass buttons and their breeches were also dark blue. When they were not on campaign, they all wore white stockings.

Grenadiers

The grenadiers' bearskin caps had a blue bag with white lacing and a white hanging tassel.

NCOs

The *sergenti* had two bands of imitation gold lace on their cuffs. In the grenadier company the *sergenti* wore the bearskin cap with a blue bonnet with imitation either silver or gold lacing and an imitation silver or gold hanging tassel.

Officers

The officers' hats had a silver tassel, lace and loop, with a deep blue cockade and a gold button. Their coats had gold lace on the seams, cuffs, and pockets, and gilt buttons. The officers' bearskin cap had a blue bag with silver lacing and a silver hanging tassel. It is not certain that the officers coats had the lapels. A portrait of *Colonnello* Christoph Daniel Birkoltz von Schoulembourg in his regimental uniform

Company colour, *Reggimento Alemanno di Schulenburg*. (Author's Illustration)

does not have lapels, but 10 buttons placed in pairs with a lot of fine floral embroidery and very large lace embroidery on the cuffs. One can imagine that junior officers had the lapels, but not the senior captains and above.

Tamburi and Pifferi

The *tamburi*, *pifferi* and musicians wore red coats with yellow cuffs and lining, with a yellow waistcoat, red breeches and brass buttons. Their lace, if any, is unknown. The drum is described as white with blue flames. The grenadier *tamburi* and *pifferi* wore bearskins.

Company Colours

On the Obverse, a white cross, in each quarter there were three large red flames and two small black flames issuing from the inner angle and four large yellow counter flames issuing from the exterior angle. The standard had a thin white border all around, including the stave edge. The reverse was identical in mirror image. The sleeve was yellow and the staves were painted red, studded with brass nails in a spiral design. The spear shaped finial was gilded as was the cone shaped ferrule which was secured with a ring. The cords and tassels were yellow and gold. During the battle of Madonna dell'Olmo, the regiment drew heavy enemy artillery fire and the colours of the first battalion were literally torn to shreds by the shot.

Reggimento Alemanno di Rehbinder (Bourgsdorff, 1743)

In 1740 the regiment consisted of 1,200 officers in men in two battalions. This rose to 1,400 officers and men in two battalions in 1743 and remained as such until 1747. The *colonnello* of the Regiment under Charles Emmanuel III was Baron Bernard Otto Rehbinder of Estonia, but it was Guillaume IV, the adoptive son of Baron Rehbinder, who was the active commander from 1723. His mother was Irish, Mary O'Moore, Oge of Mordha, the widow of Baron Bourgsdorff of Juliers. In fact, he was only officially named *colonnello* in 1743. Baron Leutrum became the *colonnello* in 1749.

Service

The regiment entered the war in the spring of 1742 when they marched to Parma and Piacenza in the company of *Schulenburg*. In August, the first battalion was in garrison inside the small citadel of Parma, while the second battalion was in Piedmont, near the city of Rivoli. From this camp, in November the second battalion reached the front in Savoy, just in time to resist the Spanish invasion.

In January 1743, the regiment returned to Piedmont. The first battalion moved from its quarters at Parma and fought at the Battle of Camposanto (8 February 1743). During the second phase of the battle, three Spanish infantry brigades (*Guardia*, *Irlanda* and *Flandes*) smashed through the front line of the right wing of the Austro-Piedmontese army. From the second line *generali* d'Apremont and Leutrum led a counter charge with three battalions – *Savoye*, *Piemont* and *Rhebinder*. The right wing of the Spanish line was broken and compelled to withdraw.

During this action the Spanish *Guadalaxara* regiment was cut off from the rest of the army and forced to surrender.

Before the end of the year cannon fire was again heard over the Alps when a combined Spanish-French army tried to descend into the Piedmont from the Varaita valley but the Sabaudian army stopped its advance at Chateau Dauphin (8–10 October 1743). The first battalion of *Rehbinder* was in the centre of the valley, under the village of Castello, while the second battalion held the line further up to the Vallanta ravine.

In December 1743 Rhebinder died and the administration duties now fell under the *Ufficio del Soldo* (Finance Office) while the regiment became *Bourgsdorff*, the name of new commander.

In the spring 1744 *Bourgsdorff* arrived at the entrenched camp of the citadel and port of Villefranche-sur-Mer. On 20 April they faced the Franco–Spanish offensive. The grenadiers of *Bourgsdorff* were able to recapture the lost redoubts on Mont Gros and the Col de Villefranche with an enveloping movement in coordination with the grenadiers of *Saluce*, *Tarentaise* and *Guibert*.

Reggimento Alemanno di Rehbinder/Bourgsdorff; 1. Officer. 2. *Sergente*. 3. *Fuciliere*. 4. *Granatiere*. *Reggimento Alemanno di Baden*; 5. Officer. 6. *Sergente*. 7. *Fuciliere*. 8. *Granatiere*. (Author's Illustration)

Following the surrender of the Place, *Bourgsdorff* was placed inside the port of Oneglia. From there they returned to Piedmont, again in the Varaita valley, to see the combined Franco-Spanish army win the bloody struggle at the Battle of Pierrelongue on 19 July 1744.

The two battalions of the regiment were then divided; the first battalion was present in the main army and it fought at the Battle of Madonna dell'Olmo (September 30, 1744), in order to break the siege of Cuneo. The battalion was placed on the left wing. This battle was lost, but the siege of Cuneo is broken.

The follow year *Bourgsdorff* played very little part during the efforts to stop de Maillebois' offensive but both battalions were present during Leutrum's counter offensive in spring 1746. From 5–8 March 1746 they were present during the victorious siege of the city of Asti. In November of the same year the second battalion fought in the west, in the offensive in Provence. In 1747 both battalions were reunited around the port of Oneglia in the Ligurian theatre.

Uniforms

The fusilier companies wore a black tricorn with a dark blue cockade on the left brim, with a black loop and a pewter button, and white lace border. The men are shown with white neck stocks in 1744 and 1747. They wore a deep blue coat, with red lapels from 1748. The coat had eight pewter buttons on each side of the coat, three on the cuffs. The coat had horizontal pockets, each with three buttons. The coat had a red collar, cuffs, lapels, linings and turn backs. Their waistcoats and breeches were deep blue. When they were not on campaign, they all wore white stockings.

Arms

Exceptionally, the fusiliers of this regiment were permitted to carry swords with a yellow wool/gold sword knot (*dragona*); these were carried on a separate frog from the bayonet.

Grenadiers

The grenadiers' bearskin caps had a red bag with white lacing and a white hanging tassel.

NCOs

In the grenadier company the NCOs wore the bearskin cap which had a red bag with imitation silver lacing and an imitation silver hanging tassel.

Officers

The officers' tricorns had silver lace border and loop, a Savoy blue cockade, and silver button. The officers' coats and waistcoats had silver lacing. The officers' bearskin caps had a red bag with silver lacing and a silver hanging tassel.

Tamburi and Pifferi

As *Bourgsdorff*, the *tamburi* wore the regimental uniform, but with the addition of silver lace on the seams, pockets and around the cuffs, and probably down the edges of the coat, worn with a deep blue waistcoat and breeches. The grenadier *tamburi* and *pifferi* wore bearskins.

Company colours, *Reggimento Alemanno di Rehbinder/ Bourgsdorff*. The top colour was carried at the beginning of the war. It was replaced by the colour below, but exactly when is not clear. (Author's Illustrations)

Company Colours

This regiment had a special privilege of having the king's monogram on their company colours, an honour granted to Baron Rehbinder by Victor Amadeus II. Although the design was frequently modified it kept the same basic form. In 1733 the colour called '*Rehbinder Ancien*' had on the obverse a white cross on a red field. In the centre of the cross there was a gold crowned (with white pearls and the cross of St Maurice and a red cap), a white baroque shield within a gold frame bearing the royal monogram by supported by two rampant gold lions with their heads turned towards the exterior on each side. The reverse was identical in mirror image. In the first quarter there was a gold floral cartouche bearing a red cross on a green hill. The standard had a thin white border all around, including the stave edge. The sleeve was crimson, and the stave was painted yellow or gilded, studded with brass nails in a spiral design. The spear shaped finial was gilded as was the cone shaped ferrule which was secured with a ring. The cords and tassels were gold.

From 1744 the colour called '*Rehbinder Modern*' had a white cross on a red field. In the centre of the cross there was a large royal monogram, surmounted by a large gold crown with white pearls and the Cross of St Maurice botonny, without the red cap. In the first quarter there was a gold floral cartouche with a white field bearing a red cross on a blue hill, around the inside of the cartouche there was a white scroll inscribed with 'IN HOC SIGNO VINCES'. The reverse was identical in mirror image. The standard had a thin white border all around, including the stave edge. The sleeve was crimson and the stave was painted red and studded with brass nails placed in a linear design. The spear shaped finial was gilded as was the cone shaped ferrule which was secured with a ring. The cords and tassels were red and gold. By 1747, the crown had regained its red cap.

Reggimento Alemanno di Baden

This regiment was raised in 1742 and disbanded in 1749. In 1743 the regiment consisted of 1,400 officers and men in two battalions and remained as such until 1747. The *colonello* of the regiment under Charles Emmanuel III was Prince Karl Wilhelm Eugen of Baden-Dourlac and Hochberg, but the regiment was commanded by a *colonnello luogotenente*.

Service

The regiment was ready for action by the second half of 1742. In the summer it fought its first combat during the Spanish offensive. The first battalion was camped near the gap on Mount Cenis, ready to descend into Savoy in the counter offensive against the invading Spanish army. In November the Spanish pressure against the province of Savoy was mounting and from its barracks in Turin the second battalion marched to reach the Savoy front.

In January 1743, after about 100 days of continual fighting, the regiment, who had been heavily proven, returned to Piedmont to rest. Before the end of the year, they were again in action in the Alps when a combined Franco-Spanish army tried to penetrate into Piedmont from the Varaita calley, but the Sabaudian army stopped its advance at Chateau Dauphin (8–10 October 1743). The regiment held them further up the Vallanta ravine, brigaded with the second battalion of *Rehbinder*.

The enemy was repulsed but the following year they launched a greater and better planned offensive. The army led by the Prince de Conti made a number of feints in different Alpine valleys, but the main enemy's main thrust was in the Stura di Demonte valley, more to the south. The regiment marched to the head of the Maira valley. The two battalions were divided at the Battle of Madonna dell'Olmo (30 September 1744), which was fought to break the Siege of Cuneo. The first battalion was placed on the right wing, in the second line. In this sector an artillery battery was lost. The *Brigata Piemonte* (*Vercelli*, *Kalbermatten*, *Lombardia*, *Baden*, *Torino*, *Piemonte*), under the command of Martin de Challant, attacked the French brigades of Lyonnais and Stainville, and the cannons were recovered just in front of the church of Madonna dell'Olmo. Although they had lost the battle, the Siege of Cuneo had been raised.

The following year the regiment played little part during the efforts to stop de Maillebois' offensive but both battalions of the regiment were reunited and were present during the Leutrum's counter offensive in the spring of 1746. In November 1746 the first battalion fought in the west, during the offensive on Provence. At the beginning of February 1749, at the end of the offensive in Provence, the regiment was disbanded.

Uniforms

The fusilier companies wore a black tricorn with a dark blue cockade on the left brim, with a black loop and a brass button, and yellow lace border. The men wore black neck stocks. They wore a deep blue coat with a collar and lapels. The coat had eight brass buttons on each side of the coat, in pairs, with three on the cuffs. The coat had horizontal pockets, each with three buttons. All the button holes were stitched with white thread. The coat had a horizontal pocket on each side, each with three buttons. The coat had a red collar, cuffs, linings and turn backs. Their waistcoats and breeches were red. When they were not on campaign, they all wore white stockings.

Grenadiers

The grenadiers' bearskin cap had a red bag with yellow lacing and a yellow hanging tassel.

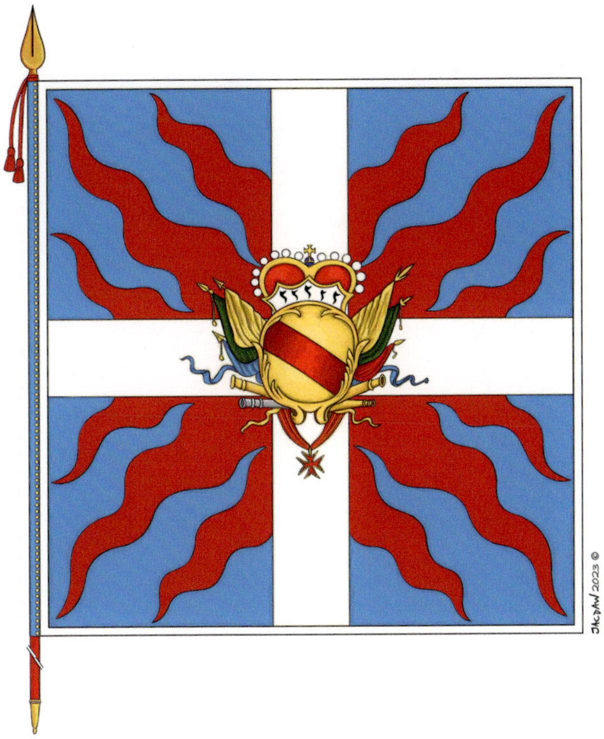

Company colour, *Reggimento Alemanno di Baden*. (Author's Illustration)

NCOs

In the grenadier company the NCOs wore the bearskin cap which had a red bag with imitation silver lacing and an imitation silver hanging tassel.

Officers

The officers' tricorns had a gold lace border and loop, a Savoy blue cockade, and gold button. The officers' coats and waistcoats had gold lacing. The officers' bearskin cap had a red bag with gold lacing and a gold hanging tassel.

Tamburi and Pifferi

The *tamburi*'s coat was bright green with red cuffs and lining, it eventually gained a red collar as well. It was worn with a green waistcoat and breeches. The buttons were silver. The lace, if any, is unknown. The grenadier *tamburi* and *pifferi* wore bearskins.

Company Colours

Obverse, on a blue field there was a white cross. In each quarter has three red flames issuing from the inner angle of the quarter. The coat of arms of the Margrave of Baden were placed in the centre of the cross. Below the shield, hanging from a blue ribbon, was an eight-pointed gold edged red cross of the Order of Loyalty. The reverse was identical in mirror image. The standard had a thin white border all around, including the stave edge. The sleeve was blue, and the staves were painted red and studded with brass nails in a spiral design. The spear shaped finial was gilded as was the cone shaped ferrule which was secured with a ring. The cords and tassels were red. Note the 1747 album has inversed the colours in the quarters.

The Regiments of Italian Infantry

Reggimento Italiano di Sardegna

The *Reggimento Italiano di Sardegna* was raised in 1744. In 1751 the regiment was re-classed as a national infantry regiment as the King was now the officially recognised sovereign of Sardinia. In 1744 the regiment consisted of 700 officers and men in one battalion. This rose to 800 officers and men in 1747.

The *colonnello* of the regiment under Charles Emmanuel III was Bernardino Antonio Genovese Cervellon, Duca di San Pietro from 26 July 1744.

Service

The regiment landed in Piedmont at the end of 1744, just in time to be employed during the futile attempts to stop de Maillebois' offensive. In 1745 *Sardegna* defended the city of Acqui Terme in the south of Piedmont against a Spanish column of Don Felipe's Army. On 14 July, the fortress was forced to surrender. The following year the regiment was transferred to the Mediterranean theatre where it guarded the southern borders of the Kingdom of Sardinia from the fortress of Ventimiglia until the end of the war.

Uniforms

The fusilier companies wore a black tricorn with a dark blue cockade on the left brim, with a black loop and a brass button, and yellow lace border. The regiment wore red neck stocks. They wore a greyish-white coat with a black collar. The coat had six brass buttons on each side, grouped as one, two and three, with three on the cuffs. The coat had horizontal pockets, each with three buttons, and had black cuffs, and white linings and turn backs. Their waistcoats and breeches were white. When they were not on campaign, they all wore white stockings.

Grenadiers

The grenadiers' bearskin caps had a black bag with yellow lacing and a yellow hanging tassel.

NCOs

In the grenadier company the NCOs wore the bearskin cap which had a black bag with imitation gold lacing and an imitation gold hanging tassel.

Officers

The officers' tricorns had a gold lace border and loop, a Savoy blue cockade and a gold button. The officers' coats

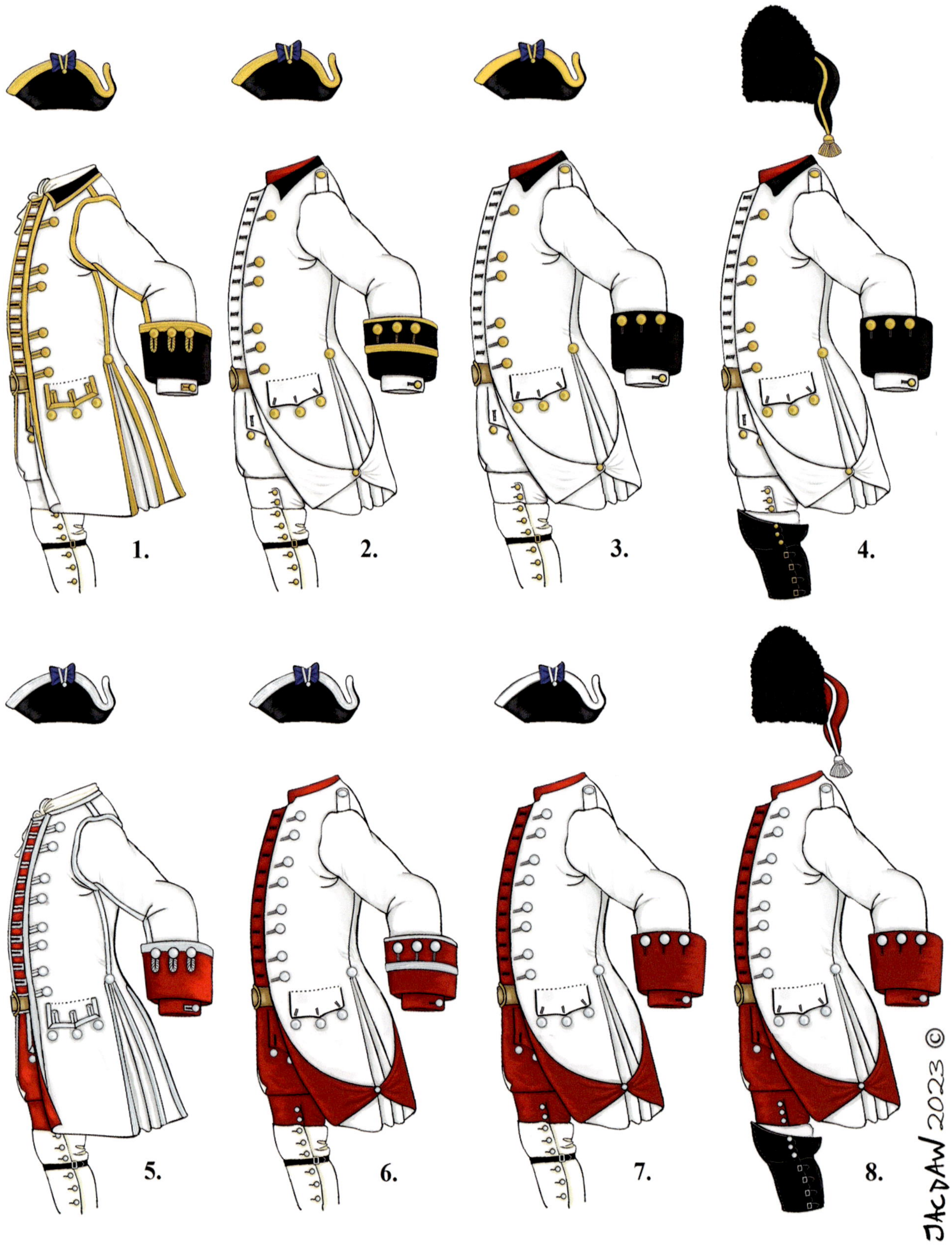

Reggimento Italiano di Sardegna; 1. Officer. 2. *Sergente*. 3. *Fuciliere*. 4. *Granatiere*. *Reggimento Italiano di Sicilia*; 5. Officer. 6. *Sergente*. 7. *Fuciliere*. 8. *Granatiere*. (Author's Illustration)

Company colour, *Reggimento Italiano di Sardegna*. (Author's Illustration)

and waistcoats had gold lacing. The officers' bearskin caps had a red bag with gold lacing and a gold hanging tassel.

Tamburi and Pifferi

The *tamburi*, *pifferi* and musicians wore the Royal Livery with white waistcoats and breeches. The grenadier *tamburi* and *pifferi* wore bearskins as well.

Company Colour

Obverse, in the centre there was a white cross. The quarters one and four were red with three flames black, white and black issuing from outer angle towards the centre. The quarters two and three were blue with three flames black, white and black issuing from outer angle towards the centre. In the first quarter was the arms of Sardinia. The reverse was identical in mirror image. The standard had a thin white border all around, including the stave edge. The sleeve was red and the stave was painted red and studded with brass nails in a spiral design. The spear shaped finial was gilded as was the cone shaped butt which was secured with a ring. The cords and tassels were blue.

Reggimento Italiano di Sicilia

The *Reggimento Italiano di Sicilia* was formed in 1722 from two existing Sicilian units originally created in 1714. The regiment was disbanded in 1751. In 1740 the regiment consisted of 600 officers and men in one battalion. This rose to 1,400 officers and men divided into two battalions in 1743, and remained as such until 1747. In 1749 the second battalion was disbanded. The *colonnelli* of the regiment under Charles Emmanuel III were the Chevalier Giuseppe La Guidara from 1735 to 1745, who was succeeded by Federico Martinengo, Conte da Barco, from 1745 until they were disbanded.

Service

In 1744, they were present at Villefranche, where they were forced to surrender. They were present at the Battle of the Assiette in 1747.

Uniforms

The fusilier companies wore a black tricorn with a dark blue cockade on the left brim, with a black loop and a pewter button, and white lace border. The regiment wore red neck stocks. They wore a greyish-white coat without a collar. The coat had eight pewter buttons, grouped in twos on each side of the coat, with three on the cuffs. The coat had horizontal pockets, each with three buttons and had red cuffs and lining. Their waistcoats were red with pewter buttons and their breeches were also red. When they were not on campaign, they all wore white stockings.

Grenadiers

The grenadiers' bearskin caps had a red bag with white lacing and a white hanging tassel.

NCOs

The NCOs had their buttonholes stitched with white bave, their distinctions and hat lace were silver. In the grenadier company the NCOs wore the bearskin cap which had a red bag with imitation silver lacing and an imitation silver hanging tassel.

Officers

The officers' tricorns had a silver lace border and loop, a Savoy blue cockade and a silver button. The officers' coats had silver lace seams, buttonholes and rank distinctions, with silver buttons. The officers' bearskin caps had a red bag with silver lacing and a silver hanging tassel.

Tamburi and Pifferi

The *tamburi*, *pifferi* and musicians wore the Royal Livery with red waistcoats and breeches. The grenadier *tamburi* and *pifferi* wore bearskins as well.

Company Colour

In the centre there was a white cross. Each quarter was red with a white flame issuing from each angle towards the centre, but without touching each other. In the first quarter was the arms of Sicily. The reverse was identical in mirror

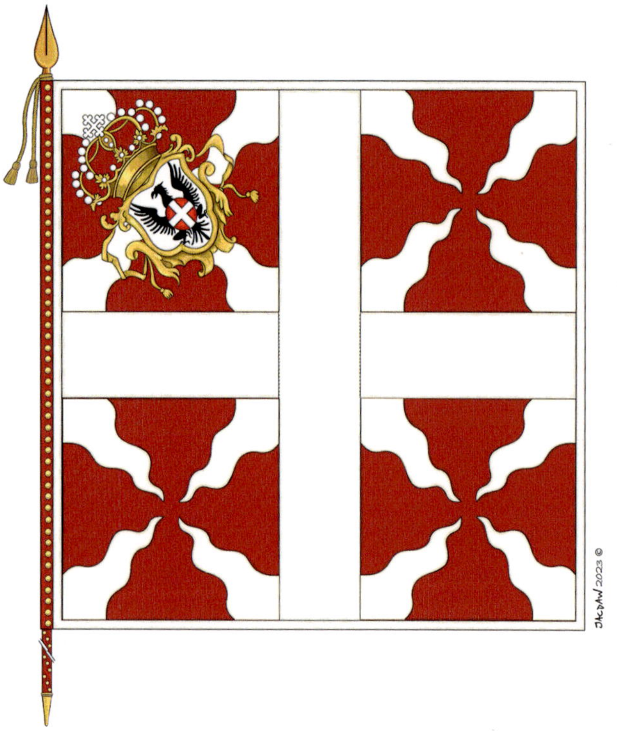

Company colour, *Reggimento Italiano di Sicilia* (Author's Illustration)

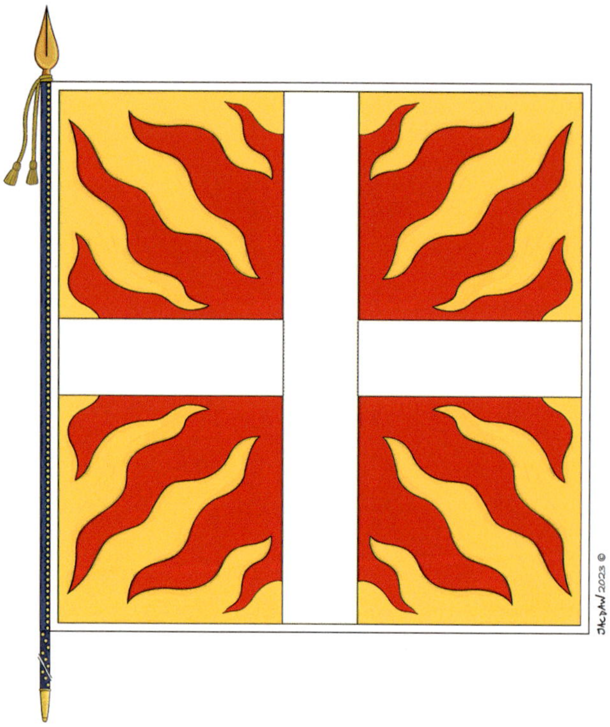

Company colour, *Reggimento Italiano di Lombardia.* (Author's Illustration)

image. This colour originally belonged to the *Reggimento Valguarnera*, which, became *Sicilia* in 1732.

The standard had a thin white border all around, including the stave edge. The sleeve and the stave were both red and the stave was studded with brass nails in a spiral design. The spear shaped finial was gilded as was the cone shaped ferrule which was secured with a ring. The cords and tassels were gold. They lost a company colour at the Battle of Villefranche, which was conserved in Madrid's Ameria Reale until 1884, when it was lost in a fire.

Reggimento Italiano di Lombardia

The *Reggimento Italiano di Lombardia* was raised in 1734 and disbanded in 1751. In 1740 the regiment consisted of 600 officers and men in one battalion. This rose to 1,400 officers and men divided into two battalions in 1743, and remained as such until 1747. The *colonnelli* of the regiment under Charles Emmanuel III were Victor Amedeo Filiberto Costa della Trinità from 1734. He was succeeded by Carlo Maurizio Maria Costa della Trinità from 1744 to 1748.

Service

The regiment was at Val Maira in 1744.

Uniforms

The fusilier companies wore a black tricorn with a dark blue cockade on the left brim, with a black loop and a pewter button, and white lace border. The regiment wore red neck stocks, but they had black neck stocks by 1747. They wore a greyish-white coat without a collar. The coat had nine pewter buttons, grouped in threes on each side, with three on the cuffs. The coat had horizontal pockets, each with three buttons and had mustard yellow cuffs, linings and turn backs. Their waistcoats were mustard yellow with pewter buttons and their breeches were white. When they were not on campaign, they all wore white stockings.

Grenadiers

The grenadiers' bearskin caps had a yellow bag with white lacing and a white hanging tassel.

NCOs

In the grenadier company the NCOs wore the bearskin cap which had a yellow bag with imitation silver lacing and an imitation silver hanging tassel.

Officers

The officers' tricorns had a silver lace border and loop, a Savoy blue cockade and a silver button. The officers' coats and waistcoats had wide and ornate silver lace.[2] The officers' bearskin caps had a yellow bag with silver lacing and a silver hanging tassel.

2 According to a contemporary portrait of Conte Vittorio Costa della Trinità, *colonnello* of *Reggimento Lombardia* in 1734.

Tamburi and Pifferi

The *tamburi, pifferi* and musicians wore the Royal Livery with mustard-yellow waistcoats and white breeches. The grenadier *tamburi* and *pifferi* wore bearskins as well.

Company Colour

Obverse, in the centre there was a white cross. Each quarter was red with four yellow flames issuing from the outer angle. The reverse was identical in mirror image. The standard had a thin white border all around, including the stave edge. The sleeve was sky blue and the stave was painted sky blue and studded with brass nails in a spiral design. The spear shaped finial was gilded as was the cone shaped ferrule which was secured with a ring. The cords and tassels were gold. Note the 1747 manuscript show different numbers of flames which is an error.

Reggimento Italiano di Corsica

The *Reggimento Italiano di Corsica* was officially established on 11 July 1744 with a capitulation between the Count of Rivarola and the King's minister, Count Bogino.

As a foreign regiment, it had pay equal to the Swiss and commands were given in Italian. It was to be made up of three battalions of 10 companies each, but only eight companies could be raised, half of which always lacked *capitani*. In 1747 it consisted of a single fusilier battalion of Corsicans, with some Italians and Genoese. In October 1750, having failed to complete the regiment with Corsicans, the regiment was sent to Sardinia and the free companies of pardoned deserters who served on that island were incorporated into it. The regiment was disbanded on 15 May 1751.

The *colonnelli* of the regiment under Charles Emmanuel III were Domenico, conte di Rivarola di Bastia, from August 1744. In 1748 he was succeeded by the Cavaliere della Vella (Villa?), who in turn was succeeded by Francesco Allerio Matra in April 1749 until they were disbanded.

Service

There is no service record as the regiment was never completed or went on campaign.

Uniforms

The fusilier companies wore a black tricorn with a dark blue cockade on the left brim, with a black loop and a brass button, and yellow lace border. The regiment wore red neck stocks. They wore a greyish-white collarless coat, the cuffs and lining were the same colour. The coat had eight brass buttons, grouped in twos on each side, with three on the cuffs, also grouped in twos. The coat had horizontal pockets, each with three buttons. Their waistcoats were red with brass buttons, also grouped in twos, and their breeches were red. When they were not on campaign, they all wore white stockings.

Grenadiers

The grenadiers' bearskin caps would have had a red bag with yellow lacing and a yellow hanging tassel, but as the regiment was never completed and they never appear to have had a grenadier company this bearskin is somewhat doubtful.

NCOs

If there had been a grenadier company, then the NCOs would have worn the bearskin cap with had a red bag, with imitation gold lacing, and an imitation gold hanging tassel.

Officers

The officers' tricorns had a gold lace border and loop, a Savoy blue cockade, and gold buttons. The officers' coats had gold lacing on their coats and waistcoats. The officers' bearskin caps would have had a red bag with gold lacing and a gold hanging tassel, had the company been formed.

Tamburi and Pifferi

The *tamburi, pifferi* and musicians wore the Royal Livery with red waistcoats and breeches.

Company Colour

Obverse, in the centre there was a white cross. Each quarter had seven flames issuing from the two outer sides of the quarter towards the centre of the cross; they were red, white, red, white, red, white, and red. In the first quarter was the arms of Corsica.[3] The reverse was identical in mirror image. The standard had a thin white border all around, including the stave edge. In 1744 the sleeve was in red cloth and the stave was painted red and decorated with brass studs in a spiral pattern, but the 1747 manuscript shows both the sleeve and stave, without studs, coloured light blue. The spear shaped finial was gilded as was the cone shaped ferrule which was secured with a ring. The cords and tassels were red.

3 Legend has it that the moor's head was blindfolded until 1755, when the Corsican patriot Pascal Paoli raised the blindfold so that symbolically the Corsican people could see – today it is shown as a headband. Others attribute the change to Gian Pietro Gafforio in 1745 as a sign of freedom from the servitude to Genoa. The reconstruction shows the correct version according to the 1747 manuscript. This detail probably applied to the arms on the colour of the Sardinian regiment as well.

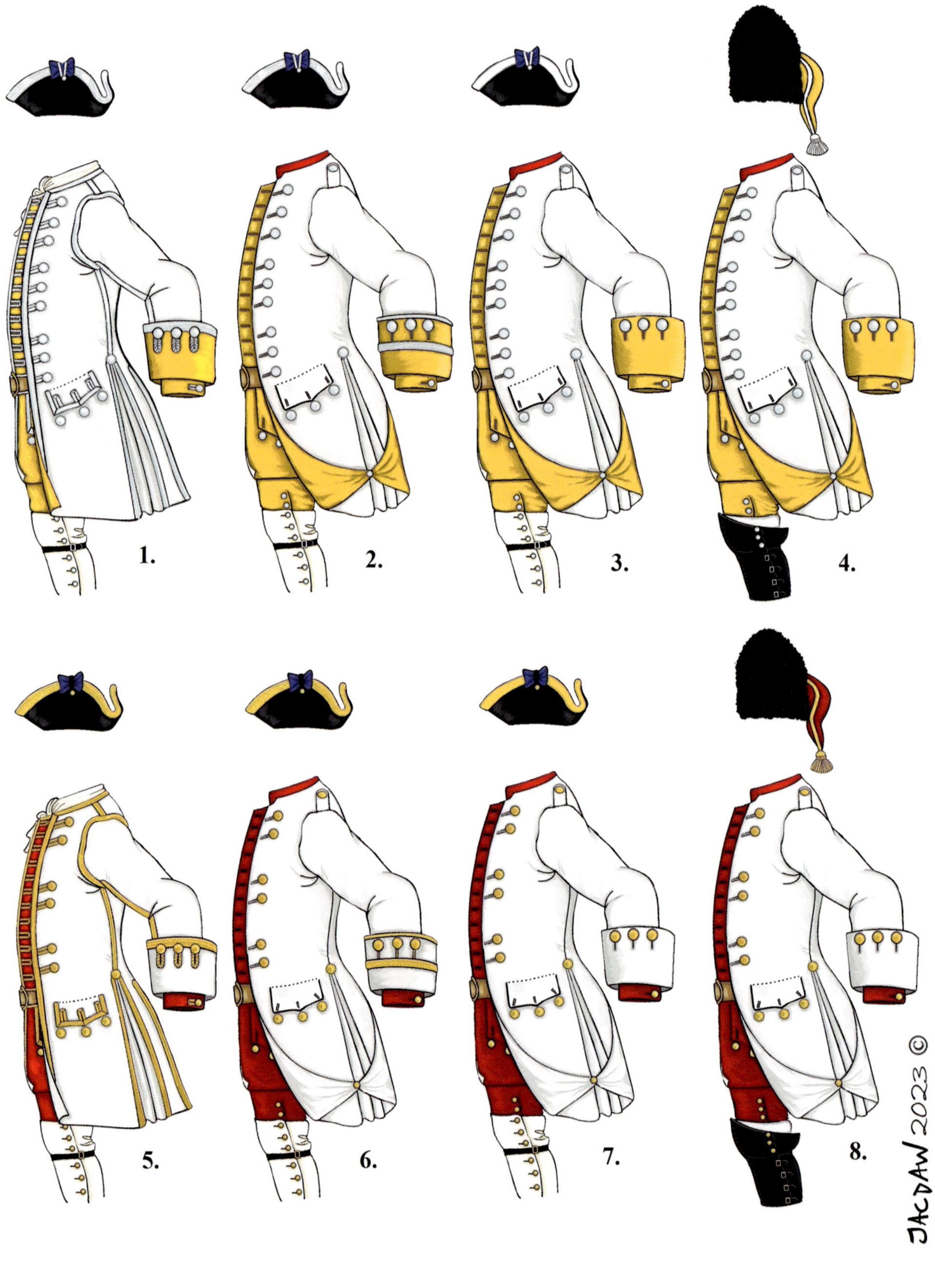

Reggimento Italiano di Lombardia; 1. Officer. 2. *Sergente*. 3. *Fuciliere*. 4. *Granatiere*. *Reggimento Italiano di Corsica*; 5. Officer. 6. *Sergente*. 7. *Fuciliere*. 8. *Granatiere*. This is the theoretical grenadier uniform, but due problems of recruitment, it is unlikely the grenadier company was ever formed and uniformed. (Author's Illustration)

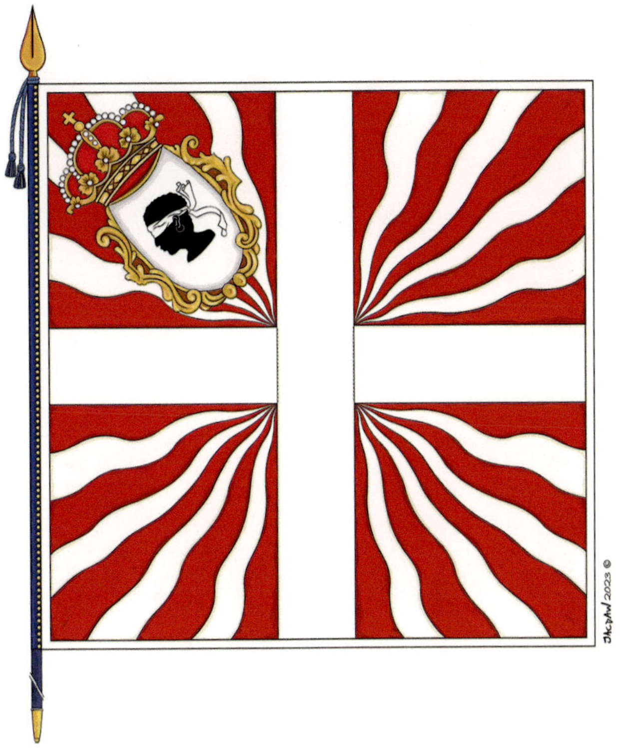

Company Colour, *Reggimento Italiano di Corsica*. (Author's Illustration)

Reggimento Straniera Misto di Audibert (Monfort 1746)

This regiment was first raised in 1703. By 1740 the regiment was composed of soldiers of mixed nationalities, but originally it had been recruited from French Huguenot refugees, with some Dutch and Irish, and even a few Englishmen; it was effectively a Protestant foreign legion. The regimental language was French and after the Seven Years War it was converted into a Catholic Regiment. In 1740 the regiment consisted of 1,200 officers and men in two battalions. This rose to 1,400 officers and men in two battalions in 1743, and remained as such until 1747.

The *colonnelli* of the regiment under Charles Emmanuel III were Jean Pierre Audibert from March 1739, and he was succeeded by the Chevalier Guillaume IV de Budé, Baron de Monfort, de Varache, de Genève, from April 1746.

Service

In 1742 only the first battalion was in the field, campaigning in north-eastern Italy in the plains of the valley of the Po. In September the first and second battalions marched to the Alps. The first battalion left the camp of Novalesa in the Susa valley and were sent to defend Mount Cenis, while the second battalion was placed inside the newly built fortress of Fenestrelle ready to reach Modane from Val du Roue and to undertake a campaign in Savoy against the invading Spanish army. In January 1743 after a cold winter campaign, Savoy was abandoned and the regiment retreated into Piedmont.

The regiment stayed on the alpine front until the summer of 1743, when it was sent to the Varaita valley. Posted above the village of Chateau, the regiment successfully stopped the Spanish autumn offensive. The western front remained at the centre of the war in 1744 and again the Varaita valley played a large part in the struggle. The first battalion fought inside the redoubt of Mount Cavallo (19 July 1744), and by the evening the battalion had lost 139 men.

The regiment was then attached to the main army to relieve the siege of Cuneo. The two battalions were present at the Battle of Madonna dell'Olmo (30 September 1744), were they were placed in the centre of the second line. In 1745, when Maillebois' offensive achieved its climax with the Battle of Bassignana (27 September), *Audibert* was placed on the right of Sardinian line, defending the plain before the village of Pietramarazzi. The following year they were present in Leutrum's army. In April the regiment received a new *colonnello*, Jean du Monfort de Varache, and they were renamed *Monfort*.

The two battalions were then separated. The first battalion fought in the south-west in the Mediterranean theatre during the invasion of Provence (30 November 1746–3 February 1747). While the operations on the Ligurian front were concentrated on Genoa, a French offensive was launched in the Susa valley. Immediately both battalions marched into the Alps. The first battalion controlled the Fattières and Finestre gaps in order to support the army which was entrenched on the Assietta ridge (19 July 1747).

Uniforms

The fusilier companies wore a black tricorn with a dark blue cockade on the left brim, with a black loop and a pewter button, and white lace border. The regiment wore white neck stocks in 1744, but they are shown with red neck stocks in 1747. They wore a greyish-white collarless coat with olive green linings, cuffs and turn backs and an olive-green waistcoat and breeches. The coat had eight tin or pewter buttons, placed in four pairs on both sides, with horizontal pockets and three buttons on the cuffs. When the regiment became *Montfort*, the uniform was slightly modified with the addition of an olive-green collar and the coat now had nine pewter buttons which were placed in three rows of three. When they were not on campaign, they all wore white stockings.

Grenadiers

The grenadiers' bearskin caps had a green bag with white lacing and a white hanging tassel

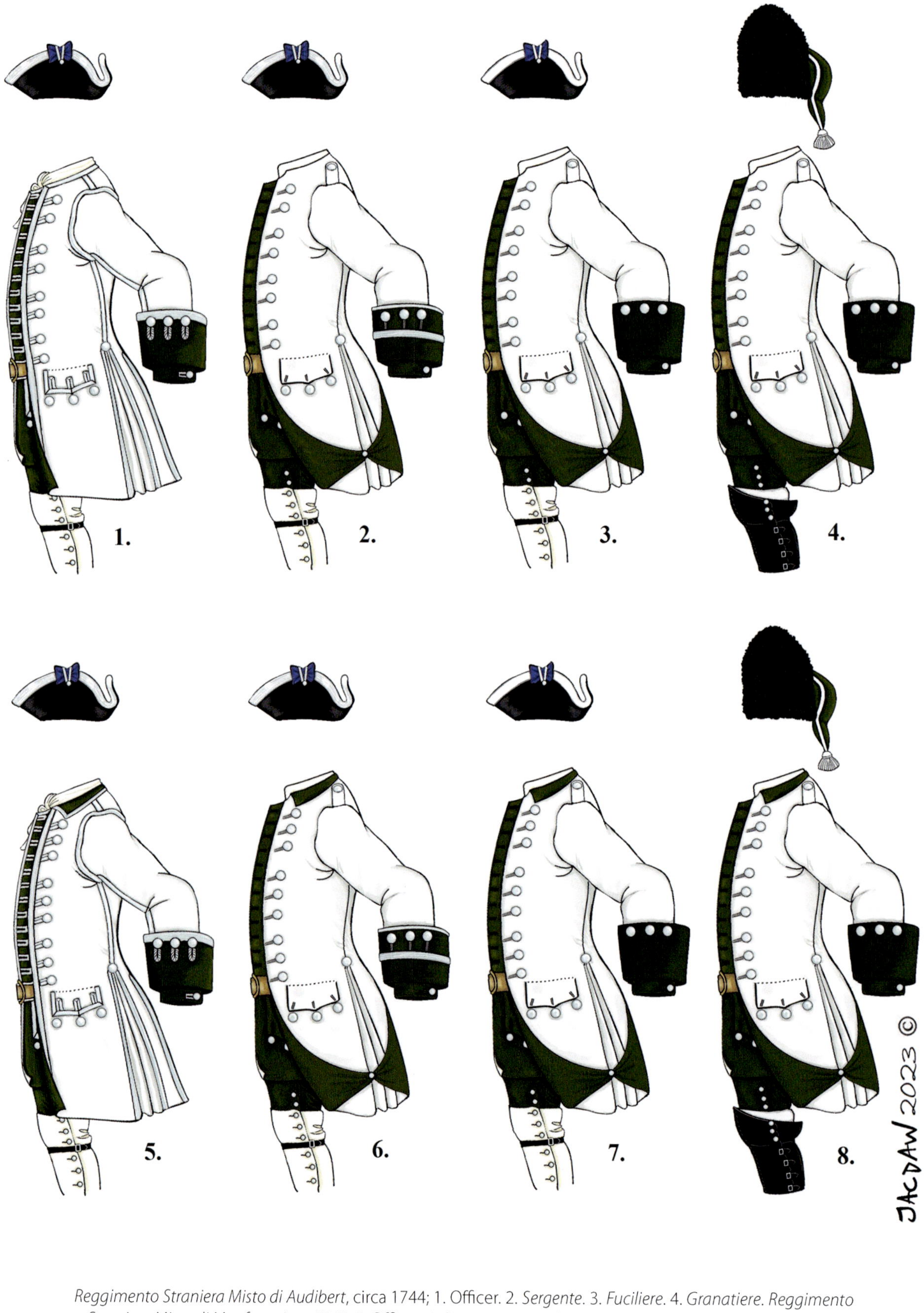

Reggimento Straniera Misto di Audibert, circa 1744; 1. Officer. 2. *Sergente*. 3. *Fuciliere*. 4. *Granatiere*. *Reggimento Straniera Misto di Monfort*, circa 1747; 5. Officer. 6. *Sergente*. 7. *Fuciliere*. 8. *Granatiere*. (Author's Illustration)

NCOs
The NCOs had their buttonholes stitched with white *bave*, and their hat lace and rank distinctions were silver. In the grenadier company the NCOs wore the bearskin cap which had a green bag with imitation silver lacing and an imitation silver hanging tassel.

Officers
The officers' tricorns had a silver lace border and loop, a Savoy blue cockade, and silver button. The officers' coats had silver lace seams, buttonholes and rank distinctions, with silver buttons. The officers' bearskin caps had a green bag with silver lacing and a silver hanging tassel.

Tamburi and Pifferi
The *tamburi* wore green coats, with green cuffs and lining, and white waistcoats and breeches. The regiment had a *tamburo maggiore*. In 1747 the drum is shown with a red case and a seme of white crosses with green hoops. As *Monfort*, the coat was garnished with royal livery lace. The grenadier *tamburi* and *pifferi* wore bearskins.

Company Colours
The company colours were the same for *Audibert* and *Monfort*. The obverse had a red field with a white cross, three dark green flames that issuing from the centre, black on the corners formed by the cross. The reverse was identical in mirror image. The standard had a thin white border (binding) all around the standard, including the staff edge. The sleeve was dark green, and the stave was painted red and studded with brass nails in a spiral design. The spear shaped finial was gilded as was the cone shaped ferrule which was secured with a ring. The cords and tassels were red.

Reggimento Straniera Misto di Audibert (*Monfort* 1746). (Author's Illustration)

9

The Line Cavalry Regiments

Organisation

In 1740 there were two line cavalry regiments, the *Reggimento Piemonte Reale Cavalleria* and the *Reggimento Piemonte Savoia Cavalleria*. In wartime both regiments consisted of two squadrons, each squadron was composed of five companies of 75 men giving a total of 750 men per regiment in theory. These were the *colonnello*'s company, the *luogotenente colonnello*'s company, the *maggiore*'s company and seven *capitano*'s companies.

From 1744 the regimental staff was comprised of the *colonnello*, a *luogotenente colonnello*, a *maggiore*, an *aiutane maggiore*, a *quartiermastro*, a *cappellano*, a *chirurgo maggiore*, a *brigadie rmaggiore*, a *prevosto*, *servente al prevosto* and a *timballiere*. The *colonnello*'s company comprised of the *colonnello*, a *capitano*, a *luogotenente*, a *cornetta*, a *maresciallo d'alloggio*, five *brigadieri*, a *trombettiere*, a *Maniscalco*, five *carabiniere*, and 44 *cavaliere*.

The *luogotenente colonnello*'s and *maggiore*'s companies comprised of the *luogotenente colonnello* or *maggiore*, a *capitano*, a *luogotenente*, a *cornetta*, a *maresciallo d'alloggio*, four *brigadieri*, a *trombettiere*, a *maniscalco*, five *carabinieri*, and 44 *cavaliere*. The other companies comprised of a *capitano*, a *luogotenente*, a *cornetta*, a *maresciallo d'alloggio*, four *brigadieri*, a *trombettiere*, a *maniscalco*, five *carabinieri*, and 44 *cavaliere*. Companies were reduced to a total of 45 men at the end of the war.

In 1744 one company from each regiment were converted to carabiniers, the only change being they exchanged their standard carbines for the new rifled carbines, but there are some doubts about this as some texts give just five men per company armed with carbines and not grouped into a special company. In 1748, there were still 10 companies, and one was still designated a carabineer company.

Their uniform was similar in cut to those of the infantry but with minor differences. Their coat and waistcoat were to last for 38 months, and they had a new pair of breeches every year, but their socks had to last for two years. They received a new hat every year. Their harness had to last for eight years in peacetime but was replaced every six years in times of war.

NCOs wore the same uniform as the men, but probably of a better quality. Their rank distinctions were the same as the infantry, with metallic lace for the *brigadieri* and woollen galloon for the *sottobrigadieri*.

The officers wore a sash of blue and gold silk with two gold hanging tassels, one on each end of the sash; these were blue with a gold central stripe for *cornetto* and *luogotenenti*, gold with a blue stripe down the centre for *capitani*. They were armed with a pair of pistols and a sword.

Originally, when on campaign both the troopers and the officers changed their cloth uniform coats for one of buff leather worn over their regimental coats, with the cuffs turned back over them. But it appears that they were not used between 1741 to 1748, and they were then re-issued. Both of the regiments had a pair of kettle drums.

At this time there was no organized veterinary service at all. Any care was entrusted to the company's farriers. This was also true for the dragoons and the artillery train.

The remounts for the cavalry and dragoon regiments were no longer the responsibility of the *capitani*, but supplied directly by the state.

Horse Furniture

The saddle was a standard model for the period, made of buff leather with a padded seat. Sometime around the end of the war they appear to have started to put a sheepskin over the saddle. The harness was of blackened leather with steel fittings, bridle, bit and stirrups and there was a bucket for the musket butt. The NCOs blankets had a simple metallic border in the button colour. The officers' lace was, for the three most senior officers, two broad gold or silver metallic laces and fringes, *capitani* had one broad gold/silver metallic lace and fringe, while junior officers had just one gold/silver thinner metallic lace border, and no fringe. The holster caps and corners of the housings were also embroidered with a gold/silver metallic crowned regimental cypher

Arms and Equipment

The Piedmontese cavalry started the war still using an older model of sword: the brass hilted model 1695 as shown in the Embser manuscript. It had a simple straight double edged, 42cm blade without a fuller. It was mounted in a single bar cast brass hilt (for the men). Embser also drew another model with two branched knuckle bow.

This cavalry sword was replaced with a new steel hilted sword (M1740) based on the Austrian '*Pallasch*', but with a single-edged blade. It had originally been designed in 1738, but this early design was rejected, so another model was presented and accepted but was only produced in 1740. Since only 500 were made initially and there is no indication of any more being made, this implies that not every cavalryman received the new '*Pallaso*' sword. The 1747 manuscript only shows the new model. It had a large double shell, the overall length was 98cm, and it had a black leather scabbard with a brass chape. Exactly when and who received them is not clear, but at the earliest they were probably issued at the end of 1740, when the troops went into winter quarters. The sword was carried on a buff leather waist belt, worn over the waistcoat, but under the coat.

The troopers had a carbine belt made of buff leather. They were armed with a pair of M 1727 pistols '*alla tedesca*' (German style) with a calibre of 17.5mm, and they were 55cm long and weighed 1.25kg They were carried in black leather holsters on the saddle brow.

A small cartridge box was carried on a thin buff leather strap, slung over the right shoulder, giving them a cross belted appearance. They carried a model 1735 musket and, as mentioned above, five men per company were issued with the new 1743 model carbine. Before the war, in 1737, five men per company in both the cavalry and the dragoons had been issued with the first rifled carbines. After the Battle of Camposanto, where they did not perform very well, it was decided to group the carabineers together in a composite unit. This six-company unit was sent into action ant the Battle of Pietralunga with disastrous results. They were used as a rear guard with the idea that the long range of the carbines would slow the enemy down from a distance but they suddenly found themselves confronted by a massive attack and they only had large calibre musket balls for the rifled guns which took too long to load in these circumstances and no sub-calibre shot, which would have enabled them to fire quicker and possibly avoid defeat. Following this and a second incident at Bassignana, the Sabaudian command decided to withdraw the rifled carbines and made little use of rifled carbines again until the Napoleonic wars. The high command had failed to understand their importance and in particular how to use them tactically.

Standards

In principle, each regiment had 10 standards, of which one was the *colonnello*'s (blue) standard. These standards were quite small, around 60 centimetres in the fly by 60 centimetres by the stave, excluding the fringes.

The field for the *colonnello*'s standard was deep sky blue (*turchino*) and the field of the company standards was crimson red (*cremisi*). The actual colours are open to debate as all the different manuscripts show a variation in the shades, from a light pastel to a deeper colour. The only surviving company standard is of an earlier model, from around 1730, which shows a more reddish colour, as does the 1747 manuscript.

They were made of a heavy silk damask. All the decoration appears to have been embroidered with coloured and metallic silk thread. The fringes were made of metallic thread. They were nailed to the lance with gilded tacks. The fluted wooden staffs or lances were painted with medium or sky blue oil paint for the *colonnello*'s and crimson red oil paint for the company guidons. The cords were probably gold intertwined with azure blue for all. The sash or cravats were blue with a gold fringe. The finials were made from steel or tin, engraved with kings crowned arms and then gold plated.

Horses

In Piedmont, due to the poverty of the local farms, it was always difficult to procure the 4–5,000 horses needed to mount all the cavalry and dragoon regiments as well as enough draught horses for the artillery. Horses were always a serious problem for the Piedmontese army which, despite all the efforts they made to create native breeds, they were always forced to buy many of them from abroad, especially from Germany or Denmark.

But when they bought the horses, they were carefully selected, horses with brindle coats, dun coloured and greys, with frills at the knee and with too much white on the head were rejected. This concerned not only the cavalry, but also the dragoon and draught horses. To get the best possible uniformity, the individual squadrons had all horses of the same colour. The *timballiere*, who were traditionally a privilege of the cavalry regiments, only rode grey or white horses, as did the *trombetti*.

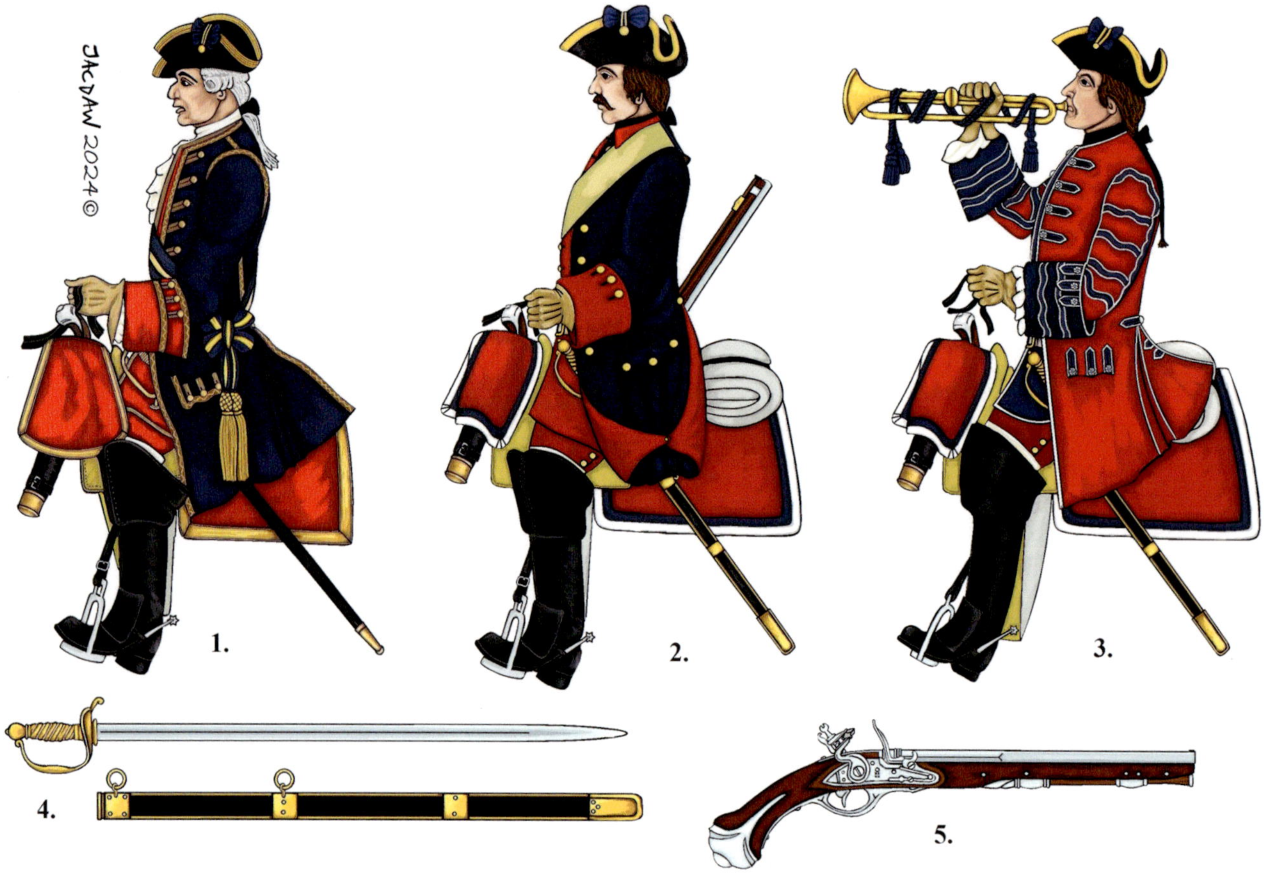

Reggimento Piemonte Reale Cavalleria; 1. Officer. 2. *Cavaliere* 3. *Trombettiere*. 4. Cavalry sword M1695. 5. Cavalry pistol M1727, '*alla Tedesca*' (German style), made in Turin from parts imported from Suhl. (Author's Illustration)

Reggimento Piemonte Reale Cavalleria

The *Reggimento Piemonte Reale Cavalleria* was first raised in 1692 from some companies of *Gendarmi*. In 1738 they had 500 men, but only 333 horses. By 1747 they had 650 men and only 600 horses. The *colonnelli* of the regiment under Charles Emmanuel III were in 1733 Chevalier Francesco Ignazio Filippi, who was succeeded by Chevalier Renato Ignazio Roero [Rovero] di Revello from January 1742 until 1755.

Service

In 1744 regiment fought at Battle of Madonna dell'Olmo, and in 1745 it was present at the siege of Valenza and fought in the Battle of Bassignana.

Uniforms

The *cavalieri* wore a black tricorn with a dark blue cockade on the left brim, with a black loop and a brass button, and yellow/gilt lace border. Their service dress uniform from 1736 consisted of a dark blue coat. The coat had seven brass buttons, with three on the cuffs. The coat had horizontal pockets, each with three buttons, and red cuffs, linings, and turn backs. The coat had a shoulder strap on the left shoulder which held the carbine belt in place and was secured by a button. The regiment wore black neck stocks. Their waistcoat and breeches were red and they wore black cavalry boots.

NCOs

The *brigadieri* wore a black tricorn with a dark blue cockade on the left brim, with a gold loop and a gilt button, and gold lace border.

Officers

The officers' tricorns had a gold lace border and loop, with a deep blue cockade, and a gilt button. The officers' coats had gold lace and gilt buttons.

Trombetti and Timballiere

The *trombetti* and *timballiere* all wore the Royal Livery. The lace was probably applied differently for the *trombetti* and *timballiere*.

The trumpet had blue or blue and silver cords. The trumpet and drum banners were crimson with a gold fringe, there decoration is unknown, but they probably had a motif similar to the standard on them. The trumpet banners were probably not carried on campaign.

Horse Furniture

The housings and holster caps were red with a broad white lace border piped blue with a wavy line down the centre embroidered in red. NCOs metallic border and officers' lace was gold. The holster caps and corners of the housings were also embroidered with a gold metallic crowned regimental cypher, in this case 'PR'.

Squadron Standards

These standards (often referred to as company standards) were issued in 1730. Each of the squadrons carried a square standard, mounted on red or blue fluted jousting style lances with gold fringes, blue cords and knots and a gilt finial and ferrule. The standards had a blue taffeta cravat with a gold fringe; although it is probable that only *colonnello*'s standard had this, not the ordinary companies, this maybe so for the trumpet banners as well.

The *colonnello*'s company standard had a Turkish blue damask field, the obverse was charged with the crowned full coat of arms of the King of Sardinia, supported by gold lions and in each angle a trophy of arms including a helmet, breastplate and two stands of flags bearing crosses in gold. The reverse had a white rampant or prancing horse looking left, with a scroll inscribed with 'VENUSTUS ET AUDAX' (Handsome and Audacious) in gold lettering, with, in each angle, a trophy of arms including a helmet, breastplate and two stands of flags bearing crosses in gold. The other three standards had the same motifs obverse and reverse, but on a crimson damask field and with gold fringes, and blue cords and knots and a gilt finial and ferrule.

The standard was carried with the aid of a bandoleer which had a carabiner. It was made of leather and covered in velvet, probably blue for the *colonnello*'s standard and red for the squadron standards and edged and embroidered with gold lace. It was joined by a ring and a swivel spring clip by two gilded metal plates.

Cavalry standards, *Reggimento Piemonte Reale Cavalleria*. Top, company standard, obverse. Bottom, the company standard, reverse. The *colonnello*'s standard was identical, but on a light sky-blue field. The staves or more exactly, lances, were painted the same colour as their standard. (Author's Illustration)

Reggimento Savoia Cavalleria

The *Reggimento Savoia Cavalleria* were first raised in 1692 from the regiments of Cavaglià and None, the first commanders of the two regiments that were formed, merging eight existing companies of *Gendarmi* which had just been reformed. Briefly disbanded in 1699 they were reformed in 1701. In 1738 they had 400 men and 500 horses. In 1747 they only had 333 men and 650 horses. The c*olonnelli* of the regiment under Charles Emmanuel III was the Chevalier Giuseppe Duchesne di Lignana, from 1736 to1747, when he was succeeded by Vassallo Giovanni Angelo Sclarandi.

Service

In 1742 the regiment was at Modena and Mirandola. In 1743 they fought at the Battle of Camposanto. In 1744, they were at the Battle of Madonna dell'Olmo and the Siege of Cuneo. In 1745 they were at the Battle of Bassignana and the liberation of Alessandria. In 1746 they distinguished themselves at the Battle of Tidone where they charged the *Gallispans* several times.

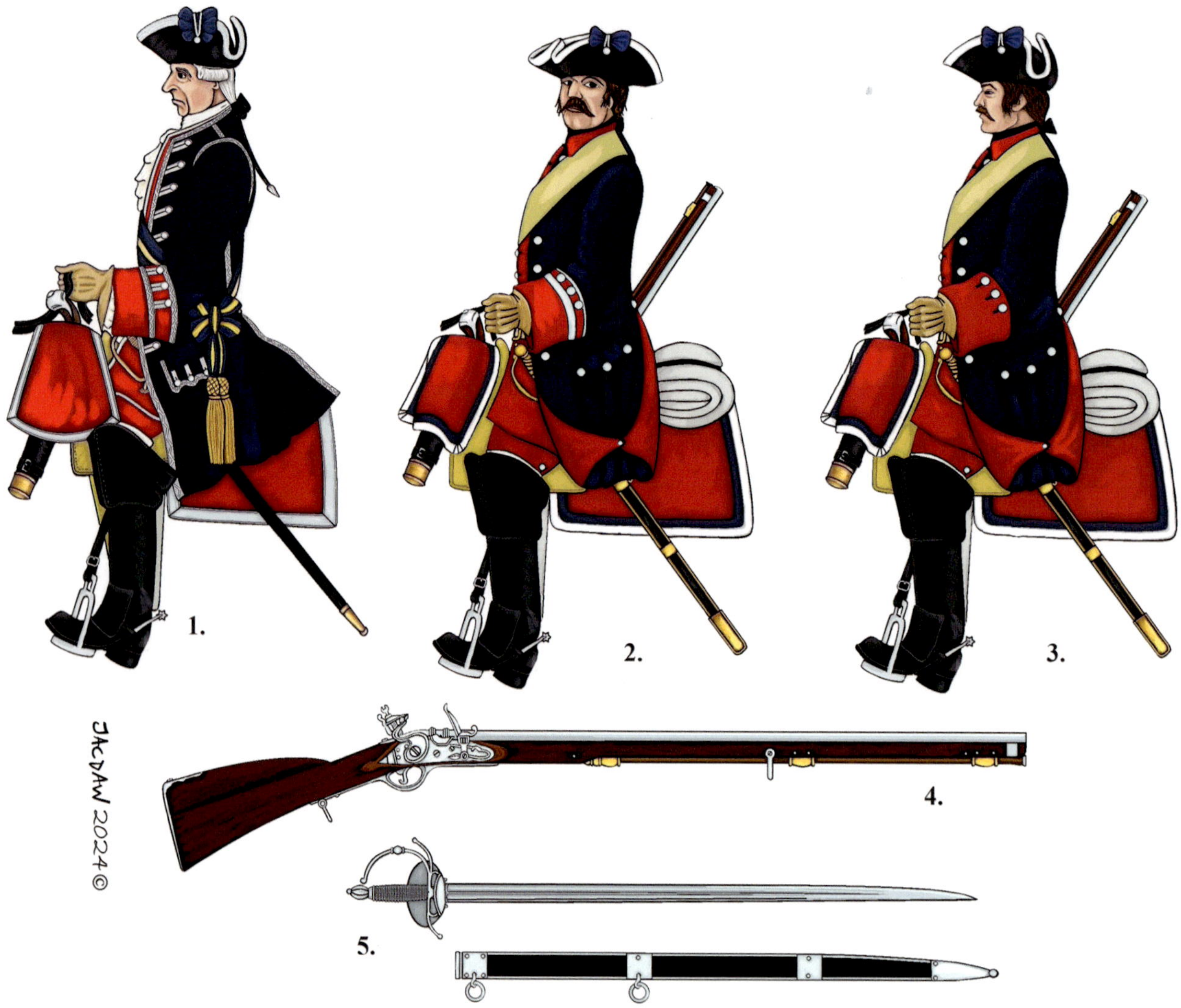

Reggimento Savoia Cavalleria; 1. Officer. 2. *Maresciale di Logis*, note the cuff lacing. 3. *Cavaliere*. 4. Smoothbore Cavalry Musket M 1735, there was also a rifled version. 5. Cavalry sword M 1740, a '*Pallasch*' style all steel construction, only 500 were made so probably not in general use. (Author's Illustration)

Uniforms

The *cavalieri* wore a black tricorn with a dark blue cockade on the left brim, with a black loop and a pewter button, and white lace border. The regiment wore black neck stocks. Their service dress uniform from consisted of a dark blue coat. The coat had seven pewter buttons on the coat, with three on the cuffs. The coat had horizontal pockets, each with three buttons and red cuffs, linings, and turn backs. The coat had a shoulder strap on the left shoulder which held the carbine belt in place and was secured by a button. Their waistcoats and their breeches were red, and they wore black cavalry boots.

Horse Furniture

The housings and holster caps were red with a broad white lace border, edged and with a wavy line in the centre embroidered in blue. The *cavalieri* and *trombetti* carried a grey cloak lined blue, rolled up and attached to the saddle. The holster caps and corners of the housings were also embroidered with a silver metallic crowned regimental cypher, in this case 'SC'.

NCOs

They *brigadieri* wore a black tricorn with a dark blue cockade on the left brim, with a silver loop and a pewter button, and silver lace border.

Officers

The officers' coats had silver lace and buttons, and their tricorn had a dark blue cockade on the left brim, with a silver loop and a silver button, and silver lace border.

Trombetti and Timballiere

The *trombetti* and *timballiere* wore the Royal Livery; the trumpet had blue cords and tassels. The trumpet and drum banners were blue with a gold fringe, decoration unknown, but probably had a motif similar to the standard.

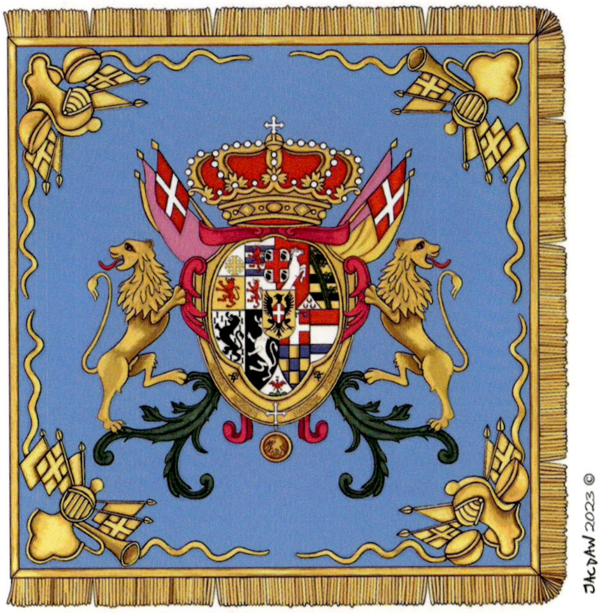

Cavalry standards, *Reggimento Savoia Cavalleria*. Top, the *colonnello*'s standard, obverse. The reverse was the same as the ordnance or company standard, but on a light sky-blue field. Bottom, the company standard, reverse. The obverse was the same as the *colonnello*'s standard, but on a crimson red field. The lances were painted the same colour as their standard. Although the original illustrations have been followed, the blue was probably much darker. (Author's Illustration)

Squadron Standards

These standards were issued in 1731. Each of the squadrons had a square standard, carried on blue fluted wooden jousting style lances with gold fringes, cords and knots and a gilt finial and ferrule. The first or *colonnello*'s company had a Turkish blue damask field. The obverse was charged with the crowned full coat of arms of the King of Sardinia, supported by gold lions and in each angle a trophy of arms including a helmet, breastplate and two stands of flags bearing crosses in gold. On the reverse, a gold tree in leaf on a green turf, over the tree a white scroll inscribed with the motto 'SECTA & LIGATA REFLORET', (cut, and tied, it blooms again) in each angle a trophy of arms including a helmet, breastplate and two stands of flags bearing crosses in gold. Sometimes the turf is coloured gold as well. The other company standards had the same motifs obverse and reverse but on a crimson damask field.

The standard was carried with the aid of a bandoleer which had a carabiner. It was made of leather and covered in velvet, probably blue for the colonel's standard and red for the squadron standards and edged and embroidered with silver lace. It was joined by a ring and a swivel and spring clip by two gilded metal plates.

10

The Dragoon Regiments

Organisation

There were four regiments of dragoons, who each had a wartime strength of some 650 men, of which only 600 were classed as mounted, in 10 companies divided into two squadrons with the same number of staff as the cavalry regiments. A fifth unit was raised, the *Corpo di Dragons di Sardegna*, composed of only three weak companies, some 200 men strong all told, who were stationed on the island of Sardinia performing mainly police, coastal patrol, and anti-smuggling duties.

From 1744 the regimental staff was comprised of the *colonnello*, a *luogotenente colonnello*, a *maggiore*, an *aiutane maggiore*, a *furieri*, a *quartiermastro*, a *cappellano*, a *chirurgo maggiore*, a *brigadie rmaggiore*, a *tamburo maggiore*, a *prevosto*, and *servente al prevosto*. The *Reggimento Dragoni di Sua Maestà* also had a *timballiere*. The *colonnello*'s company comprised of the *colonnello,* a *capitano*, a *luogotenente*, a *cornetta*, a *maresciallo d'alloggio*, five *brigadieres*, a *tamburo*, a *maniscalco*, five *carabinieri*, and 44 *dragoni*.

The *luogotenente colonnello*'s and *maggiore*'s companies comprised of the *luogotenente colonnello* or *maggiore*, a *capitano*, a *luogotenente*, a *cornetta*, a *maresciallo d'alloggio*, four *brigadiere*, a *trombettiere*, a *maniscalco*, five *carabiniere*, and 44 *dragoni*. The other companies comprised of a *capitano*, a *luogotenente*, a *cornetta*, a *maresciallo d'alloggio*, four *brigadiere*, a *tamburo*, a *maniscalco*, five *carabinieri*, and 44 *dragoni*. The other seven companies composed of a *capitano*, a *cornetta*, a *maresciallo d'alloggio*, four *brigadieri*, a *tamburo*, a *maniscalco* five *carabinieri* and 44 *dragoni*. The companies were reduced to 45 men (including NCOs etc.) at the end of the war.

Being mounted infantry, the dragoons had a *tamburo maggiore*. He was in charge of leading the band when they were reunited and to teach the *tamburi* their beats and calls. A *tamburo maggiore* of dragoons carried a mace and wore a richly embroidered bandolier, adorned with a silver plate bearing the arms of the regiment. How this functioned when he was mounted is not clear, so this was probably limited to service on foot and parades.

One company of each regiment appears to have been detached and used to police the territory, so the regiments were never complete when on the field of battle.

Piedmontese dragoons could often still be found fighting on foot. Due to region's terrain and a lack of horses, this occurred more frequently than in most other countries.

Uniforms

Their red uniforms were basically of the same cut as the infantry, but can be divided into two periods: the 1730–1740 uniform and the 1740–1754 uniform. The basic difference was that the new uniform had eight buttons placed in pairs and two red shoulder straps, lined in the regimental distinctive colour, one on each shoulder, and the coat lost its fall down collar. Pockets and cuffs had four buttons. The dragoons wore a woollen fatigue cap, probably the same as the French model – a red bag with a distinctive coloured turn-up. There is scant information on the dragoons' shoulder knots. *Genevois* had a white shoulder knot earlier in the period, *La Regina* and *Sardegna* definitely did not have them as they were raised later, but for the other two regiments there is no information.

The dragoons wore black leather shoes and leather gaiters with reinforced knee protection, which were fastened with 12 brass buckles; nine up to the knee and three above the knee with a garter strap in-between. They had an large red cloak, lined in the regimental colour.

Another item of clothing that may have been unofficially continued is the dragoons' sashes, worn at the waist and tied on the left. In a letter to the *Ufficio del Soldo* of 1738 states: 'To relieve the soldiers of the expense, which they had to contribute to, of the maintenance of the sashes, they allowed that they were lacking and were no longer replaced because they were useless.'[1] Despite this order, however, in the illustrations representing the dragoons, from the eighteenth century they are still often represented with the red sashes around their waist.

1 *Ufficio del Soldo*, Archivio di Stato Torino.

NCOs' Distinctions

In 1736, the rank of *brigadieri*, was distinguished by gold or silver braid, laced or stitched button holes on their coat, and two laces on their cuffs – one on the border and one around the cuff, two thirds of the way down (this one is generally shown as larger than the one on the edge of the cuff). Their tricorn probably had metallic lace as well. The *carabinieri* (future *granatieri*) were only awarded distinctions on their coat from 1741. This consisted of a narrow yellow or white lace border on their cuffs, more or less the same as the *caporali* for all the regiments except *Sua Maestà*, who had gold metallic lace.

Officers' Uniforms

There were no clear instructions or regulations regarding officers' dress before the 1750 regulations were edited, just a letter from the King in 1735 which simply said that 'the officers' uniforms should be as simple as possible, the only concession being that they could use silver or gilt buttons. The sashes should not have too much gold on them, moderation is the watch word.'[2] With such simple and unregulated instructions, at least the senior officers added gold or silver lace on their coats and waistcoats, if not all officers.

If contemporary portraits are to be believed, the *colonnello* wore a breast and back plate, at least on parade. The officers' coats and waistcoats had button-colour metallic lace on their seams, buttonholes and around their pockets and cuffs, with gilt or silver buttons. The officers' principal badges of rank were a sash of blue and/or gold silk with two gold hanging tassels, one on each end of the sash; these were blue with a gold central stripe for *cornetto* and *luogotenenti*, and a larger gold stripe down the centre for *capitani*. They were armed with a pair of pistols and a sword. The officers usually appear to have preferred a French style '*Epée à la Mousquetaire*'.

Arms and Equipment

The dragoon sabre (*Sabro da Dragoni con fornimento in ferro alla Vallona*) M 1737 was slightly curved and was a little shorter than the cavalry model: 1.13m overall with a 95cm blade. It had a double branched steel Walloon style hilt and shell guard and was carried in reinforced black leather scabbard that was 96 cm long and wider than the blade. It was made of wood, covered in black leather, equipped with an iron locket and chape. The chape was approximately 15cm long with a small sphere on the point of the chape. None of these early models have survived. This model had replaced the previous M 1732 single branched brass hilted model by 1740. It was carried on a buff leather waist belt, which had a brass oval buckle, along with the bayonet in a separate frog, worn over the waistcoat, but under the coat.

The dragoons used a Piedmontese M 1726 Fusil, but it was slightly shorter than the standard infantry model. It was carried on a wide shoulder bandoleer of buff leather. When the musket was slung from the saddle, barrel upright, it had a fluffy cloth tompion to protect it from the rain. This was made in the regimental colours; red plus the facing colour.

They had a small cartridge box with a buff leather flap that was carried on a thin belt of buff leather over the right shoulder; this gave them a cross belted appearance. By 1750 a larger cartridge box is shown with a black leather flap.

By 1743 five men per company of dragoons were issued with the new rifled carbine and grouped in a unit called the *carabinieri*. They were identifiable by their natural leather ventral pouch which contained the necessary accessories to maintain their new weapon. They also had a thin button coloured galloon around their cuff to distinguish their elite status.

The dragoon's bayonet was the new M 1731 socket model which had replaced the older antiquated plug bayonet. They also carried a pair of M 1726 dragoon pistols, of either French or Piedmontese origin, which were carried in holsters attached to the saddle.

Horse Furniture

The saddle was a standard model for the period, made of natural buff yellow leather. Sometime around the end of the war they appear to have started to put a sheepskin or an off-white woollen blanket over the saddle.

The harness was of blackened leather with steel fittings and there was a bucket for the musket butt. The early housings and holster caps were red with a thin blue and white silk lace border. The 1741 regulations confirmed this, but the galloon was now a little larger, this was the same model for all the regiments. The *dragoni* and *tamburo* carried a red cloak, lined in the facing colour, rolled up and attached to the saddle.

In 1749 each regiment received their own regimental lace border. The NCOs had a simple metallic border.

The officers' housings had metallic lace in the button colour which was, for the three most senior officers, two broad metallic laces and fringes, the *capitani* had one broad metallic lace and fringe, while the junior officers only had one broad metallic lace border and no fringe.

2 *Ufficio Generale del Soldo* followed by a *Regio Bigilietto*, Archivio di Stato Torino.

Guidons

The design of the dragoon guidons dates back to the 1732 contract with the princes (but which the ministry only received the following year). They are described in detail in the annex to the contract. Therefore, we know that they were light blue for the *colonnello*'s and crimson for the company guidons. However, the actual colours are open to debate as all the different manuscripts show a variation in the shades, from a light pastel to a deeper colour. The only surviving company guidon is of an earlier model, from around 1730, and shows a more reddish hue, as does the 1747 manuscript. As regards the blue, but we do know that the 1766 model was dark blue, as this is clearly noted, and it infers that the earlier models were of a lighter colour.

The guidons were made of silk damask. All the decoration appears to have been embroidered in coloured and metallic silk. The followed a fairly standard model, on the obverse the greater arms of Sardinia and on the reverse the regimental insignia, although some could have a variation. The fringes were made of metallic thread. They were nailed to the lance with gilded tacks.

The fluted wooden staffs / lances were painted with medium /sky blue oil paint for the colonel and crimson red oil paint for the Ordnance or company guidons. It probably had a gilded hand grip to clip on the bandoleer.

In principle, each regiment had 10 guidons, of which one was the *colonnello*'s (blue) guidon, except *Sardegna* who only had one guidon, and according to the wardrobe accounts it was *colonnello*'s. The guidons were quite small, around 85cm in the fly by 50cm by the stave, excluding the fringes.

The cords were probably gold intertwined with azure blue for all. The sash or cravats were blue with a gold fringe. The finials were made from steel or tin, engraved with the Kings' crowned arms and then gold plated.

Reggimento di Dragoni di Sua Maestà

The *Reggimento di Dragoni di Sua Maestà* was the most prestigious of the dragoon regiments, with a long tradition of valorous service. The regiment was first raised in 1683 as the *Dragoni di Verrua*, and originally known as the *Dragoni Rossi* (Red Dragoons), because of the colour of their coats. In 1738 they had 500 men and 333 horses, by 1747 they had 650 men and 600 horses.

During the battle for the liberation of Turin in September 1706, the regiment captured the kettledrums of the French *Bartillat* cavalry regiment. The Duke Vittorio Amadeus II then authorised the regiment to adopt a *timballiere* to beat the kettle drums they had taken from the enemy.

In addition to the *timballiere*, the regiment also had the privilege of a marching band, made up of eight players: two bassoons, two hunting horns and four oboes. This band, known as the little or '*petite*' band could, on special occasions, be combined with the *timballiere* and the *tamburi* to make up the big band. This regiment also recorded as having some musicians who played Hautboys, but this probably refers to the oboes listed above.

The *colonnelli* of the regiment under Charles Emmanuel III were Ludovico Piccone, Conte della Perosa from 1731. He was succeeded by Giovanni Battista Benedetto Saluzzo, Conte della Manta di Verzuolo in 1740.

Service

In 1743, the regiment fought at the Battle of Casteldelfino, and at the Siege of Villafranca in 1744. In 1746, the regiment was at the Battle of Tidone near Piacenza, where in a combat together with the Austrian cavalry it captured the guidons of the Spanish *Lusitania* dragoons and the French *Dauphin* dragoons. In May 1747, they led the assault on the Genoese fortress of Masone, and a company was detached to form a composite squadron of carabiniers.

Uniforms

The regiment wore a black tricorn with a dark blue cockade on the left brim, with a black loop and a brass button, and yellow/gilt lace border. They wore black neck stocks. Their service dress uniform consisted of a red coat with royal blue cuffs, linings and turn backs. The coat had eight brass buttons placed in pairs, with four on the cuffs. The coat had horizontal pockets, each with four buttons. There were shoulder straps on both shoulders which held the musket and cartridge pouch in place. These were secured with buttons. The waistcoat and their breeches were royal blue. The musket tompion was red and blue.

Officers

The officers' black tricorns had gold lace and a gilt button. The officers' coats had gold lace and gilt buttons. The officers wore a sash of blue and/or gold silk with two gold hanging tassels, one on each end of the sash.

Tamburi

The *tamburi* wore the Royal Livery. The drum case was painted plain blue with blue hoops. The drum had red cords and an off whitened leather shoulder belt; in full dress they had a red shoulder belt with three bands of livery lace. The waistcoat and their breeches were royal blue.

As mentioned above, the regiment owned a pair of copper kettledrums which they had captured from the French *Bartillat* cavalry regiment in 1706 including the banners. They kept the original French banners (still conserved to this day in Turin), which were red charged

These are the uniforms of circa 1743–1747. Some modifications may have been made after this date, but most likely after the end of the war. *Reggimento di Dragoni di Sua Maestà*; 1. Officer. 2. *Dragoni*. 3. *Tamburo*. *Reggimento di Dragoni di Sua Altezza Reale* (formerly *del Genevois*); 4. Officer. 5. *Dragoni*, note the sheepskin on the saddle. A white shoulder knot (*lesse*), these were worn by the dragoons and NCOs of this regiment, possibly the *tamburi* and officers as well, but this is unconfirmed. 6. *Tamburo*. (Author's Illustration)

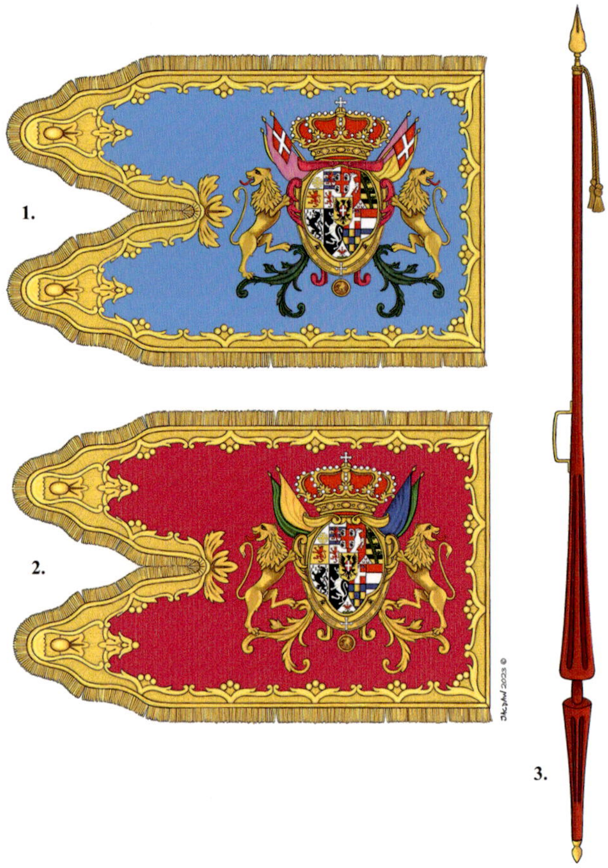

Guidons, *Reggimento di Dragoni di Sua Maestà*. 1. *Colonnello*'s guidon, both the obverse and reverse were identical, but with the arms orientated correctly. The original manuscript shows the crown's cap as yellow, which could be an error of the colourist and the traditional red has been shown. 2. Company Guidon, both the obverse and reverse were identical, but with the arms orientated correctly. 3. The wooden fluted lance was painted crimson red for the company guidons and painted sky blue for the *colonnello*'s. The finial was made of steel and gilded. The illustrations show different models, but as no original from exactly this period has been conserved which one was actually made is not known. It would have had a 'cravat' or sash attached to the finial and cords, according to the descriptions in the wardrobe accounts it was blue with a gold fringe. None have survived. The original illustrations have been followed, but the blue was probably much darker. (Author's Illustration)

with *colonel*'s armorials. The embroidery, fringes and tassels were gold with silver.[3]

Horse Furniture

The housings and holster caps were red bordered with a broad blue and white silk galloon. From 1749 they had a broad regimental white lace border, embroidered with a wavy blue line in the centre bordered in blue. The NCOs had a simple metallic border in the button colour. The officers' lace was gold. The *dragoni* and *tamburi* carried a red cloak lined blue rolled up and attached behind the saddle. The holster covers and corners of the housings were also embroidered with a gold metallic crowned regimental cypher, in this case 'SM'.

Guidons

These guidons were issued in 1733. Each of the squadrons had a swallow-tailed guidon, carried on fluted red jousting style lances with gold fringes, cords and knots and a gilt finial and ferrule. The *colonnello*'s guidon was mounted on a blue lance. They are shown with blue lances in 1747. The *colonnello*'s guidon had a medium dark blue field with an intricate double gold lace border and fringe. In the centre were the full crowned arms of the King of Sardinia, obverse and reverse were the same. The company guidons had the same motifs on the obverse and reverse, but on a crimson field.

The guidon was carried with the aid of a bandoleer which had a carabiner. It was made of leather and covered in velvet, probably blue for the *colonnello*'s guidon and red for the others, and edged and embroidered with gold lace. It was joined by a ring and a swivel spring clip by two gilded metal plates.

Reggimento di Dragoni di Son Altesse Royale

The *Reggimento di Dragoni di Son Altesse Royale* was first raised in 1689 as the *Reggimento di Dragoni del Genevois* and were originally known as the Green Dragoons (*Dragons Verts*), because of the colour of their coats but they later adopted the standard red. In 1740 they were renamed *Son Altesse Royale* since it came under the command of Victor Amadeus, Prince of Piemont, (the future King Victor Amadeus III). In 1738 they had 500 men and 333 horses, by 1747 they had 650 men and 600 horses.

Service

Between 1742 and 1743 they were present at Tidone, Imola and at the Battle of Casteldelfino. In 1744 they were at the Siege of Villefranche-sur-Mer, the Siege of Nice, Bellino, the Battle of Madonna dell'Olmo, and the Siege de Cuneo in 1744. In 1745 they fought at the Battle of Bassignana.

Uniforms

The men wore a black tricorn with a dark blue cockade on the left brim. with a black loop and a pewter button. and white lace border. They wore black neck stocks. Their service dress uniform consisted of a red coat with green cuffs, linings and turn backs. The coat had eight pewter buttons on the coat, placed in pairs, with four on the cuffs. The coat had horizontal pockets, each with four buttons.

3 See Charles d'Hozier, l'*Armorial général de France*, 1696, for the arms of Jehan de Bartillat. The original kettledrum banners of Bartillat Cavalerie are conserved in the Armeria Reale in Turin, ref. 0200/201.

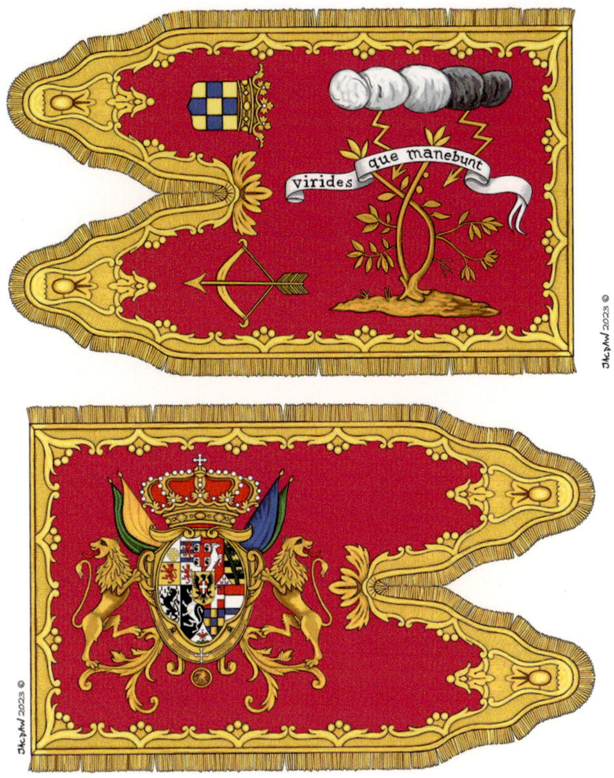

Company guidon, *Reggimento di Dragoni di Son Altesse Royale.* (Author's Illustration)

Guidons

These guidons were issued in 1733. Each of the companies had swallow tailed guidons, shown as being carried on blue fluted jousting style lances (1745) with gold fringes, cords and knots and a gilt finial and ferrule. The *colonnello*'s guidon weas mounted on a blue lance. A contemporary print also shows them with lances painted gold.

On the reverse of the *colonnello*'s guidon there was a golden tree in leaf on a green ground, in between the tree and the cloud, there was a white scroll inscribed with the motto 'VIRIDISQUE MANEBUNT' under a storm cloud and flashes of golden lightning.[4] In 1745 version, the scroll passes in front of the tree. In the 1740 version, the scroll passes in front of the tree and the top tail has a shield chequered or and azure with a gold ducal crown; on the bottom tail a gold bow and arrow. The other company guidons had the same motifs on the obverse and reverse but on a red field.

Different contemporary manuscripts show variations of the reverse, some with the arms of the Comte de Genève and a crossbow, some with a natural-coloured tree other versions a golden tree, but as only one stand was made it is impossible to know exactly which one was the exact model. The illustration is based on the 1747 version.

There were shoulder straps on both shoulders which held the carbine belt and cartridge pouch in place. These were secured with buttons. Their waistcoat and their breeches were green. The musket tompion was red and green.

Officers

The officers' black tricorns had silver lace and a silver button. The officers' coats had silver lace and silver buttons. The officers wore a sash of blue and/or gold silk with two gold hanging tassels, one on each end of the sash.

Tamburi

The *tamburi* wore the Royal Livery. The drum case was painted red with white crosses and blue rims. The drum had natural-coloured cords and an off-white leather shoulder belt. In full dress they had a red shoulder belt with three bands of livery lace. Their waistcoat and their breeches were apple green.

Horse Furniture

The housings and holster caps were red bordered with a broad blue and white silk galloon. From 1749 they had a simple blue lace border. The NCOs had a simple metallic border. The The *dragoni* and *tamburi* carried a red cloak lined green rolled up and attached behind the saddle. The officers' lace was silver. The holster caps and corners of the housings were also embroidered with a silver metallic crowned regimental cypher, in this case 'DG'.

Reggimento di Dragoni di Piemonte

The *Reggimento di Dragoni di Piemonte* was first raised in 1690 as *Dragoni di Macello* and originally known as the Yellow Dragoons because of the colour of their coats.

The *Dragoni di Piemonte* had five squadrons, each of two companies. In 1738 they had 500 men and 333 horses, by 1747 they had 650 men and 600 horses. Of the 10 companies, one of these was in reserve and another one was the depot company.

The *colonnelli* of the regiment under Charles Emmanuel III were Tommaso Solaro, Count di Moretta, from 1736, who was succeeded by Augustin Martin de Challant in 1742, who in turn was succeeded in turn by Vittorio Amedeo, Count Maffei, in 1747.

Service

In 1742 the regiment fought in Italy and Savoy, with the first half of the year being spent campaigning against the Spanish army in the Padania plain. In late summer a Spanish offensive was launched against Savoy, and Charles Emmanuel III launched a counter offensive. The Regiment was attached to La Salle's column.

In January 1743, the regiment returned to Piedmont, leaving Savoy to the Spanish. During the enemy offensive

4 The regimental motto translates to 'and they will always remain green', in reference to their facings.

against the Varaita valley, in autumn 1743, the regiment was on the plain around Saluce, while a company was detached and entrenched at Villaretto during the combats from 24 September to 10 October, around the village of Chateau Dauphin.

In 1744 the regiment was again in the area of Saluzzo, ready to reach the valley from where the main Franco-Spanish offensive was launched. Conti's army broke through the front of the Alps in the Stura and Varaita valleys, capturing, for the second time, the Fort of Demonte and then besieging Cuneo. The King tried to break the siege, and he moved his army to the fields of Madonna dell'Olmo (30 September 1744). The cavalry was on the right of the Piedmontese line. The regiment was situated in the centre of the infantry's front line, to close a gap in the front. The chevaux de frises of the grenadiers were placed before the cavalry, so the enemy's mounted forces had no possibility of closing. There was only an exchange of fire.

In 1745 at Bassignana (27 September), the regiment faced, with the rest of the Sabaudian army, de Maillebois' offensive. All the six Piedmontese mounted regiments (two cavalry and four of dragoons) were on the left, around the village of Bassignana. They tried to stop the advance of the enemy, but the regiments were forced to withdraw on Valenza. During this movement, the *Dragoni di Piemonte* was at the end of the column and near the village of Pelizzari, where they had to face three enemy columns alone: Arembourg's, Pignatelli's and Gage's. After a short and violent defence, during which the company led by *Capitano* Della Villa was destroyed, many dragoons surrendered. Two regimental guidons were lost on this occasion. The rifled carbines were blamed for this disaster.

In 1746 the regiment was present in Leutrum's army, first patrolling the country around Moncalieri, then present before the walls of Asti during the short siege (6–7 March 1746). The dragoons escorted Leutrum's advance to the Citadel of Alessandria.

The cavalry was then employed in the campaign around the cities of Alessandria and Valenza.

After the Battle of Plaisance (16 June 1746) the regiment was part of a brigade that was detached on the right side of the river Po, where they were able to fight in the Battle of the Tidone (10 August 1746). The Piedmontese had their most succesful day of the entire war; they first blocked the *Gallispan* counterattack, they then faced three French squadrons and the infantry line. Then, with some Austrian dragoons, they charged the enemy cavalry three times, taking many prisoners and two guidons.

After this engagement the regiment were dismounted and placed in the trenches around the Fortress of Tortona (from 20 August until the 27 November 1746). They were then remounted and were sent to patrol the western mountain front until the end of the war in 1748.

Uniforms

The regiment wore a black tricorn with a dark blue cockade on the left brim, with a black loop and a pewter button, and a white lace border. They wore black neck stocks. Their service dress uniform consisted of a red coat with white cuffs, linings and turn backs. The coat had eight pewter buttons placed in pairs, with four on the cuffs, and a flap with four small buttons. The coat had horizontal pockets, each with four buttons. T There were shoulder straps on both shoulders which held the musket and cartridge pouch in place. These were secured with buttons. Their waistcoat and breeches were originally white, but changed to red from 1740. The musket tompion was red and white.

Officers

The officers' black tricorns had silver lace and a silver button. The officers' coats had silver lace and silver buttons. The officers wore a sash of blue and/or gold silk with two gold hanging tassels.

Tamburi

The *tamburi* wore the the Royal Livery. The drum case and hoops were painted blue, as were the hoops. The drum had red cords and an off whitened leather shoulder belt; in full dress they had a red shoulder belt with three bands of livery lace and edged silver. Their waistcoat and their breeches were red.

Horse Furniture

The housings and holster caps were red bordered with a broad blue and white silk galloon. From 1749 they had a regimental lace of blue bordered white. The NCOs had a simple metallic border in the button colour. The *dragoni* and *tamburi* carried a red cloak lined white rolled up and attached behind the saddle. The officers' lace was silver. The holster caps and corners of the housings were also embroidered with a silver metallic crowned regimental cypher, in this case 'DP'.

Guidons

The regiment received new guidons in 1723 and these appear to have been replaced in 1746. Each of the companies had swallow tailed guidons, carried on red fluted jousting style lances with gold fringes, cords and knots and a gilt finial and ferrule. The *colonnello*'s guidon had a blue lance. All the lances were shown painted blue in 1747, but this could possibly be a copyist's error.

In 1744 the *colonnello*'s guidon had a blue field with an intricate gold double lace border and fringe. On the obverse, in the centre were the full crowned arms of the King of Sardinia.

On the reverse, in the centre, were the Ducal crowned arms of Savoy-Piedmont. The 1745 versions show a stand

Reggimento di Dragoni di Piemonte, circa 1743–1747; 1. Officer. 2. *Dragoni*, note the sheepskin on the saddle. 3. *Tamburo*. *Reggimento di Dragoni della Regina* circa 1743–1747. 4. Officer. 5. *Dragoni*, note the sheepskin on the saddle. 6. *Tamburo*. (Author's Illustration)

Company guidon, *Reggimento di Dragoni di Piemonte*. The obverse of the company guidons bore the crowned royal arms and supporters and, on the reverse, were the arms of Piemonte under a prince's crown on a crimson red field. The *colonnello*'s guidon bore the same motifs, but placed on sky blue field. The illustration is based on the 1747 version. (Author's Illustration)

of colours issuing from each side of the crown. The other company guidons had the same motifs obverse and reverse, but on a crimson/red field.

In 1740 version there were no supporters, but a stand of colours is shown issuing from each side of the base of the shield and crimson ribbons. The different contemporary manuscripts show different variations of the reverse, one with the arms of Piemonte in a simple gold baroque frame and ribbons, one with a simple gold baroque frame and ribbons over a trophy of colours, one with royal supporters of gold lions, one with royal supporters of gold lions and trophies of colours, but as only one stand was made it is impossible to know which was the exact model was actually made.

The standard was carried with the aid of a bandoleer which had a carabiner. It was made of leather and covered in velvet, probably blue for the *colonnello*'s guidon and red for the others, edged and embroidered with gold lace. It was joined by a ring and a swivel spring clip by two gilded metal plates.

Reggimento di Dragoni della Regina

The *Reggimento di Dragoni della Regina* were raised in 1736 from a disbanded hussar company, which had been originally raised in 1734. In 1738 they had 500 men and 333 horses, by 1747 they had 650 men and 600 horses.

The *colonnelli* of the regiment under Charles Emmanuel III were Barone Cesare Grimaldi di Boglio from 1736, who was succeeded by Centorio Filippo Perucard D'Annecy, Chevalier di Ballone, in 1742. He was severely wounded at the Battle of Camposanto on 8 February 1743, and died on 10 February. His successor was Gaetano Francesco San Martino d'Agliè, Marchese di San Germano, from 1743 to 1763.

Service

The regiment was at the Battle of Camposanto on 8 February 1743. In 1744 they fought at the Battle of Madonna dell'Olmo.

Uniforms

The regiment wore a black tricorn with a dark blue cockade on the left brim, with a black loop and a pewter button, and a white lace border. They wore black neck stocks. Their service dress uniform consisted of a red coat with sky blue cuffs, linings and turn backs. The coat had eight pewter buttons, placed in pairs on the coat, with four on the cuffs. The coat had horizontal pockets, each with four buttons. There were shoulder straps on both shoulders which held the musket and cartridge pouch in place. These were secured with buttons. Their waistcoat and their breeches were also sky blue. The musket tompion was red and sky blue.

Officers

The officers' black tricorns had silver lace and a silver button. The officers' coats had silver lace and silver buttons. The officers wore a sash of blue and/or gold silk with two gold hanging tassels, one on each end of the sash.

Tamburi

The *tamburi* wore the Royal Livery. The drum case was painted blue with red and orange flames and a white cross on the orange field in between the blue flames. The hoops were blue. The drum had red cords and a red leather shoulder belt; in full dress they had a red shoulder belt with three bands of livery lace. Later the hoops were blue with red stripes around the edges of the hoops. The drum had red cords and an off whitened leather shoulder belt. Their waistcoat and their breeches were sky blue.

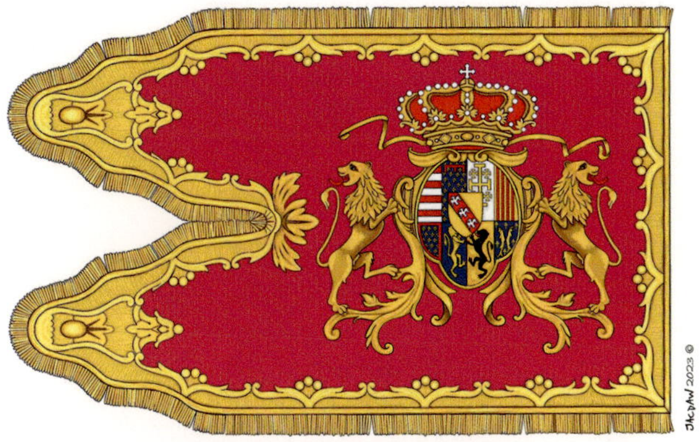

Company guidon, *Reggimento di Dragoni della Regina*. The obverse bore the crowned royal arms. The reverse bore the crowned arms of Lorraine on a crimson red field. The illustration is based on the 1744 version. (Author's Illustration)

Horse Furniture

The housings and holster caps were red, bordered with a broad blue and white silk galloon. The NCOs had a simple metallic border. The *dragoni* and *tamburi* carried a red cloak lined sky blue rolled up and attached behind the saddle. From 1749 they now had a regimental white lace which was edged in red on both sides, with a thin wavy red lace down the centre. The officers' lace was silver. The holster caps and corners of the housings were also embroidered with a silver metallic crowned regimental cypher, in this case 'DR'.

Guidons

Their guidons were issued in 1736 when the regiment was created. Each of the companies had a swallow-tailed guidon, carried on red fluted jousting style lances with gold fringes, cords and knots and a gilt finial and ferrule. The colonel's guidon had a blue lance.

In 1740, the *colonnello*'s guidon had a sky-blue field, on the obverse; in the centre were the crowned full arms of the King of Sardinia. On the reverse, were the crowned great arms of Lorraine for Queen Elisabeth Therese of Lorraine, the third wife of Charles Emanuel. The other company guidons bore the same motifs on the obverse and reverse but on a crimson/red field.

The different contemporary manuscripts show variations of the reverse, including a version with the lesser arms of Lorraine, but as only one stand was made it is impossible to know which was the exact model was finally made.

The standard was carried with the aid of a bandoleer which had a carabiner. It was made of leather and covered in velvet, probably blue with royal lace and edged with silver lace. It was joined by a ring and a swivel spring clip carabiner on two gilded metal plates.

Corpo dei Dragoni di Sardegna

The *Corpo dei Dragoni di Sardegna* was first raised in 1726. Although occasionally referred to as a regiment, it was really only an independent corps (a term often used at the time for smaller bodies of troops). In 1738 they had three weak companies, each of 66 men, in one squadron, raised from veteran invalid cavalrymen and deserters from enemy armies, and 198 horses. Their strength remained much the same in 1747. Of the nine officers, only the *cornetta* was actually Sardinian.

The commanders of this unit under Charles Emmanuel III were Tommaso Solaro del Borgo, Conte di Moretta, from 1726 to 1742, followed briefly by Gaetano Pioppis, who in turn was succeeded by Giacinto Faletti della Morra from June 1743. He was succeeded by Marchese Balestrin in July 1749.

Service

They remained as the garrison in Sardinia and served mainly as a police unit for the island against smugglers and bandits. One company was garrisoned in Cagliari, seat of the viceroy, in the complex called the *Quartiere dei Dragoons of Santa Croce* with a large stable in the old Jewish quarter.

Uniforms

The corps wore a black tricorn which had a dark blue cockade on the left brim, with a black loop and a pewter button, and a white lace border. Their service dress uniform consisted of a red coat with yellow cuffs, linings and turn backs. The coat had eight pewter buttons placed in pairs, with four on the cuffs. The coat had horizontal pockets, each with four buttons. There were shoulder straps on both shoulders which held the musket and cartridge pouch in place. These were secured with buttons. Their waistcoat and their breeches were red. The musket tompion was red and yellow.

Officers

The officers' black tricorns had silver lace and a silver button. The officers' coats had silver lace and silver buttons.

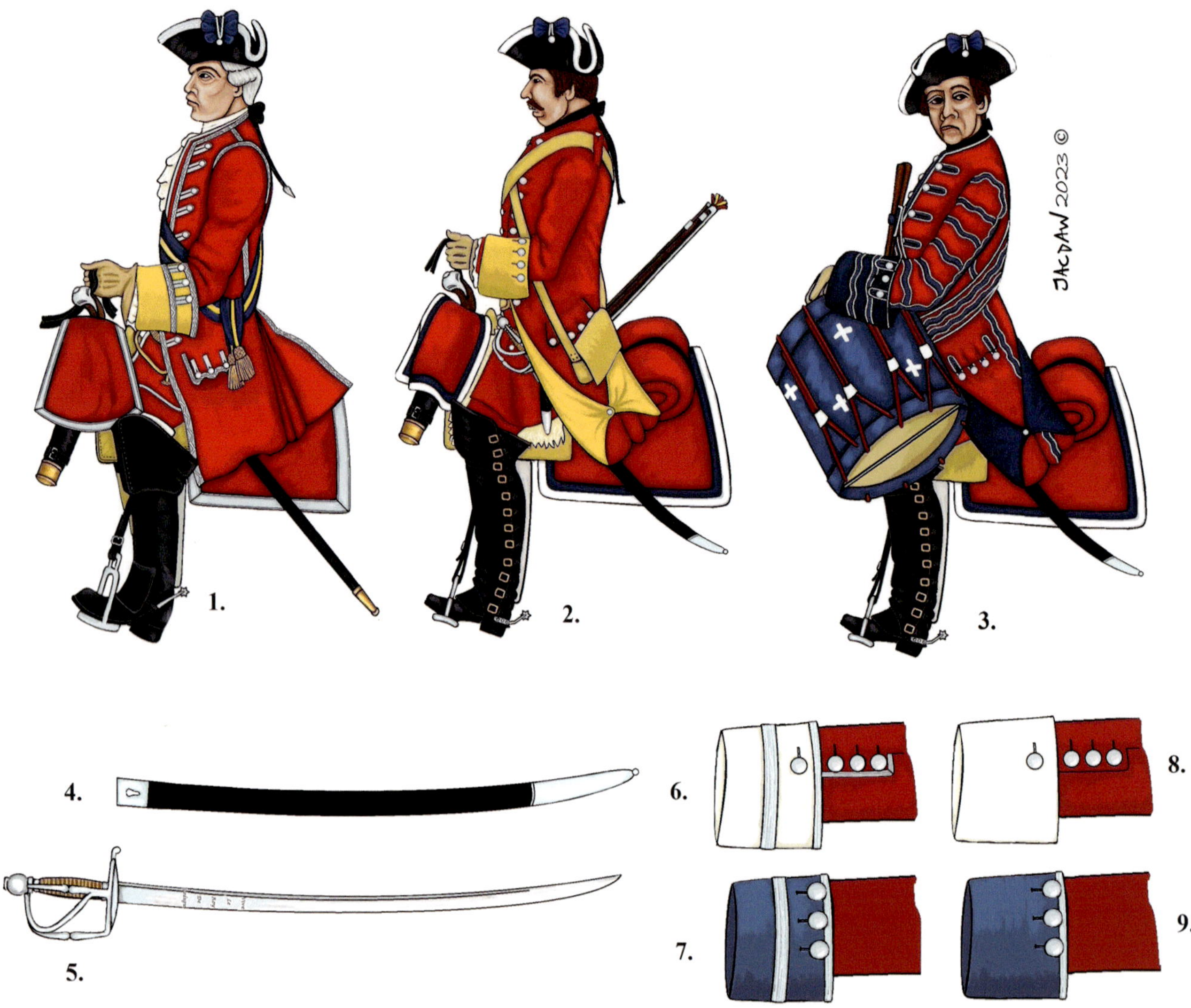

Corpo dei Dragoni di Sardegna; 1. Officer. 2. *Dragoni*, note the sheepskin on the saddle. 3. *Tamburo* 4. Scabbard. Author's reconstruction after the 1747 manuscript. 5. The M1738/1740 sabre. The blade was inscribed with the motto 'Vive Le Roy De Sardaigne'. Cuff details, *Reggimento di Dragoni di Piemonte*; 6. *Brigadiere*. 7. *Dragoni*. Cuff details, *Reggimento di Dragoni dell Regina*; 8. *Brigadiere*. 9. *Carabiniere*. (Author's Illustration)

The officers wore a sash of blue and/or gold silk with two gold hanging tassels, one on each end of the sash.

Tamburi

The *tamburi* wore the Royal Livery. The drum case was painted blue with white crosses; the hoops were blue. The drum had natural cords and a red leather shoulder belt. In full dress they had a red shoulder belt with three bands of livery lace. Later the hoops were blue with red stripes around the edges of the hoops. The drum had red cords and an off-white leather shoulder belt. The waistcoat and their breeches were mustard yellow.

Horse Furniture

The housings and holster caps were red, bordered with a broad blue and white silk galloon. From 1749 they had a regimental red lace border with a yellow stripe down the centre. The NCOs had a simple metallic border. The *dragoni* and *tamburi* carried a red cloak lined yellow, rolled up and attached behind the saddle. The officers' lace was silver. The holster covers and corners of the housings were also embroidered with a silver metallic crowned regimental cypher, in this case 'DS'.

Guidons

Theoretically each of the companies had swallow tailed guidons, carried on red fluted jousting style lances with gold fringes, cords and knots and a gilt finial and ferrule. The lances were painted blue in 1747. But only *colonnello*'s company, actually had a guidon made and issued. It was sky blue, with an intricate double gold lace border and fringe. On the obverse, in the centre were the crowned full arms of the King of Sardinia. On the reverse there was a flaming bomb on a patch of green turf with a white scroll inscribed with the motto 'IN PECTORE VIRES' on a sky-blue field.[5] The other companies guidons were designed, in both a crimson and a pale-yellow version, but they were never made and only existed on paper. The standard was carried with the aid of a bandoleer. It was made of leather and probably covered in red velvet and edged and embroidered with gold lace. It was joined by a ring and a swivel spring clip by two gilded metal plates.

Colonello's guidon, *Corpo dei Dragoni di Sardegna*. The original illustrations have been followed, but the blue was probably much darker. (Author's Illustration)

5 In the original manuscript the scroll is shown as red, but having had the chance to see the originals, the current author is of the opinion that it was an artist's error and the scroll should be white. The regimental motto translates to 'With a strong heart'.

11

The Artillery & Engineers

The artillery service in the Duchy of Savoy was first regulated on the 30 July 1625 following an edict of Duke Carlo Emanuele I of Savoy. The *Reggimento Reale Artiglieria* (Royal Regiment of Artillery) was constituted as an organised battalion in May 1691, reorganised in 1692, and then again in 1696 under Duke Victor Amadeus II. From 1743, it became the *Reggimento d'Artiglieria* and took precedence with the national regiments after *La Regina*, which also confirmed its regular status. From 1732 to 1757 the *colonnello* was Giacinto Andrea de Nicola.

From 1713, the Grand Master of the Artillery was Count Annibale Maffei who was succeeded by the Marquis Seyssel d'Aix in 1736. The *Corpo degli Ingegneri* (Corps of Engineers) was still part of the artillery regiment at this time.

Reggimento d'Artiglieria

Organisation

At the beginning of the war there were 12 companies. Of these companies only eight were artillery, each theoretically with eight guns. The other four were classed as technical companies: one was of bombardiers who were responsible for howitzers and mortars; one of sappers; one of miners; and one of labourers. There was also a detachment of volunteer gunners on Sardinia. In 1743 this company consisted of only 60 officers and men to cover the whole of the island.

The artillery service grew in numbers as needed. They began the War of the Austrian Succession with just a single battalion and ended it with two. Among the tasks of the service, in addition to manoeuvring and firing the pieces, both on campaign and in the fortresses, they were also responsible for their design, development, casting and construction. In addition to the artillery pieces, the service also dealt with other weapons, especially the muskets for all the army, as well as the bridging materials, pontoons, and the manufacture of gunpowder.

Each company was made up of 51 officers and gunners including a *capitano*, two *luogotenenti*, two *sergente*, three *caporale*, a *tamburo*, five *bombardieri*, 25 *artiglieri*, five *zappatori/minatori*, two *Maniscalco*, and five *ingegneri* or craftsmen. They probably had some help from infantry detachments to manoeuvre the guns when on campaign

The other companies were one company of sappers, one company of miners, one company of labourers, and a company of drivers for the artillery train and the commissariat wagons.

By 1747, the regiment had a strength of 1,400 men, who were divided into two battalions of eight companies each (12 of gunners, four of specialists). By 1748 three more companies of artillery had been added to the regiment.

Uniforms

The gunners wore a black tricorn with a yellow wool border and a royal blue cockade on the side, held in place by a yellow loop and a brass button. They wore red neck stocks. They had a dark blue coat, lined and cuffed in dark blue, with brass buttons which were grouped, from the top one, two and three. The cuffs had two bands of yellow lace, one on the edge and the other just below the buttons. They wore a dark blue waistcoat and breeches, and black gaiters, with black or brass buttons, and black shoes. When they were not on campaign, they wore dark blue stockings.

The *minatori* (miners) wore the same uniform, but for the mining itself, they wore a black coarse linen smock with 36 brass buttons, probably worn over their waistcoat and possibly with a fatigue bonnet or cap as well.

NCOs

The NCOs wore the same uniform as the men but with the addition of one wide and one thin band of gold lace around their cuffs for the *sergenti* and of one thin one of yellow wool for the *caporali*. The *sergenti* also had a small blue collar edged with a small gold lace, and their pockets were piped with gold lace. From in the early part of the century the NCOs had worn a scarlet waistcoat to distinguish them from the gunners, it is not clear when this dress ceased to be worn.

Arms and Equipment

The gunners wore a buff waist belt with a black belly box that had a pointed pouch flap, edged with red leather, with

Reggimento d'Artiglieria. 1. Officer. 2. *Sergente* with an elaborate partisan, '*picca da sergente bombardiere*'. 3. *Artigliere* with sponge and rammer. Note the priming flask carried on a bandoleer, the NCOs also carried these. The gunners were also armed with a musket. Note the elaborate ventral cartridge pouch. (Author's Illustration)

an oval brass badge (motif unknown). They carried a sabre, similar to the grenadiers one, in a black leather scabbard suspended from their waist belt. The sabre had a yellow wool/gold sword knot.

They were armed with either a French or Piedmontese musket. The miners' *sergenti* were also issued with blunderbusses, which was much more effective in the mines. It was made from

German manufactured parts but assembled in Turin. They also carried a black leather powder flask of priming powder with a brass nozzle suspended by mixed black, yellow and white cords, attached to a thin buff leather shoulder strap with a brass buckle. The *sergenti* also carried the ventral cartridge pouch, an NCOs version of the sabre with a gold sword knot and carried an ornate linstock called a '*Buttafuoco*'.

Officers

The officers wore a black tricorn with a gold lace border and a blue cockade on the side, held in place by a gold lace loop and a gold or brass button. Over their shoulder they had the habitual blue and gold tasselled sash. They had a dark blue coat, lined and cuffed in dark blue with a gold lace around their cuffs and pockets, a dark blue waistcoat with gold lacing, and a pair of dark blue breeches. They had black gaiters with black or brass buttons and black shoes.

Tamburi

The *tamburi* and musicians wore the Royal livery with a dark blue waistcoat and a pair of dark blue breeches. They did not have *pifferi*.

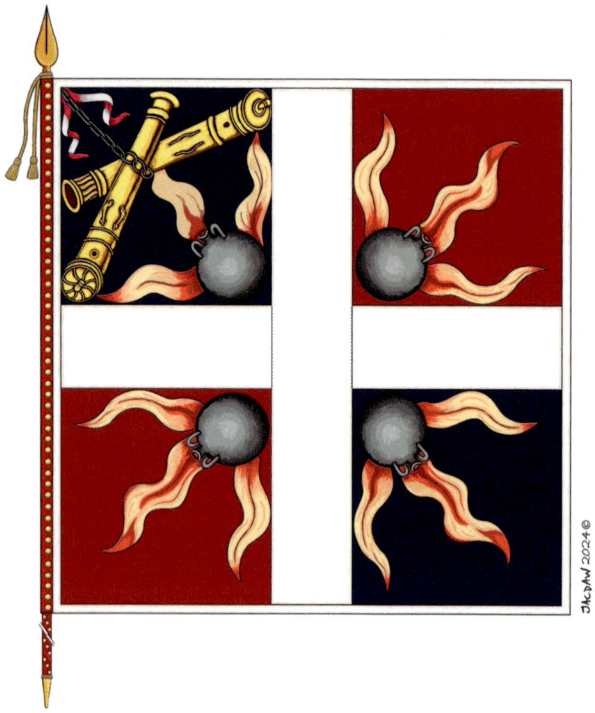

Reggimento d'Artiglieria, company colour. (Author's Illustration)

Colonnello's Colour

They had the standard blue model with a crowed black eagle. The sleeve was blue, and the stave was painted red and studded with brass nails in a spiral design. The spear shaped finial was gilded as was the cone shaped ferrule which was secured with a ring. The cords and tassels were gold.

Company Colours

Overall, a white cross, the first quarter was blue with a flaming bomb in natural colours in the angle under a pair of crossed bronze cannon barrels and a port fire and a white scroll. The fields were alternating blue and red, with a flaming bomb in corners. The obverse and reverse were identical in mirror image. The standard had a thin white border all around, including the staff edge and a red sleeve. The staves were painted red and studded with brass nails in a spiral design. The spear shaped finial was gilded as was the cone shaped ferrule. It had red cords and tassels. In the 1739 version, the flames in the red quarters were white and those in the blue quarters were red and the scroll was red and wrapped around the cannons.

The Ordnance

The weight of the Savoyard artillery used in the war is uncertain, in part due to the number differences between the individual pieces. The ordnance of the Sabaudian field artillery was closely based on a system very similar to the French Vallière system, with one important difference; the weight of the shot. In fact, a Piedmontese *libbra* (pound) was 368g instead of 489g for a French *livre*. So, the Savoyard 4-, 8-, 16- and 32-pounders were equivalent to 3-, 6-, 12- and 24-pounders in French Valliere system. The most common piece they used being 4-pounders called '*Falconetti*', basically a battalion gun. The official texts gave the preferred weight as 60 *rubbi*. An 8-pounder called a '*Falcone*' was the next most common piece. See the appendix on weights. Other various guns that existed in very limited numbers were another model 8-pounder called a '*Sagri*', as well as some 12-, 16-, 24- and 32-pounders, all named after different birds of prey.

While the administrative unit of the artillery was a company, the tactical unit was a brigade made up of a company of gunners, the guns, and drivers and other support staff. There were five brigades of field artillery, each of six guns. In 1744 there was a medium brigade with a battery of four 8-pounders and four light brigades with five 4-pounders of various origins. Some of these 4-pounders may in fact have been howitzers.

The main problem of the Savoyard artillery was its excessive weight. The 4-pounder, the lightest campaign gun, had a barrel weighing 460kg – together with the weight of the gun carriage this brought the weight up to almost a tonne. The 8-pounders had a barrel which weighed in at 920kg. Another problem was aiming, as they were still elevated with wooden levers and secured with wooden quoins, hammered in for finer sighting, like most of the artillery of the period.

At Madonna dell'Olmo when the caissons broke down with the reserves of the powder for Gioannini's guns, after an unexpected clash between the Sabaudian and the Franco-Spanish infantry for possession of the guns, they were only able to move one of the guns from its original location during the combat.

Due to the low mobility of the artillery, the necessity of field fortifications to protect the batteries was obvious, both on the western Alps and in the east where it was hilly but with plains as well. In fact, a number of encounters were concentrated on these redoubts. Once engaged, the artillery remained static for the duration of the battle; the gunners, very proud of their pieces, usually defended their guns to the last.

By 1743, the artillery brigades in battle were made up of five field pieces, this appears to have been four guns and one howitzer, commanded by a *capitano*, to be used with the infantry brigades and four short pieces to be used with the cavalry. Two or more brigades were commanded by a *maggiore* or another senior officer. During the campaign of 1743 they also used some small Coehorn type mortars in the field.

The field artillery was cast in bronze and the fortress artillery was generally cast in iron. Where the cannons were cast in iron, they were quite plain with only the reinforcing

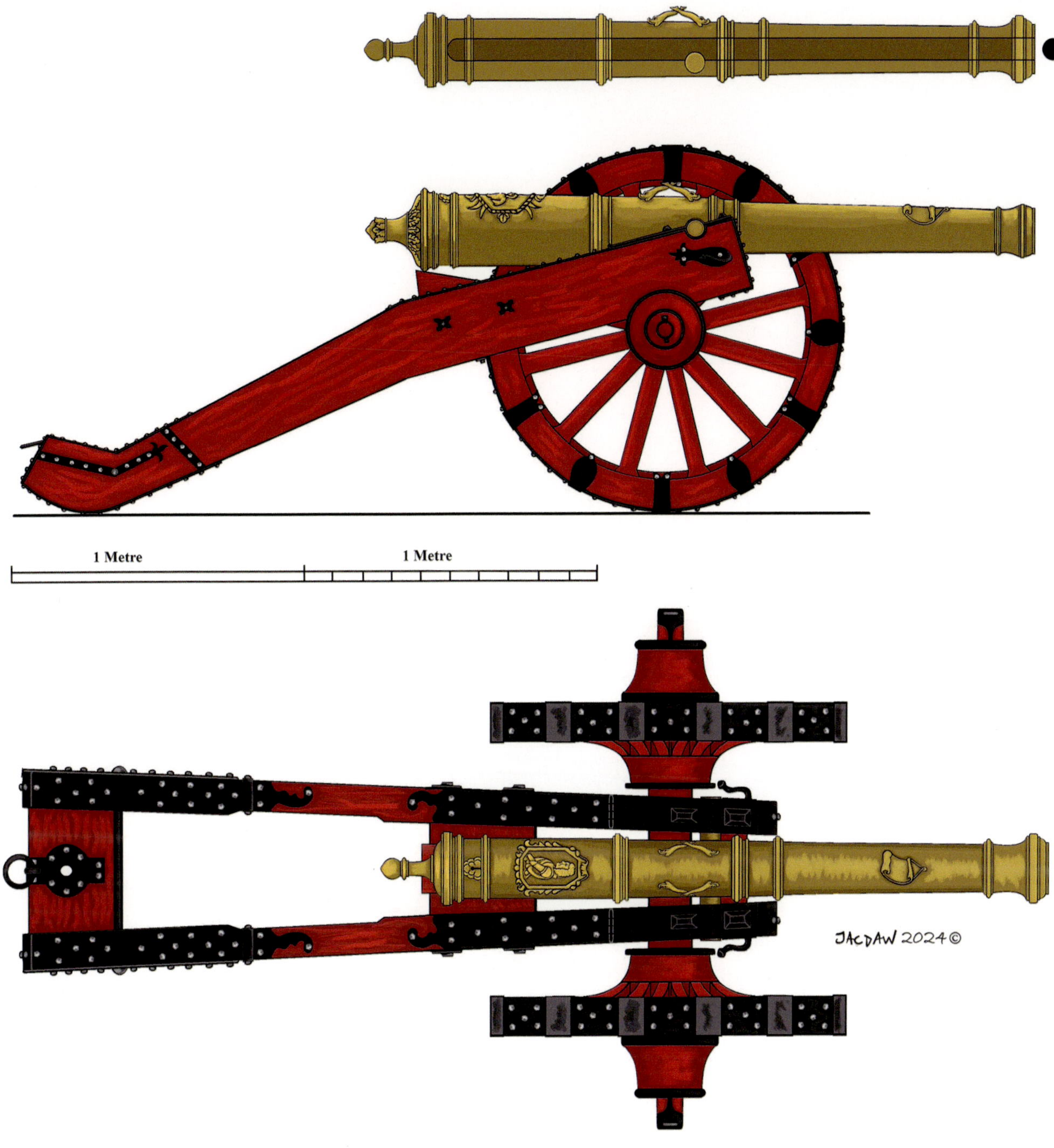

Piedmontese 4-pounder field gun. This piece is the 28 calibre Falconetto. Termed *leggero* (light), this appears to refer to the carriage as the barrels all seem to be the same, but it could refer to a shorter barrel, no data to prove this has been found. On the breech there was a portrait of the grand master of the artillery. Generally they had a plain cascabel, the lifting rings were either pairs of inter twined dolphins or simple acanthus leaves. The reconstructions of all the guns illustrated are based on the Embser and Saluzzo manuscripts, but as details are missing from the original plans some errors may have crept in. Missing details have been replaced with information from the contemporary French Valliere system. The nail and bolt heads are shown as light grey for clarity, in reality they would have been painted black like the rest of the iron work. (Author's Illustration)

rings, but the bronze field pieces were heavily decorated in a similar manner to the French artillery starting with the lifting rings in the form of stylized lions which later became acanthus leaves. Embser shows dolphins and griffons in his manuscript, so there were probably a number of variations, each one probably referring to a particular calibre, but no study of this has been found.

On the breech ring there was the name of the caster, from 1731 to 1748 this would have been Antonio Francesca of the Cebrano family, who were master casters during this period. The name would have been followed by the date of manufacture, the royal arms, and in the centre the arms of the grand master of artillery. But there were a number of variations between each class of pieces. The decoration

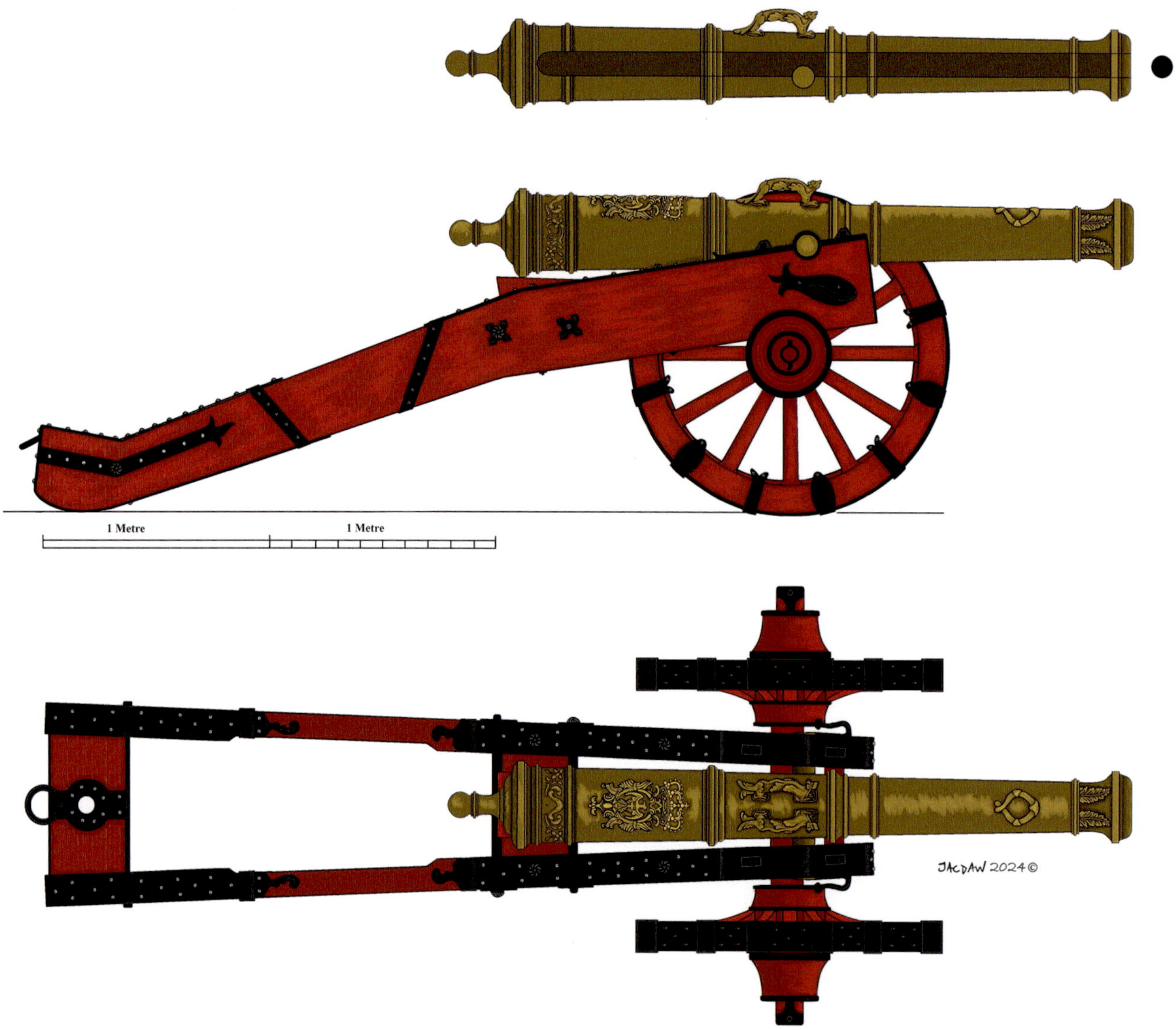

Piedmontese 8-pounder field gun. On the breech, there was a crowned eagle of Savoy, this could be replaced a crowned cross of Savoy. Generally they had a plain cascabel, although one surviving model is decorated with acanthus leaves. The lifting rings were either phantasmagorical animals or simple acanthus leaves. (Author's Illustration)

was cast with the gun and then finished with chisels (this description refers to the 8-pounder '*Falcone*' cannon). Each cannon (and heavy mortar) was named like French guns, some known names are Adone, Hiperione, Arrigo, Iuno, La Balista and Bellicoso & Il Capone (the boss).

The official colour of the gun carriages was red, but according to contemporary iconographic sources, they are occasionally shown painted a darkish red, but more frequently shown in natural brown wood with blackened ironwork for field artillery. The red paint was probably red lead/red oxide, used by many countries at the time and popular on wooden farm vehicles up to the twentieth century.

Jan Peeter Verhussen shows them as red with black ironwork in one of his paintings of the Battle of Guastualla, painted around 1743 (and in the Galleria Sabauda, Turin). By the Seven Years War they appear to have been painted grey with black ironwork, like British artillery.

The calibres adopted for the field pieces in 1750 were:

Light (Leggero) 4-pounder M 1732 Field Piece (Falconetto)
Calibre: 76mm
Length of bore: 24 calibres (1.82m)
Overall length of barrel: 1.98m
Weight of barrel: 461kg
Breech decoration: a portrait
Lifting handles: dolphins
Weight of ball: 1.475kg
Weight of carriage: 590kg
Dimension of wheel: 1.33m
Length of carriage: 2.7m (estimate)

Heavy (Pesante) 4-pounder M 1732 Field Piece (Falconetto)
Calibre: 76mm
Length of bore: 28 calibres (2.12 m)
Overall length of barrel: 2.42m
Breech decoration: a portrait of the master of the artillery
Lifting handles: pairs of intertwined dolphins
Weight of barrel: 553kg
Weight of ball:1.475kg
Weight of carriage: 590kg

Light (Leggero or Curto) 8-pounder M 1732 Field Piece (Sagro)
Calibre: 90mm
Length of bore: 24 calibres (2.17m)
Overall length of barrel: 2.43m
Breech decoration: crowned cross of Savoy or the crowned cross of Jerusalem
Lifting handles: dolphins or zoomorphic
Weight of barrel: 875kg
Weight of ball: 2.95kg
Weight of carriage: 680kg
Dimension of wheel: 1.45m
Length of carriage: 3.60m (estimate)

Heavy (Pesante) 8¼-pounder M 1732 Field Piece
Calibre: 96mm
Length of bore: 26 calibres (2.66m)
Overall length of barrel: 2.95m
Breech decoration: crowned eagle of Savoy in a baroque frame or wreath
Lifting handles: lions or griffons (zoomorphic)
Weight of barrel: 1,015kg
Weight of ball: 2.95kg
Weight of carriage: 680kg
Dimension of wheel: 145 centimetres.
Length of carriage. 3.60m (estimate)

Light (Leggero) 16-pounder M 1732 Field Piece (Quarto di Cannone)
Calibre: 123mm
Length of bore: 24 calibres (2.88m)
Overall length of barrel: 3.43m
Breech decoration: cross of Savoy under a crowned helm surrounded by a trophy of arms
Lifting handles: either dolphins or rococo leaves and stems
Weight of ball: 5.9kg
Weight of barrel: 1,640kg
Weight of carriage: 950kg
Dimension of wheel: 1.64m (estimate)
Length of carriage: 4.70m (estimate)

Heavy (Pesante) 16-pounder M 1732 Field Piece (Colubrina)
Calibre: 120 mm
Length of bore: 30 calibres (3.6m)
Overall length of barrel: 4.1m
Breech decoration: a crowned cross within a wreath
Lifting handles: dolphins or lions
Weight of barrel: 1,890kg
Weight of ball: 5.9kg
Weight of carriage: 950kg
Dimension of wheel: 1.64m (estimate)
Length of carriage: 4.7m (estimate)

32-pounder (Leggero) M 1732 Field Piece (Mezzo Cannone)
Calibre: 153 mm
Length of bore: 21 calibres (3.21m)
Overall length of barrel: 3.81m
Breech decoration: crowned cypher of King Charles Emanuele
Lifting handles: dolphins or lions
Weight of barrel: 2,770kg
Weight of ball: 11.8kg
Weight of carriage: 1,400kg
Dimension of wheel: 1.64m (estimate)
Length of carriage: 4.47m (estimate)[1]

From the 1730s the artillery had been equipped with howitzers (*Obice/Aubitz*). They were all 6-pounders with a calibre of 15.3mm. There was a long (*longo*) barrel version chambered to length of six grenades (*granate*) and a short-barrelled (*curto*) version. We have a fairly good idea what these barrels looked like from technical drawings in the Embser (1732) and Saluzzo (1740) manuscripts, but we know a lot less about the carriages.

Another piece was the Merlin or Smeriglio (the smallest of the artillery pieces) firing a 10-ounce lead shot (approximately 307g, with a diameter of 37mm). It had a length of 35 calibres and 'the thickness of the metal was adjusted to the diameter of the ball'.[2] These are closer to what we would call '*Amusettes*'.

1 The dimensions given are fairly exact for the barrels, but the carriages and limbers are the author's estimates based on different contemporary documents, which frequently contradict each other. In the kingdom at this time there were a number of different systems of measurements in use, which can create some confusion. The Piedmontese foot (*piedi*) measured 34.2cm, but the Turin foot only measured 29.3cm and it this unit that has been used to calculate (approximately) the dimensions of the artillery. In Sardinia they used yet another system. This has also rendered calculating the dimensions difficult.

The breech decorations and lifting handles given are apparently the most common, but there were many other variations as were the lengths of the barrels. Most of the larger categories had the neck of barrel decorated with acanthus leaves.

2 *Manusritto d'Embser*, 1732, p.5.

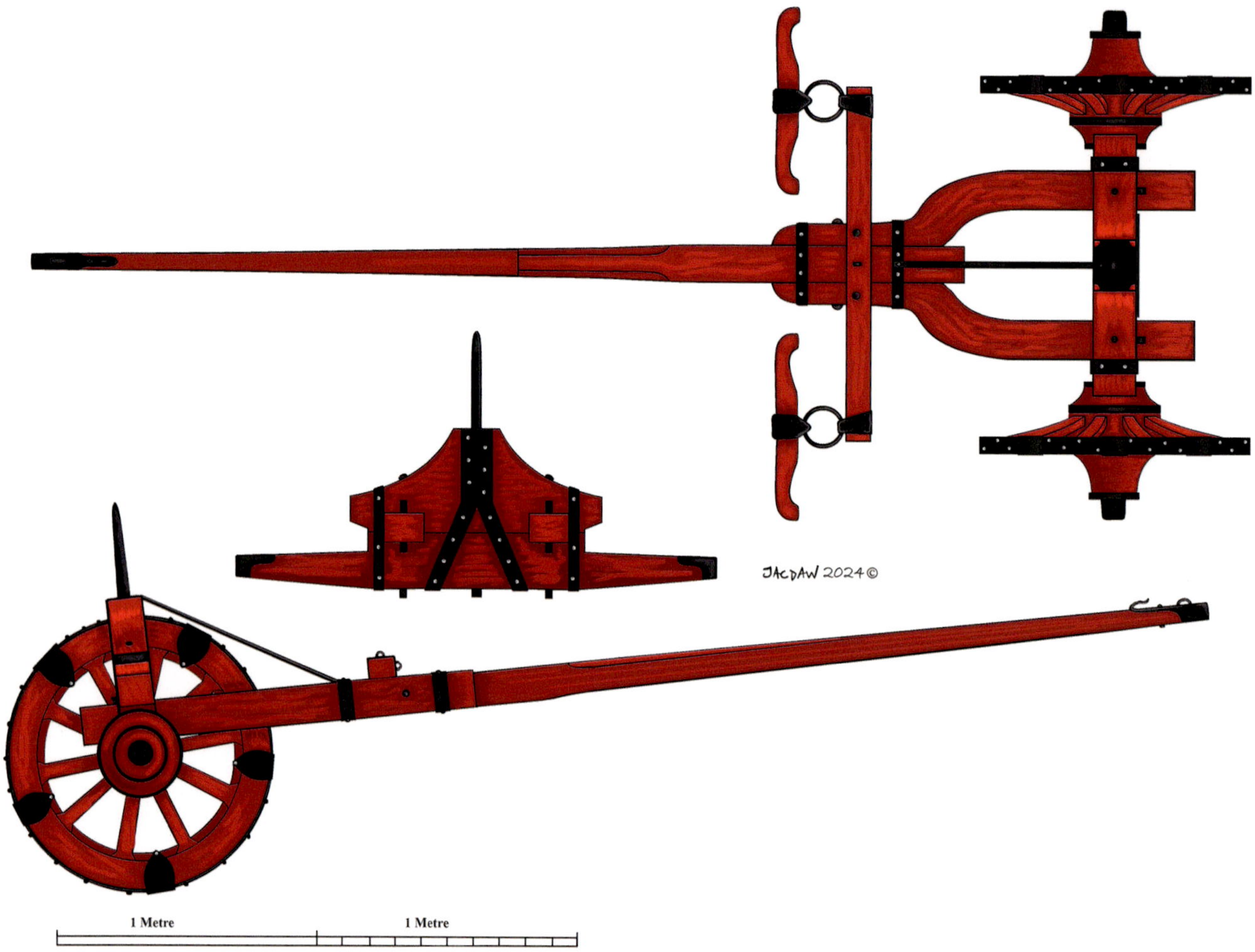

Piedmontese heavy limber. This is the standard four to six horse artillery limber, for the 4- and 8-pounder field guns and the howitzer. (Author's Illustration)

It was noted in the *Courrier d'Avignon* in a report from Turin on 9 June 1742: 'We sent more than 100 small pieces of cannon, or swivels to Nice, which must be dispersed in the gorges and mountain passes.' These were probably the Merlins.

There would have been a number of wall or rampart guns (oversized muskets), but we do not have any information on the Piedmontese version, they were possibly imported French weapons. A wall gun's barrel could be over 1.4m in length with a bore of at least 20–25mm or even more.

The usual siege park was composed of forty 32-pounders, twenty 16-pounders and 24 mortars, twelve 12-inch mortars, four 4-inch mortars and eight 6-inch mortars for '*grenades royals*'.

They used some very light guns as mountain guns (called a *porbeagle*) of two different calibres. The six of these light pieces which were used in combat in Savoy used a charge of between four to six ounces of powder. However, although the lightness of these guns made them suitable for operations in the mountains, the weight of the shot (respectively 184.2g and 491.2g), meant that the presence of these weapons was more psychological than actually effective. They subsequently concluded that the *porbeagle* was irrelevant, if not completely useless, as an infantry support weapon.

In 1743 and 1744, a light breech-loading cannon was forged with a rifled barrel, which fired a 1¼ pound ball of 38 mm calibre. This breech loading cannon was called the '*Jenner*', '*Hyenner*' or '*Gioannini*'. This cannon was the 'new invention' which was used in the campaign of 1744 and some later campaigns, but there were only some five or six of them. There was also a howitzer version designed, but there no record of it actually being made.

In 1747 a dismountable 4-pounder mountain gun was issued. Designed in Turin in 1745 by the military engineer Ignazio Giuseppe Bertola Roverda, Count d'Exilles, it could be pulled by four men. It was mounted on a small carriage, with a barrel (length 1.83m) made in two parts, joined in the centre between four iron slats which slid into rings along the sides of the barrel. It was designed to be broken down and transported on mules. It was an innovative design, but expensive and needing frequent maintenance. There were never more than a battery of four pieces available at any time, more often only two. The French also captured two of them.

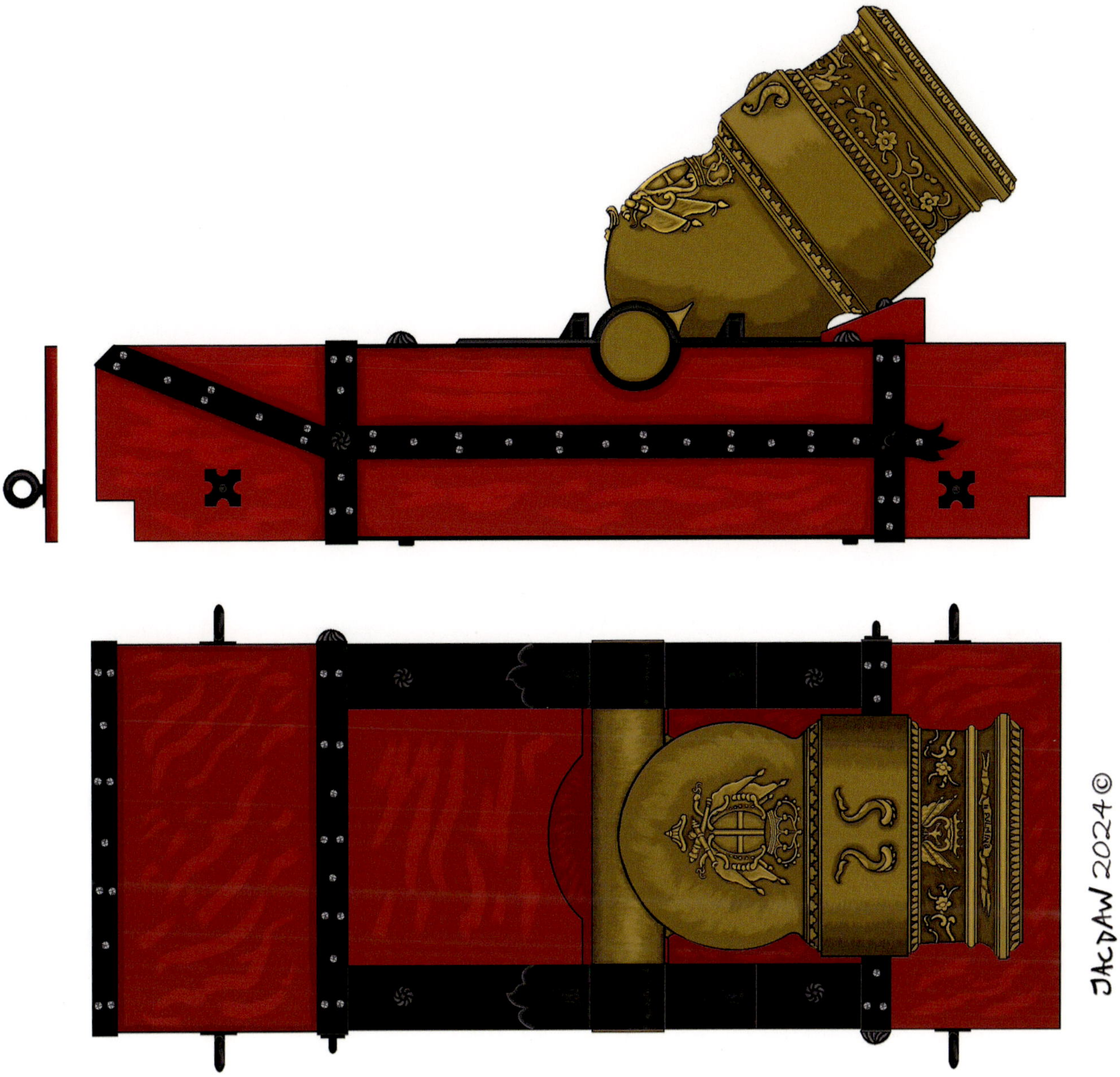

Piedmontese 12-inch mortar. This one is called '*Il Fulmina*' (the lightning). (Author's Illustration)

The Artillery Train

Although the artillery train (*treno d'artiglieria*) was basically composed of civilian contractors during the war, they were uniformed, militarised and subjected to military discipline. Surviving documents dated to 1743 and 1744 explain that the creation of four artillery brigades with campaign pieces was planned in 1743, three with 4-pounders and one with 8-pounders. Normally the brigades of 4-pounders had five guns and the 8-pounders had four pieces, so the total of number of pieces that were available to the Savoyard artillery and ready to go on campaign was only 19. In 1744 the number of brigades on campaign was raised to six: one brigade had four 8-pounders; four brigades each had five 4-pounders and finally a sixth brigade had ten 16-pound 6-ounce stones throwers (*Pietriere*).

The increase in the number of campaign pieces, in addition to the other services the artillery was in charge of (fortresses, mountains, arsenal, mines, etc.) made it necessary to create a second artillery battalion. Consequently in 1744 the corps was reorganised and raised to the strength of a regiment of two battalions.

For the same reason, the artillery train, which was responsible for moving the field guns, a mule train for moving the mountain guns and munitions, another train for the transport of bridging materials and pontoons, as well as the ammunition for the infantry and cavalry, was increased in strength as well to cope with needs of the artillery regiment.

As an example, a brigade of 4-pounder field pieces needed the following train:

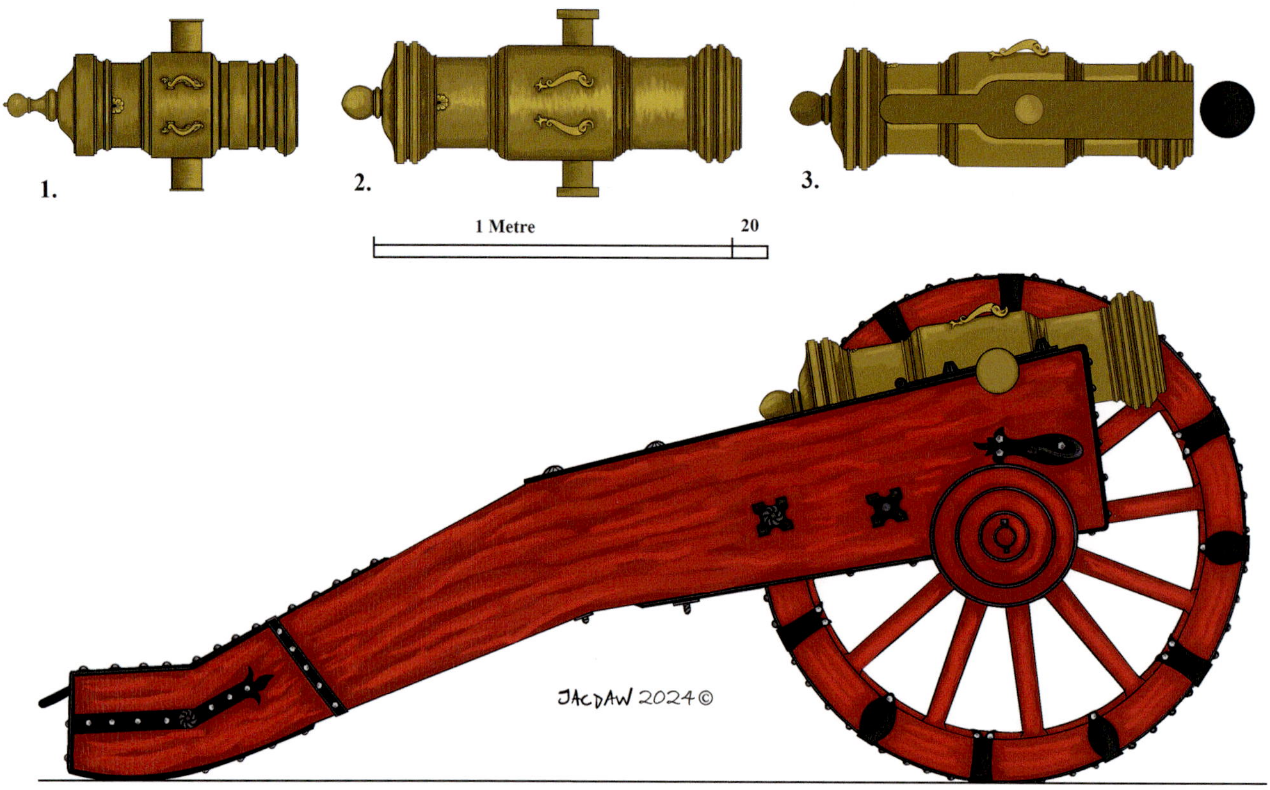

Piedmontese 6-pounder howitzer. 1. The short howitzer barrel. 2. The long howitzer barrel. 3. The long howitzer barrel section showing bore and powder chamber. The drawing of this carriage in the Embser document looks rather strange, as the recesses for the trunnions are set too far back and the central transom would impede placing the barrel. The carriage has been redrawn. The general outline has been kept, but the recesses for the trunnions are as used in France and Austria. (Author's Illustration)

20 horses for the five limbers and pieces (four for each limber)
Four horses to tow two reserve carriages (carried on a wagon)
Four horses to pull the ammunition wagon which carried the powder cartridges
Four horses for a light cart with hinged sides.
32 horses for the eight wagons carrying the cases of cannon balls
Eight horses for four light tumbrels
Two horses for towing a wagon with the campaign forge
Seven horses for the officers and *sergenti* of the train (one was in reserve)
70 mules for infantry and cavalry ammunition
Four oxen for two country-style wagons (the classic four-wheeled Piedmontese peasants' wagon)

This gave a total of 81 horses, 70 mules and four oxen to tow five guns and limbers and 17 wagons of various types.

Another contemporary document notes that to move 24 light field guns, the army needed 415 horses, 300 mules, 44 oxen and 120 vehicles, including 34 limbers, five powder wagons, five open wagons, 40 tumbrels (light two-wheel wagons), 11 peasant farm wagons pressed in to service, 20 dumpers (presumably two wheeled light farm wagons), and five field forges to move it around the country. One presumes that this insinuates that there were four brigades of 4-pounders, not three, or perhaps a battery of light 8-pounders.

Uniform and Arms

The waggoners' uniform consisted of a black tricorn with a yellow border and a blue cockade, with a loop and a brass button. They wore a double-breasted red coat, shown with light blue or white lining and turn backs, the buttons were brass.[3] The coats had slashed small blue cuffs with an elaborate red cuff flap and three brass buttons. The pockets had three brass buttons. The waistcoat and breeches were red, and they wore black laced gaiters similar to those worn by French dragoons. They were armed with an iron hilted sabre in a black leather scabbard which was carried on a buff leather waist belt worn under the coat. Their M 1742 sabre was of a special design; both the grip and base of the steel guard were all studded. The 76cm blade was also engraved, on one side with the royal arms, and a cross on the reverse surrounded by baroques floral wreaths. It was designed by the swordsmith Paolo Clavel. This replaced an older model, which also had a steel hilt.

3 The original watercolour has faded and the blue would have been much deeper.

Piedmontese army wagons. Top. A logistical '*Cartatouchia* or 'Caisson (*Cassone Logistico*). These vehicles were pulled by horses or oxen. The staff took their places at the box seat and on the rear flap. They were used for transporting cartridges and fuses. Note that on the wheels there are no steel reinforcements where the felloes join. Bottom. A general (*Cassione Compito*) service wagon. (Author's Illustration)

NCOs

The *brigadieri* were distinguished from the *carrettiere* by distinctions in galloon. Its form is not described, but it was probably similar to that of the artillery *brigadieri*. The border and loop of the tricorn were in gold galloon. In addition, a *maresciale di logis* of the artillery train wore a blue waistcoat and breeches instead of red. Also, they probably carried a better quality sabre.

There is no information of the officers' uniforms. It was possibly similar to the NCOs but of better quality and with the usual officers' distinctions. There is no information on the housings of the officers or NCOs, possibly they were red.

The Supply Train

Again, the supply train (*Treno di Provianda*) was also originally composed of civilian contractors but later during the war they were also uniformed and militarised. On campaign the supply train consisted of five brigades, each consisting of 50 wagons and 100 horses. Each brigade was

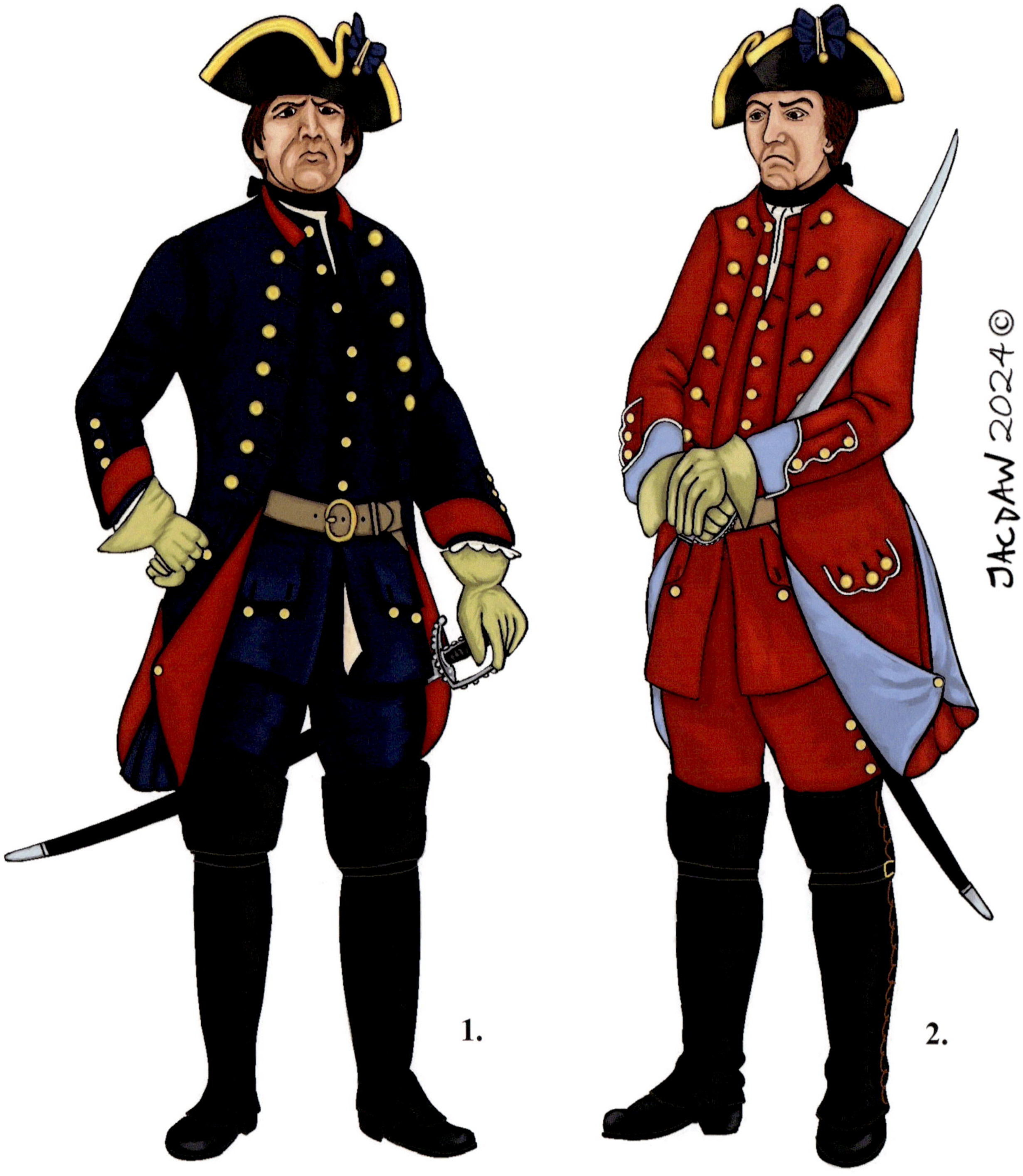

Piedmontese wagon drivers. 1. Mounted driver of the supply train. 2. Mounted driver of the artillery train. (Author's Illustration)

commanded by a *luogotenente* with a *maresciale di logis* and the overall commander of the train was a *capitano*. The officers and *brigadieri* were mounted. Each wagon in the brigade was driven by a carter or waggoner. The wagons of the brigade were divided into five groups of 10, each commanded by a *brigadier*.

In total, there were 220 wagons, and apart from some four-wheeled farm carts (*carro alla paesana*), most of them two-wheeled tumbrels (*tombarelli*). The load of each open wagon was covered with a tarpaulin which was painted with a white cross in oil paint in each of the four corners.

In each brigade there were four specialists; a *bourrigliere* (who took care of the carts), a *maniscalco* and a young assistant, and a *carradore* (a carpenter who took care of the maintenance and repair of the wagons). No mention is made of a blacksmith, but they surely had them.

Uniforms

The drivers wore a black tricorn and a blue cockade with a loop and a brass button. They wore a double-breasted blue coat with a red collar, lining, and turn backs. The coats had buttoned cuff flaps with red turned back half cuffs and brass buttons. The waistcoat and breeches were blue, and they wore black laced gaiters. They were armed with the same iron hilted sabre as the artillery train, which was carried on a buff leather waist belt worn under the coat.

Miners

As noted at the beginning of the chapter, the miners were part of the artillery regiment and as such they wore the same uniform. For work in the mines, they had a black smock (*camisacci*) which had 36 brass buttons, the exact pattern of which is unknown. They were considered specialists in underground warfare, but they were not always directly employed in mining, sapping and earthworks. That was undertaken by soldiers recruited from the garrison regiments and probably professional civilian miners, the Savoyards were particularly expert in the domain. Mining in Savoy was a major industry and an important part of the wealth of the Kingdom of Sardinia. Mining for iron ore dated back to before the arrival of the Celts, but there were also copper, silver and lead mines.

The miners had a sophisticated range of tools at their disposition; from different crowbars, mattocks, augers, shovels and pickaxes. The miners supervised the excavations and were responsible for positioning the charges and placing the fuses, as well as firing. They were armed with blunderbusses and artillery sabres.

The Corps of Engineers

The mountainous nature of the country and the complex system of fortifications guarding the mountain passes, in particular on the French border, had by necessity led to the development of a highly efficient Corps of Engineers. But they were only officially constituted into a corps in 1752. During the war they were still officially part of the artillery regiment, so theoretically they should have worn their uniform, but the 1747 album shows them in their own uniform.[4]

They are shown wearing a uniform consisting of a black tricorn with a broad gold lace border with light blue feather border around the edge, and a blue cockade, with a gold loop and button. They wore a black neck stock. Their collarless coats were grey-white with medium blue cuffs and lining, and three gold buttons with gold laced buttonholes on both sides of the coat. Their horizontal pockets had three buttons. Their waistcoats and breeches were blue, and they had soft black/brown leather riding boots. Around their waist they had a leather belt covered in blue cloth and edged in gold lace. Their swords had a red sword knot.

These engineers would probably have worn helmets and breast plates, similar to those used in the French army during sieges, when they were in the saps.

The sappers who actually carried out the work, were probably mobilised civilian labourers, who appear to have worn ordinary civilian work clothes, according to a contemporary illustration. They wore a black unlaced tricorn or round hat, a coarse short brown woollen jacket, with no cuffs or turn backs. They wore brown stockings, a red waistcoat and blue breeches – basically civilian dress – but there were probably a number of variations. Pointed bonnets were also popular with peasants and labourers, as were twill work smocks.

4 State Archives, Turin, H VIII 53.

Engineers, miners and sappers. 1. An engineer, note the light blue plumes on his tricorn and the red sword knot. 2. A miner wearing a black work smock called a *camisacco* and a bonnet, more practical than a tricorn in a tunnel, as worn by miners in Savoy. He is holding a '*Gaja*', a type of pickaxe. Authors reconstruction. 3. A sapper, simply a hired labourers wearing their own civilian clothes, note the form of the spade, typical of Piedmont. Not to scale: 4. The miners' blunderbuss called a *trombone da minatore*. The metal parts were made by Suhl of Spangemberg. Only about a 100 of them were made. 5. Another type of pickaxe '*Piccone*', with a hammer head. 6. A miners' hoe called a '*Zappa*' or '*Hauletta*'. (Author's Illustration)

12

The Militias

The Milice Vaudoise

The Vaudois, also called Valdesi or Waldenses, were mainly Occitane speaking Protestants who lived in the frontier Alpine valleys of Pellice and Chisone, in particular Angrogna, and the valleys of Saint Martin and Lucerne in Piedmont.

These communities were closely related to the French Huguenots who fled France after the revocation of the Edict of Nantes, many of whom joined them. Following their persecution, they had become hardened guerrilla combatants, defending their families from French catholic incursions. Although in the past they had suffered persecution at the hands of the Duke of Savoy, during the War of the Grand Alliance he had ensured their loyalty when he granted them liberty of faith in 1689, although they were forbidden to leave their valleys.

The *Milice Vaudoise*'s commander under Charles Emmanuel III, was *Capitano* Jean-Baptiste Rouzier, who later became a *capitano* of *Monfort* and ended his career as a *luogotenente colonnello.*

Service

They were part of the *Milizia Ordinaria*, but as they were employed as professional mountain troops it seemed best to separate them from the rest of the *Milizia*. They served in free companies of around 100 men. There were as many as 10 companies in 1744.

At the beginning of the conflict, *Capitano* Rouzier took command of around 2,000 Vaudois on the western alpine front. In the summer of 1742, he carried out a thorough reconnaissance of the Varaita and Susa valleys. This served them well during the fighting at the Battle of Casteldelfino in 1743. The 'partisans' noted at the Battle of Camposanto in 1743 were the Vaudois. Following the defeat at Pietralunga in 1744, when the army moved down to the plains, Rouzier with 1,200 of his Vaudois stayed behind and harassed the enemy's rear.

He raided as far as Queyras, burning the French villages and taking over 13,000 livres in contributions. He returned to Piedmont and hit the supply lines of the French besieging Cuneo. He and the other bands played an important part in defeating the siege. There were 600 of them at Genoa in 1747, while with another unit served as a screen around the Battle of L'Assiette, and limited the reconnaissance of the French, which led to their defeat. A battalion of 350 men helped to cover Browne's retreat from Provence.

Uniforms

Uniforms were rare and most wore their everyday work clothes with hats with field signs, gaiters, and whatever else they could acquire. Cloth bonnets or stocking caps were popular as well, usually in brown homespun, which made them less conspicuous in the mountains.

The companies wore a black tricorn with a dark blue cockade on the left brim, with a black loop and white lace border. The officers had silver lace and buttons. Contemporary illustrations show them with the imperialist field sign of sprigs of oak leaves in their tricorns.

They all wore a home spun brown collarless coat. The coat had eight buttons in cloth covered wood, and three on the cuffs. The coat had horizontal pockets, each with three buttons and it had brown cuffs and lining. Sometimes illustrations show them in coats of ticken (white linen cloth with thin blue or black stripes). They wore white cravats. Their waistcoats were red and their breeches could be blue, brown, black or red. The gaiters were black, and they had brass buttons. When they were not on campaign, they could wear white stockings.

Arms

Their principal weapon was a standard infantry musket, but they often carried hunting fire-arms. Their cartridge pouch was carried on a buff leather shoulder belt. They had a small sabre carried on a buff leather waist belt. By 1744 they had been partially rearmed with rifled muskets. Belt pistols are also mentioned, as are grenadier sabres.

However, their traditional sidearm was a rather strange weapon called a '*Beidana*', a typical village weapon used in the western Alps between the seventeenth and the end of the eighteenth century, not only by the Waldensians. It was a cross between a falchion and a cleaver type weapon. It was simply hooked over one's belt. There were many different

The *Milizia*. 1. *Milice Vaudoise*, probably the best militia Piedmont had. 2. Militia man from the province of Mondovi, note his cheap ticken jacket, brown homespun waistcoat and breeches. He also carries an old infantry sabre and an old black leather cartridge pouch. 3. *Reggimento Fisso della Città di Torino*. This well-dressed regiment, originally an infantry/militia regiment, was disbanded in 1741. 4. The Valdese Beidana (not to scale), this was a both a common sidearm as well as a tool in the valleys. (Author's Illustration)

variants and sizes, from 60–70cm long, some much cruder, others more sophisticated, and some with a full hilt and a belt hook. The grip could be simply the steel, or a wooden or horn grip. Obviously, there was no scabbard. If typical to the valleys, it was used in the surrounding provinces as well.

NCOs

Distinctions unknown, but they probably just had a silver lace around the cuffs.

Officers

The officers' tricorns had silver lace border and loop, a Savoy blue cockade and a silver button. The officers' coats and waistcoats had silver lacing, and they very likely wore blue sashes at the waist.

Musicians

The musicians wore the Royal Livery, although probably in a much-simplified style and probably not on campaign. Their instruments are not defined and although drums are not very practical in mountain warfare, but as regulated troops they were the regiment's official instrument. One may assume that they used some form of horn when they were detached from their unit, as did their French and Spanish enemies.

Colours

It is possible that some colours were carried by the Vaudois militias; they definitely had a couple during the War of the Spanish Succession. In 1706 the 'Waldenses' militia had a blue sheet with, in the centre, a candle in a gold candelabra, over an open book (the bible) under a crescent of seven gold stars, all within a thin gold cadre. Around the lower part was a wreath of green oak leaves and above a scroll bearing a motto 'LUX LUCET IN TENEBRIS' – a light in the dark. A motif used by the Huguenots around the same time. On a blue field, was a stylised silver dog under a blue scroll edged gold with the probable text 'PATIENTIA LAESA FIT FUROR' (from suffering comes fury). The reverse was identical in mirror image. This colour, which only slightly predates the war, was probably only carried when they were mustered or on parade, but not in combat.[1]

Milizia Ordinaria

Most of the *Milizia Ordinaria* (Ordinary Militia) were conscripted from the country's border provinces. They were organised into companies of 100 men, and they elected their own officers. They could then be grouped into battalions of varying strengths. These were then to be placed under the command of a regular officer, either a *capitano* or *luogotenente* with a local temporary rank of *colonnello comandante*.

The provinces of Ceva and Mondovi were able to raise as many as 10,000 men when they were needed. Generally, they were only mobilised when the country was attacked and in danger of being invaded, although some did serve in field armies. The militias of Mondovi and Monferrato both served at the Siege of Genoa in 1747. There were also some companies of militia in Sardinia.

Uniform

The militia wore a simple black tricorn with a dark blue cockade and a sprig of oak leaves. They wore a blue and white striped ticken coat with seven evenly spaced tin buttons on each side, and horizontal pockets with red cuffs and collar. They had a cloth waistcoat and a pair of breeches made from brown homespun woollen cloth. Theoretically they had white gaiters, but no doubt there would have been a number of regional variations with cheap ticken or brown cloth being used as well. Some may have had old grey-white coats as well. Some are noted as having either blue or green cuffs, but we do not know which provinces used them.

Their arms and equipment would have varied considerably from unit to unit, depending on what was in the arsenals and those who were the most active, but they would probably been issued with older muskets. The *tamburi* would have worn some form of the Ducal Livery. They probably had simple colours if any, probably just a white cross on a red field.

A later manuscript (1758), but referring to an earlier period, shows them in a simple black tricorn with a white lace border and a dark blue cockade. They had a blue coat lined and cuffed in red, with silver buttons and a red waistcoat and breeches. Their neck stock was red, and their gaiters were white. They are shown armed with musket and sword.

Corps Francs

These bands of volunteers, present in numerous reports from the Sardinian side, were not soldiers who presented themselves for specific missions, nor were they civilians who volunteered to defend their country. The figure of the volunteer had been defined by the Royal Decree of 22 June 1744, which urged the recruitment of outlaws in return for a reduction of their sentence or a royal pardon in the future. Each company should have a minimum strength of 50 and a maximum of 100 men. They were to be commanded by officers from regular units, three in all – including a *capitano*, a *luogotenente* and a *sottoluogotenenti* – who had also a drum for the transmission of orders. The combat quality of these units was not high; they lacked NCOs, and were poorly armed and disciplined.

Milizia Urbana di Torino

It should be noted that from 1741 to 1748, the *Milizia Urbana di Torino* was no longer mustered, in fact it was originally an infantry regiment. The number of companies is unknown.

Uniform

They had a simple black tricorn with a white lace border and a dark blue cockade. Their neck stock was red. Their first uniform, from around 1736, consisted of a dark blue coat with a red collar, cuffs and lining, with 10 pewter

1 Source; Gerbaix di Sonnaz. *Bandiere, Stendardi E Vessilli Dei Conti E Duchi Di Savoia*. Turin 1911.

buttons placed in pairs. They wore a red cloth waistcoat and a pair of red breeches. Theoretically they had white gaiters, but no doubt there would have been a number of regional variations with cheap ticken, grey or brown cloth probably being used as well. No doubt the *tamburi* would have worn some form of the Royal Livery.

Around 1747, they wore a red coat with seven evenly spaced tin buttons on each side and horizontal pockets with yellow cuffs, lapels, lining, and collar. Their neck stock was now black, but as in theory they were no longer mustered at this date this uniform may in fact be a post war tenue. It is possible that they were no longer mustered as such, but transferred to the provincial regiment. Their arms and equipment would have varied considerably, but they were probably armed with older model muskets. By 1747 they had a sword as well.

Colour

They only had one colour; it was a white cross on a dark blue field. In each quarter there was a bull rampant. In the first quarter there was a white scroll bearing the devise 'AUXILIUM MEUM A DOMINO' (my help comes from the lord) painted in black. The reverse was identical in mirror image. The standard had a thin yellow border all around, including the staff edge. The sleeves and the staves were painted blue and studded with brass nails in a spiral design. The spear shaped finial was gilded as was the cone shaped ferrule, which was secured with a ring. The cords and tassels were blue. This colour can probably be dated to the first half of the eighteenth century.

Colour, *Milizia Urbana di Torino*. (Author's Illustration)

13

The Invalids, Galley and Deserter Companies

Battaglione degli Invalidi

First raised in 1719. These troops were created from elderly soldiers no longer fit for field service, but who were capable of sedentary service. They were formed in July 1739 by the general staff based in Asti. Initially there were 17 companies, with 11 as garrison troops, and eight detached companies for a total of 1,164 men dispersed among the different fortresses, freeing more able troops for the field armies. The officers were generally invalids as well.

By 1740 the unit fallen to 730 officers and men in one battalion. This rose to 1,400 officers and men divided into two battalions by 1744, and in 1747 they had risen to 22 companies and nine detachments.

Uniform

The invalids wore a black unlaced tricorn with a dark blue cockade, held in place with a loop and a pewter button. Their coat was grey-white with six pewter buttons on each side, placed from the top as one, two and three. The coats had horizontal pockets with three buttons, grey-white linings and turn backs, and yellow cuffs with three pewter buttons. The waiscoats and breeches were also both grey-white and they wore white stockings. They had standard infantry arms and equipment. The *tamburi* wore a red coat with blue facings. Invalids who served in the headquarters wore a blue coat, waistcoat and breeches with red facings, and silver cloth buttons. Those assigned to the *Regio Magazzino delle Merci* (Royal Arsenal) wore a red coat with blue facings, waistcoat and breeches, with silver cloth buttons. The invalids serving the fortress artillery probably wore a uniform similar to the artillery regiment.

Compagnie delle Galere

The galley companies were raised in 1740. There were three companies of 100 men employed on the navy's galleys as marines and to keep the oarsmen in order. The three companies had a total of 320 officers and men in 1740. This rose to 348 officers and men in 1743, and remained as such until 1747. They distinguished themselves fighting alongside the British Royal Navy where they helped evacuate the Sardinian garrison from Ventimiglia, where they were besieged by the French. They were closely associated with the infantry regiment *La Marina*.

Uniforms

Their uniform was virtually the same as the infantry regiment *La Marina*. They wore a black tricorn with yellow lace border, and a dark blue cockade, held in place with a loop and a brass button. They wore a red coat lined green, with nine brass buttons on each side, grouped in threes, horizontal pockets with three buttons, and olive green cuffs with three brass buttons. Their coat was not turned back. Their olive green waistcoat had nine buttons, grouped in threes, and their breeches were also olive green. They had a black neck stock and white stockings.

The officers wore blue naval uniforms which had gold lace and gilt buttons. The *tamburi* would have worn the Royal Livery with olive green waistcoat and breeches.

Arms and Equipment

They were armed with the standard infantry musket. On their waist belt they had a black ventral cartridge box and carried a brass hilted sabre in a black leather scabbard. They do not appear to have been issued with colours at this time.

Compagnia Franca dei Disertori Graziati.

These free companies of 'pardoned deserters' from different enemy armies were first raised in 1741. The company eventually consisted of 500 officers and men and remained as such until 1747. They were to be the basis of a light infantry unit. It is highly unlikely they had any grenadiers. Of highly questionable military value and obviously mistrusted, they were always kept short of munitions. They were eventually sent to Sardinia, out of harm's way, and some were enrolled into the islands dragoon companies.

Baron Leutrum said of them; 'How can I employ these villains. It is a waste of good officers to command them. They are not to be trusted, either as pickets or to guard the

The Invalid, Galley and Deserter Companies. 1. *Battaglione degli Invalidi*. This was the standard uniform and they could also wear gaiters of white or ticken cloth. The officers would have worn the same uniform, but with officers' attributes. 2. *Compagnie delle Galere*. 3. *Compagnia Franca dei Disertori Graziati*. (Author's Illustration)

baggage, as they would steal it, I am minded to send them to the Prince Philippe [the Spanish commander] in chains and be done with them.'[1]

Uniform

The unit wore a black tricorn with a white lace border, and a dark blue cockade, held in place with a loop and a pewter button. The officers had silver lace and button on their hats.

Their coats was grey-white with seven evenly spaced buttons on each side and vertical pockets with three buttons. It had red linings and turn backs with red cuffs (with three brass buttons), waistcoat and breeches. They wore a black neck stock and white gaiters. If they had *tamburi*, they would have worn some form of the Royal Livery. They carried the standard infantry arms and equipment. They did not have any known colours.

Micheletti Sardi

This Sardinian unit consisted of one company of 80 men. They were classed as a regular unit and not *Milizia*. They had been recruited from Sardinian bandits who had been pardoned. Their commander was Giovanni Battista Melis. Apparently, when they came up against the *Gallispans* they ran away and deserted to a man. This incident added fuel to the resistance to forming a real light infantry corps from them.

1 Stephen Manley, *The War of the Austrian Succession. Part VIII* (Eckington: Potsdam Publications, 1998), p.11

Uniforms

Although some modern authors show the *Micheletti Sardi* with their coats slung over their shoulders like the French and Spanish mountain troops, contemporary Piedmontese illustrations show them wearing their coats normally.

The companies wore a black tricorn with a dark blue cockade on the left brim, with a black loop and a pewter button, and white lace border. The officers probably had silver lace and buttons on their hats.

They wore a dark medium blue collarless coat that had eight pewter buttons on each side of the coat, and three on the cuffs. The coat had horizontal pockets, each with three pewter buttons, and red cuffs, linings, and turn backs. They wore white cravats. Their waistcoats and breeches were red, with pewter buttons. The gaiters were white with brass buttons. When they were not on campaign, they all wore white stockings.

Arms

They used a ventral cartridge case in black leather, on the waist belt they also carried two pistols, a bayonet, and a sabre in a black leather scabbard. Although some appear to have kept their oriental style sabre (*coltellaccio*), which did not have a handguard and was carried in a simple light brown leather scabbard. The blade was around 50cm long. It vaguely resembled the Turkish Yatağan, but without a reversed blade. The blades appear to have been old blades which had been re-used. The Sardinian militia also carried these sabres.

NCOs

NCO distinctions unknown, but they probably just had a gold or silver lace around their cuffs.

Officers

The officers' tricorns had a gold lace border and loop, a Savoy blue cockade with a gold button. The officers' coats and waistcoats had gold lace and they very likely wore blue sashes at the waist.

Musicians

The musicians wore the same dress as the men. Their instruments are not defined and drums are not very practical in mountain warfare so one must assume that they used some form of horn, as did their French and Spanish enemies.

Colours

They did not have any known colours.

Gendarmes de la Ville de Turin

This was a para-military police unit who were created for enforcing public order.

Uniform

Around 1745, the *gendarmes* wore a black tricorn with a red lace border (silver for officers), and a dark blue cockade, held in place with a loop and a pewter button. They wore a grey coat with red lapels, seven evenly spaced buttons on each side, and horizontal pockets with three buttons. Their waistcoat, breeches and stockings were grey.

They wore a red bandolier with white stitched edges, embroidered with a black eagle charged with an oval red shield with a white cross, and the arms of Savoy on the front and back (no cartridge pouch). They were armed with muskets, but no swords.

Appendices

Appendix 1

Selected Orders of Battle

Battle of Camposanto, 8 February 1743

The Austrians and Piedmont-Sardinians

Generalfeldmarschall von Traun
Strength: 9,000 infantry, 3,000 cavalry, 24 cannons

Advance Guard

Croats, Partentantenkorps
Esclavones Croat Battalion
Austrian HRiv Havor Hussar Regiment, three Squadrons
Austrian Heavy Artillery Battery.

Right Wing

Generalleutnant Schulenburg
Generalfeldwatchmeister Baron Pestaluzzi
Austrian IR11 Alt-Wallis Infantry Regiment, three battalions with four cannons
Austrian IR22 Roth Infantry Regiment, two battalions with two cannons
Austrian Field Battery; two 12-pounders, three 6-pounders and one howitzer

Left Wing

Generalleutnant Pallavicini (DC)
Generalfeldwatchmeister Graf Novati
Austrian IR4 Hoch und Deutschmeister Infantry Regiment, two battalions
Austrian IR6 Traun Infantry Regiment, three battalions

Generalleutnant Aspremont

Regiment Schulenburg, one battalion, Regiment Savoy, one battalion
Austrian Field Artillery Battery; two 12-pounders, three 6-pounders, one howitzer
Piedmontese field Artillery battery; ten 10-pounders (actually probably 8-pounders)
Infantry Regiment Savoy, two battalions

Left Wing Cavalry,

Generalleutnant Payersberg
Cavalry Brigade Petrasuti
Austrian KR20 Miglio Cuirassier Regiment, six squadrons
Austrian CR2 Savoye Cuirassier Regiment, three squadrons
Austrian Dragoon Regiment Aspremont-Linden (Von Savoyen), six squadrons

Second Line Right Wing,

Croat light infantry
Austrian HRv Grenz Hussar Regiment
Insurrectio Huszaren

Second Line Centre,

Luogotenente Generale Pestaluzzi
Austrian IR 20 Diesbach Infantry Regiment, three battalions
Austrian IR 25 Piccolomini Infantry Regiment, three battalions
Baron Leutrom
Regiment Rhebinder, one battalion
Regiment Diesbach (Piedmontese service)
Regiment Piedmont, two battalions
A Sardinian Light Artillery Battery.

Second Line Left Wing

Feldmarschallleutnant Ciceri
Cavalry Brigade St Pierre
Austrian Berlichingen Cuirassier Kreis Regiment, six squadrons
Dragoon Regiment La Regina, three squadrons.

Reserve Cavalry Corps

Elite companies of all the cavalry regiments present
Piedmontese Militia

Battle of Pietralunga, 17 July 1744

Piedmontese

Overall Commander: *Maggiore Generale* Charles Philibert du Verger
Overall Strength: arround 4,000 men
Garrison Redoubt Strength four battalions, around 2,400 men
Two battalions Regiment Roquin, *Colonnello* Agustine Roquin
One battalion Regiment Audibert, *Colonnello* Pierre Audibert
One battalion Regiment Saluces, *Colonnello* Giuseppe Faletto di Castagnole
Artillery: two 4 pounders

Reserve corps from Villaret

Strength three battalions, around 1,600 men
Commanded by Marquis Francois de Seyssel
Regiment Guardie, 2nd battalion, *Colonnello* Giuseppe Osasco, Comte de Roque
Regiment Guibert, 2nd battalion, Alexander Guibert de Saissac
Regiment Savoie, 1st battalion, *Colonnello* Charles Philibert du Verger

Battle of Assietta, 19 July 1747

Overall Commander; *Luogotenente Generale* Giovanni Battista Cacherano di Bricherasio

Hill of L'Assiette

Officer Commanding *Maggiore Generale* Alcanti, assisted by *Generalmajor* Count Antonio Colleredo, (commander of the Austrian contingent)

Right Wing

Regiment Meyer, one battalion, *Colonnello* Adrian Meyer of Harrisau
Regiment Traun, one battalion (Austrian)
Regiment Hagenbach, one battalion (Austrian)
Regiment Forgatz, one battalion, *Oberstlieutenant* Dracskovitz (Austrian)

Left Wing

Regiment Casale, one battalion, *Colonnello Luogotenente* Guiseppe Damiano di Priocca
Regiment Colloredo, one battalion (Austrian)

Redoubt of L'Assiette

Regiment Gardie, one battalion, *Colonnello Luogotenente* Paolo Novarina, Count of San Sebastien
Note: There were two small guns inside the redoubt.

Hill of the Gran Serin

Officer Commanding: *Colonnello* Comte de Martinengo
Regiment Kalbermatten, two battalions, *Colonnello* Bruno de Kalbermatten
Regiment Roy, one battalion, *Colonnello* Charles Antoine Roy
The Light Corps, environ 500 men
The Milice Vaudois, *Maggiore* Jean Perron
The Milices of Pragelat
The Volunteers of Piedmont

Other troops present, but not engaged

Regiment Chiablais, one battalion

Order of battle of the Sabaudian Field Army in the Alps, July 1744

Corps of Val Varaita

Commander: *Luogotenente Generale* Seyssel d'Aix
Strength: 12,600 men
Brigade Guardie
Two battalions *Guardie*, two battalions *Audibert*, one battalion *Tarantasia*
Brigade Savoia
Two battalions *Savoia*, three battalions *Roguin*
Brigade Saluzzo
One battalion *Saluzzo*, one battalion *Casale*, two battalions *Reydt*
Brigade La Regina
One battalion *La Regina*, two battalions *Guibert*, one battalion *Mondovì*

Corps of Valle Stura, at Cuneo

Commander: *Luogotenente Generale* Pallavicini
Strength: 7,070 men
Two battalions *Piemonte*, two battalions *Monferrato*, two battalions *Schulemburg*, two battalions *Kalbermatten*, one battalion *Chiablese*, one battalion *Nizza*, one battalion *Guibert*

Corps of Val Maira,

Commander: *Maggiore Generale* Cumiana
Strength: 2,100 men
One battalion *Lombardia*, one battalion *Fucilieri*, one battalion *Baden*

Corps of Alta Valle Po

Commander: *Luogotenente Colonnello* d'Isola
Strength: 700 men
One battalion *Saluzzo*

Corps of Val Chisone

Commander: *Maggiore Generale* Leutrum at Fenestrelle
Strength: 5,713 men
One battalion *Fucilieri*, one battalion *La Marina*, one battalion *Pinerolo*, one battalion *Kalbermatt*, one battalion *Burgsdorff*
One battalion *Reydt*
Three reserve battalions (*Pinerolo, Mondovì, Reydt*)

Corps of Val Sesia

Commander: *Luogotenente Generale* Bertone
Strength: 1,200
One battalion *La Marina*, one battalion *Kalbermatten*

In Iverea and the valley of Aosta

Strength: 971 men.
Ivrea; one battalion *Vercelli*
Aosta; reserve companies of Aosta

Total strength: 30,354 men

Appendix 2

Medical Services

The *Servizio Sanitario* of the army was the responsibility of the *Intendente Generale*.

In each of the regiments there was a *chirurgo maggiore* with a number of medical orderlies. In addition to their salary, the *chirurgo maggiore* received an annual fee for each soldier in the regiment. It was prescribed that he should always have the medicine chest with him.

The sick who could not follow the regiment were admitted to hospitals, which were divided into campaign or flying hospitals, which always closely followed the troops, and permanent hospitals. In peacetime, sick soldiers were treated in civilian hospitals, or in hospitals called *spedali reali*, which were reserved for them and run by contractors. The administration of and treatment in these hospitals left much to be desired, and the sick often lacked medicines, blankets, and even beds. Nor were the sick treated better in the wartime hospitals, where corruption and embezzlement was rife.

In wartime, the hospital service depended on the general army administration. A hospital was created, which was generally based in a locality along the lines of communication of the troops, and a flying hospital was in immediate contact with the operational troops. Regulations for these were laid down in 1735 with other minor regulations added in 1746.

Each hospital had a director with related administrative staff; doctors, surgeons, apothecaries, nurses, cooks, laundresses, mattress makers, chaplains and gravediggers. In the 1747 budget, the medical personnel for the royal and flying hospitals accompanying the troops in campaign operations was established as follows:

18 Doctors
60 Surgeons
40 Chief Nurses
400 Nurses

In addition to these, there were 30 other surgeons attached to the army. The budget also provided for all the costs of medicines and necessary materials. Officers were appointed from each regiment to visit the nearby hospitals, both to check on the men from their regiment and the conditions at the hospital. They were then expected to write a report for their commanders.

Many soldiers undergoing treatment were sent to the Baths of Acqui and the spa of Vinadio, which were state establishments whose staff were paid from the military budget.

Appendix 3

Food and Rations

Unfortunately, we do not have a great deal of information on the Piedmontese army's rations and culinary practices.

For the Alpine campaign of 1747 the Ministry of War decided that the quantities to be supplied to an infantry battalion of 410 men for 15 days should be: 6,200 rations of biscuit (3,100kg); 4,435 litres of wine; 590kg of rice; 461kg of lard; 50.6kg of oil; 359.58kg of cheese; and 55.32kg of salt. The individual supply therefore consisted of 15 rations (for 15 days) of biscuit (7.5 kg), 10.81 litres of wine, 1.4kg of rice, 1.12kg of lard, 0.87kg of cheese, 0.13 kg of salt. In total, each soldier had at his disposal 11.02kg of food and just little less than 11 litres of wine, the latter was used as a food substitute more than a simple beverage.

Every day, each soldier could consume 0.5kg of biscuit, and 0.226kg of cheese and rice, to be washed down with 0.72 litres of wine. It was certainly not a generous meal, especially for men who had to work on the construction of field fortifications at high altitude. We can assume that a good part of their pay went into the pockets of local suppliers who guaranteed the troops the necessary supplementary additions to their rations.

Appendix 4

Infantry Regiment Uniforms

National Regiments

	Coat	Cuffs & lining	Waistcoat & Breeches	Pockets	Buttons	Hat lace	Neck stock	Grenadier bearskin
Guardie	Deep blue, 7 buttons	Crimson red	Crimson red, piped yellow	Horizontal, 3 buttons	Brass, yellow buttonholes	Yellow/ Gold	Red, black in 1747	Red bag laced yellow
Savoia	Grey-white, 8 buttons	Blue	Blue	Vertical, 3 buttons	Pewter	Silver/ White	Red	Blue bag laced white
Monferrato	Grey-white, 7 buttons	Blue	Blue	Horizontal, 3 buttons	Pewter	Silver/ White	Red	Blue bag laced white
Piedmont	Grey-white, 7 buttons	Red	Red	Horizontal, 3 buttons	Pewter	Silver/ White	Red	Red bag laced white
Saluzzo	Grey-white, 9 buttons, 3 by 3	Red	Red	Horizontal, 3 buttons	Pewter	Silver/ White	Red	Red bag laced white
Fucilieri	Grey-white, 7 buttons	Red	Red	Horizontal, 3 buttons,	Brass Gilt	Yellow/ Gold	Red	Red bag laced yellow
La Marina	Red, 7 buttons	Olive Green	Olive green	Horizontal, 3 buttons	Brass Gilt	Yellow/ Gold	Red	Green bag laced yellow
La Regina	Grey-white, 9 buttons, 3 by 3	Red, 6 buttons	Red	Horizontal, 3 buttons	Brass Gilt	Yellow/ Gold	Red	Red bag laced yellow

Provincial Regiments

	Coat	Cuffs & lining	Waistcoat & Breeches	Pockets	Buttons	Hat lace	Neck stock	Grenadier bearskin
Chiablese	Grey-white, 8 buttons	Red, 3 buttons	Red	Vertical, 3 buttons	Pewter	Silver/ White	Red	Red laced white
Tarantasia	Grey-white, 9 buttons, 3 by 3	Red, 6 buttons	Red	Vertical, 3 buttons	Brass	Yellow/ Gold	Red	Red laced yellow
Aosta	Grey-white, 8 buttons, in pairs	Red, 3 buttons	Red	Vertical, 3 buttons	Pewter	Silver/ White	Red	Red bag laced white
Torino	Grey-white, 8 buttons	Blue, 3 buttons	Blue	Vertical, 3 buttons	Brass	Yellow/ Gold	Red	Blue bag laced yellow
Mondovi	Grey-white, 6 buttons, 1, 2, 3	Blue, 3 buttons	Blue	Horizontal, 3 buttons	Pewter	Silver/ White	Red	Blue bag laced white
Vercelli	Grey-white, 6 buttons, 1, 2, 3	Red, 3 buttons	Red	Vertical, 3 buttons	Pewter	Silver/ White	Red	Red bag laced white
Asti	Grey-white, 6 buttons, 1, 2, 3	Red, 3 buttons	Red	Horizontal, 3 buttons	Pewter	Silver/ White	Red	Red bag laced white

	Coat	Cuffs & lining	Waistcoat & Breeches	Pockets	Buttons	Hat lace	Neck stock	Grenadier bearskin
Casale	Grey-white, 6 buttons, 1, 2, 3	Red, 3 buttons	Red	Vertical, 3 buttons	Brass	Yellow/ Gold	Red	Red laced yellow
Nizza	Grey-white, 6 buttons, 1, 2, 3	Blue, 3 buttons	Blue	Vertical, 3 buttons	Pewter	Silver/ White	Red	Blue bag laced white
Pinerolo	Grey-white, 6 buttons, 1, 2, 3	Blue, 3 buttons	Blue	Horizontal, 3 buttons	Pewter	Silver/ White	Red	Blue bag laced white

Foreign Regiments

	Coat	Cuffs & lining	Waistcoat & Breeches	Pockets	Buttons	Hat lace	Neck stock	Grenadier bearskin
Swiss Reitmann/ Kalbermatten	Dark Blue, 8 buttons, yellow collar	Yellow, 3 buttons,	Dark blue white button holes	Horizontal, 3 buttons	Pewter, white button holes	Silver/ White	Black	Yellow white lace
Swiss Guibert/ Uttinger	Dark Blue, 8 buttons, blue collar	Red, 3 buttons, red lapels	Dark blue white button holes	Horizontal, 3 buttons	Pewter	Silver/ White	Black	Red bag laced white
Swiss Diesbach/Roi	Dark Blue, 8 buttons, red collar	Red, 3 buttons,	Dark blue white button holes	Horizontal, 3 buttons	Pewter, white button holes	Silver/ White	Black	Red bag laced white
Swiss Reydt/ Salis	Red, 8 buttons, in pairs, black collar,	Black, 4 buttons	Red	Horizontal, 3 buttons	Brass Gilt	Yellow/ Gold	Black	Red bag laced yellow
Swiss Keller	Dark Blue, 8 buttons. Red collar	Red, 3 buttons, white button holes	Red, white button holes	Horizontal, 3 buttons	Pewter, white button holes	Silver/ White	Black	Red bag laced white
Swiss Meyer	Dark Blue, 8 buttons, in pairs	Red, 3 buttons	Red	Double vertical, 3 buttons on each	Brass/Gilt	Yellow/ Gold	Black	Red bag laced yellow
German Schulemburg	Dark Blue, 3 buttons on lapel, white collar	White, including half lapels	Dark Blue	Horizontal, 3 buttons	Pewter, white button holes	Silver/ White	Black	Blue bag laced white
Foreign Regiments	Coat	Cuffs & lining	Waistcoat & Breeches	Pockets	Buttons	Hat lace	Neck stock	Grenadier bearskin bonnet
German Rhebinder/ Bursdorff	Dark Blue, red collar and lapels, 3 buttons	Red, 3 buttons	Dark blue	Horizontal, 3 buttons	Brass/Gilt, yellow button holes	Yellow/ Gold	White	Red bag laced yellow

	Coat	Cuffs & lining	Waistcoat & Breeches	Pockets	Buttons	Hat lace	Neck stock	Grenadier bearskin
German Baden	Dark Blue, 8 buttons, in pairs	Red, 3 buttons	Dark blue	Horizontal, 3 buttons	Brass/Gilt,	Yellow/ Gold	Black	Red bag laced yellow
Italian Sardegna	Grey-white, 6 buttons, 1, 2, 3. Black collar	Black, 3 buttons	Grey-white	Horizontal 3 buttons	Brass	Yellow/ Gold	Red,	Black bag laced yellow
Italian Sicilia	Grey-white, 8 buttons, in pairs	Red, 3 buttons	Red	Horizontal 3 buttons	Pewter	Silver/ White	Red	Red bag laced white
Italian Lombardia	Grey-white, 9 buttons, 3 by 3	Yellow, 3 buttons	Yellow	Horizontal 3 buttons	Pewter	Silver/ White	Red	yellow bag laced white
Italian Corsica	Grey-white, 6 buttons, in pairs	White, 3 buttons	Red	Horizontal 3 buttons	Brass	Yellow/ Gold	Red	No grenadiers

Bibliography

Contemporary Iconography

Jan Peeter Verhussen, Battle of Guastalla (during the battle) c.1743. Galleria Sabauda, Turin

Jan Peeter Verhussen, Guardia del Corpo c.1744. Private collection

Giovanni Michele Graneri, Deer hunting in Sardinia Granieri c. 1747. Palazzo Madama, Turin

Giovanni Michele Graneri, Market Piazza del Muncipio, Torino 1740. Palazzo Madama, Turin

Livre d'esquis des drapeaux de tous les régiments d'infanterie au service de S M Charles Emmanuel II (sic) Roi de Sardaigne. Par le Tapissier Nicolas Lauro. *c*.1734-1736, Ref. Ms.mil 431. Biblioteca Reale, Torino.

Manuscrit: *Disegno ufficiale di modello approvato dal conte Della Rocca per la bandiera del Battaglione di Artigleria dato 13 guigno*. De la Roque. Sezione IV, Ordini Generali Misti. Archivio di Stato di Torino.

Livre des Etendards des regs de cavalerie & dragons au service de S M Charles Emmanuel Roi de Sardaigne. Pour SE Mr. le Baron, & Marechal Rehbinder. Le 10 Mars 1740. Album designed by Giuseppe Ozeletti. Ref. Ms.mil 432. Bibliothèque Réale, Torino.

Livre des Drapeaux d'Infanterie au service de S M Charles Emmanuel Roi de Sardaigne 1744. Album designed by Giuseppe Ozeletti. (Biblioteca Antica 1.27.1) Archivio di Stato di Torino.

Livre des Etendards des regs de Cavalerie & Dragons au service de S M Charles Emmanuel Roi de Sardaigne 1744. Album designed by Giuseppe Ozeletti. Ref. H II 38, Archivio di Stato di Torino.

Livre des Etendards de Cavalerie & Dragons au Service de SM Charles Emanuel Roy de Sardaigne. Album designed by Giuseppe Ozeletti. 1745. Ref. Ms.mil 157a, Bibliothèque Réale, Torino.

Livre des Etendards des Gardes du Corps, Cavalerie & Dragons au Service de S.M. Roy de Sardaigne. Album designed by Giuseppe Ozeletti. 1745. Ref. Ms.mil 147, Bibliothèque Réale, Torino.

Livre de uniformes de Troupes reglеès de SM avec les Drapeaux, Ètendards ou Guidons de chaque Corps 1747. Manuscript Mil. HVIIII 53. Archivio di Stato di Torino, 1747.

Maximilien Henri, Marquis de Saint-Simon, *Histoire de la guerre des Alpes ou campagne de 1744 par les armées combinées d'Espagne et de France, commandées par SAR l'infant Don Philippe et SAS le Prince de Conti* (Amsterdam: Marc Michel Rey, 1770).

Manuscript D'Embser, Scuola d'applicazione d'arma, Torino 1732.

(Giovanni Battista d'Embser, *Dizzionario Istruttivo di tutte le Robbe appartenenti all'Artiglieria* and *Dissegni d'ogni sorta de Cannoni et Mortari*. Manuscript Mil. HVIII 53. L'Archivio di Stato di Torino, 1747.

Manuscript Saluzzo 191. Raccolta di Artiglieri Esercito Sardo c. 1740. Attributed to Generale Bertola. Bandiera (unica) e figurini delle uniformi indossate dalla Milizia Urbana di Torino. La bandiera è quella ancora attualmente in uso da parte della Città. Da notare che dal 1748 al 1772 la milizia torinese non fu più radunata per cui la bandiera è probabilmente databile alla prima metà del XVIII secolo. Giovanni Maria Genta, circa 1772, BR Ms. Mil 134. Archivio Stato di Torino.

Contemporary Printed Sources

Minutoli, Daniel, *Relation des Campagnes faites par S.M. et par ses Généraux avec des Corps Séparés dans les années 1742 et 1748*, Torino, Biblioteca Reale, Manoscritto Militare 155.

Printed Sources

Ales, Stefano, *Le Regie Truppe Sarde 1750-1773* (Milano: serie Electa, Editrice Militaire Italiana 1989)

Ales, Stefano, *Insegne Militari Preunitarie Italiane* (Roma: Stato Maggiore Dell'Esercito, 2001)

Ales, S., & M. Fiorentino, 'Les Piedmontese (1) à la Bataille de l'assiette, 19 Juillet 1747', *Tradition*, No.130, 1998

Ales, S., & M. Fiorentino, 'Les Piedmontese (2) à la Bataille de l'assiette, 19 Juillet 1747', *Tradition*, No.132. 1998

Arvers de Vault, P., *Les guerres des Alpes -Guerre de Succession d'Autriche 1742-1748* (Paris: Librairie Militaire, Berger Levrault, 1892)

Badone, Giovanni Cerino, *Il volto di Marte. L'esercito sabaudo e la realtà del campo di battaglia* (Torino: Fondazione Filippo Burzio. Borsa di Studio "Vittorio Chiusano", 2011)

Badone, Giovanni Cerino & Eugenio Garoglio *La battaglia dell'Assietta* (Torino: Edizioni del Capricorno, 2021)

Badone Giovanni, Cerino, *You have to die in Piedmont* (Warwick: Helion, 2023)

Belaubre, J., and C. P. Goldberg, *Les armées qui combattirent Louis XIV* (Paris: the author, 1970)

Bianchi, Paola, *Huguenots in the Army of Savoy-Piedmont Protestant Soldiers and Civilians in the Savoyard State in the Seventeenth and Eighteenth Century* (Turin, University of Turin, 2007)

Bianchi, Paola, *Onore e Mestiere. Le Riforme Militari nel Piemonte del Settecento* (Torino: S. Zamorani, 2002)

Boeri, Giancarlo, *The Army of the Duke of Savoy (1688-1713)* (The Pike and Shot Society, 2013)

Boeri, G.C., & Giovanni Cerino Badone, 'Uomini di Guerra. Biografie di colonnelli e comandanti di corpo sabaudi in servizio attivo durante la Guerra di Successione Austriaca (1742-1748)', *Bollettino*, 2009

Boeri, Giancarlo, Guglielmo Aimaretti, & Roberto Vela, *La guerra di Sardegna e di Sicilia 1717-1720* (Zanica: Soldiershop Publishing, 2017–2024)

Brancaccio, Nicola, *L'Esercito del Vecchio Piemonte tome I (1560-1814)* (Roma: Stabilimento Poligrafico, 1922)

Browning, R., *The War of the Austrian Succession* (New York: St. Martin's Griffin, 1993)

Canestrier, P., *Histoire Militaire de Nice* (Nice: Imprimerie de l'Eclaireur, 1932)

Cerino-Badone, Giovanni, '"Les Enfants de la Gloire", Strategie, tattiche e dottrine di impiego degli eserciti sabaudo e francese nella Guerra di Successione Austriaca (1742-1748)', *Armi Antiche*, 2008, pp. 53–87

Cerino-Badone, Giovanni, '"I portinai delle Alpi", Strategie, tattiche e dottrine di impiego dell'esercito sabaudo nella Guerra di Successione Austriaca (1742-1748), *Armi Antiche*, 2007, pp.105–165

Cerino-Badone, Giovanni, *An Army inside the Army. The Swiss regiments of the Sabaudian army 1741-1750* (Unpublished)

Compan, André, *Histoire de Nice & de son Comté* (Nice: Editions Serre, 1982)

Choulot, Vicomte Paul de, & Gabriel Maximilien Ferrero *Histoire de L'Armee Sarde* (Turin: Chez Bocca, Libraire du Roi, 1845)

Alembert & Diderot, *L'Encyclopédie, Blason Art Héraldique* (Paris: c. 1780)

Fox-Davies, A.C. *A Complete Guide to Heraldry* (London: Nelson, 1954)

Kühn, August, *Materialien zum Spanischen Erbfolgekrieg; Teil 10 Heerestung des Herzogs Victor Amadeus II von Savoyen-Piemont* (Private publication, c.1980)

Garino, Pierre-Robert, *Armorial du Comté de Nice* (Nice: Serre Editeur, 2000)

Gysin, N., 'Les troupes suisses dans le royaume de Sardaigne', *Revue Militaire Suisse*, Band 59, 1914

Loriga, Sabina, *Soldats. Un Laboratoire disciplinaire: L'armée Piémontaise au XVIIIe siècle* (Paris: Les Belles Lettres, collection Histoire, 2007)

Lupo, Maurizio *Le Lame del Re. Sabri & Spade dell'Armata Sabauda dal 1560 al 1831* (Torino: Centro Studi Piemontesi, 2007)

Manley, S., *The War of the Austrian Succession. A Wargamer's Guide Part VIII. The Uniforms of the Armies of the Italian States 1740-1748* (New Jersey: OMM, 2006)

Moris, Henri, *Operations militaires dans les alpes et les apennines pendant la guerre de la succession d'Autriche 1742-1748* (Paris: Baudoin, 1886)

Montu, Carlo, *Storia dell'artiglieria italiana* (Rome: XII Edita a cura della rivista d'Artiglieria e Genio, 1934)

Kannik, Preuben, *Military Uniforms of the World in Colour* (London: Blandfod Press, 1968)

Knötel, Richard, H. Knötel & H. Sieg, *Uniforms of the World (Handbuch der Uniformkunde).* (London: Arms & Armour Press, 1980 re-print)

Mackinnon, C., *The Observers Book of Heraldry* (London: Warne, 1972)

Ricchiardi, E., *Il Costume Militare Sabaudo, Carlo Emanuele III 1730-1773* (Torino: Ed. Lucchetti, 2000)

Ricchiardi, E., *Bandiere e Stendardi dell'Esercito Sardo 1713-1801* (Torino: Centro Studi Piemontesi, 2006)

Ricchiardi, E., *L'Esercito Sardo nel 1744, Varaita* (Torino: unpublished study, 2010)

Ricchiardi, E., 'Regno di Sardegna: Uniformi e bandiere dei reggimenti 'alemanni' al soldo di Carlo Emanuele III (1730-1773)', Bollettino, 1980

Ricchiardi, E., 'Regno di Sardegna. Uniformi della Guardia Svizzera (1740-1831)', *Bollettino*, 1985

Chiappa, E., *The Swiss ordinance regiment Guibert*, *Bollettino*, 1973

Ricchiardi, E. 'Sul "Bonetto", copricapo tipico dei granatieri dell'Esercito Sardo. Prima partie (1685-1813)', *Bollettino*, 1990

Rocca, Roger, 'Régiments Niçois dans l'armée Sarde au XVIIIe siècle "Nizza & La Marine', *Lou Sourgentin*, No.165, March 2005

Rochat, Michel, *Drapeaux Flammés des Régiments Suisses au Service de la France de 1672 à 1792* (Lausanne: Delachaux et Niestlé, 1994)

Sabatini, Carlo, *Motti Militari* (Rome: Stato Maggiore dell'Esercito Ufficio Storico, 2007)

Saluces, Comte Alexandre de, *Histoire Militaire du Piémont, Tome Premier* (Turin: Chez Pierre Joseph Pic, 1818)

San Giorgio, *Armi Antiche, Armature e Militaria*. (Torino: Auction catalogue, 2009)

Sconfienza, R., *La Campagna Gallispana del 1744* (Oxford: Storia E Archeologia Militare Di Un Anno Di Guerra Fra Piemonte E Delfinato, 2012)

Sonnaz, Gerbaix de, *Bandiere, stendardi e vessilli di Casa Savoia* (Turin, Roux Frassati, 1911)

Sonnaz, Gerbaix di, *Stendardi E Vessilli Dei Conti E Duchi Di Savoia* (Turin: Frassati, 1911)

Vallière, P. de, *Honneur et Fidélité. Histoire des Suisses au service Étranger* (Lausanne: Les Editions d'Art Suisse ancient, 1940)

von Bruckner, A. und B., *Schweizer Fahnen Buch* (St. Gallen: Zollikofer, 1942)

Wilkinson, S., The Defence of Piédmont, 1742-1748. A Prelude to the study of Napoleon. (Oxford: Clarendon Press, 1927)

Wise Terry, *Military Flags of the World 1618-1900* (New York: Blandford/Arco, 1978)

Zalou, Reinat, 'La Bataille de Fort Thaon', *Lou Sourgentin*, No.165, March 2005

Wilson, P., 'The Piedmontese Army 1689-1748', *Practical Wargamer*, May/June 1990

From Reason to Revolution – Warfare 1721-1815

http://www.helion.co.uk/series/from-reason-to-revolution-1721-1815.php

The 'From Reason to Revolution' series covers the period of military history 1721–1815, an era in which fortress-based strategy and linear battles gave way to the nation-in-arms and the beginnings of total war.

This era saw the evolution and growth of light troops of all arms, and of increasingly flexible command systems to cope with the growing armies fielded by nations able to mobilise far greater proportions of their manpower than ever before. Many of these developments were fired by the great political upheavals of the era, with revolutions in America and France bringing about social change which in turn fed back into the military sphere as whole nations readied themselves for war. Only in the closing years of the period, as the reactionary powers began to regain the upper hand, did a military synthesis of the best of the old and the new become possible.

The series examines the military and naval history of the period in a greater degree of detail than has hitherto been attempted, and has a very wide brief, with the intention of covering all aspects from the battles, campaigns, logistics, and tactics, to the personalities, armies, uniforms, and equipment.

Submissions

The publishers would be pleased to receive submissions for this series. Please email reasontorevolution@helion.co.uk, or write to Helion & Company Limited, Unit 8 Amherst Business Centre, Budbrooke Road, Warwick, CV34 5WE

You may also be interested in:

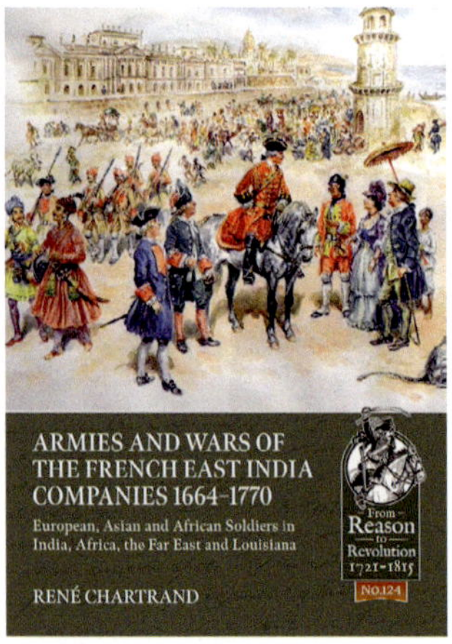

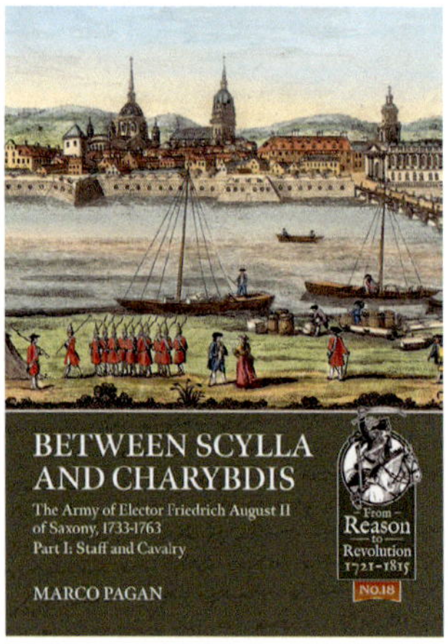

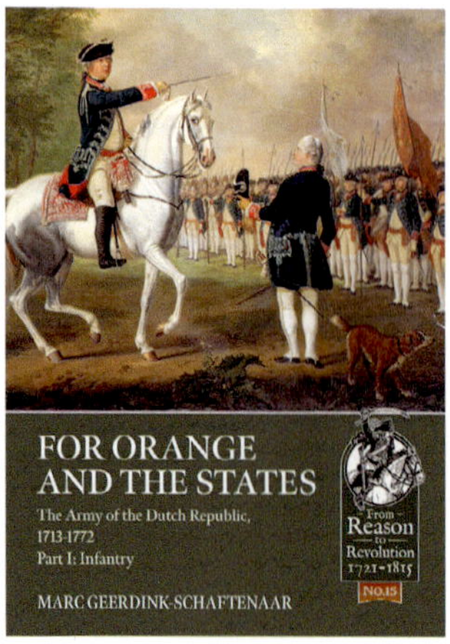

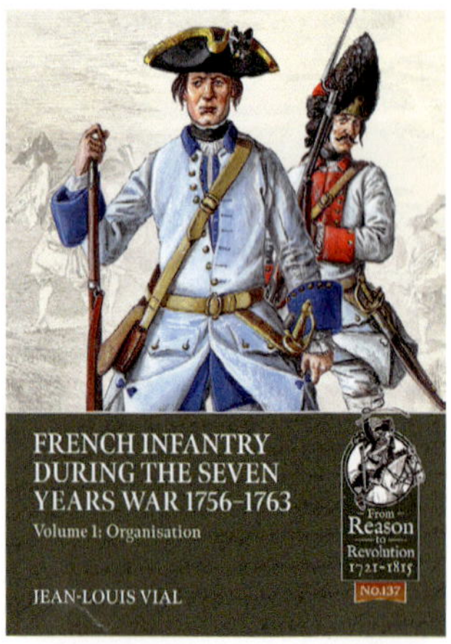

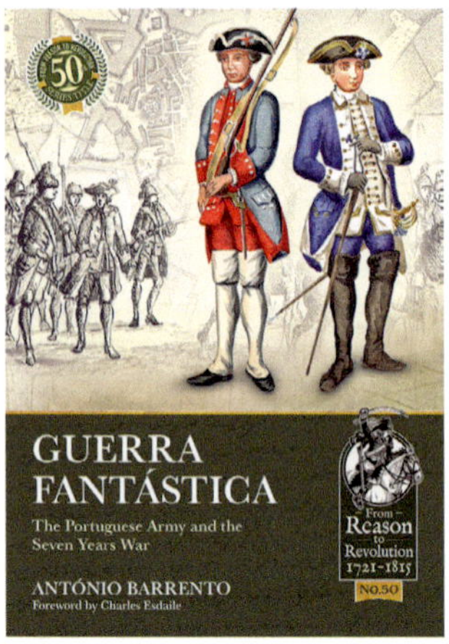

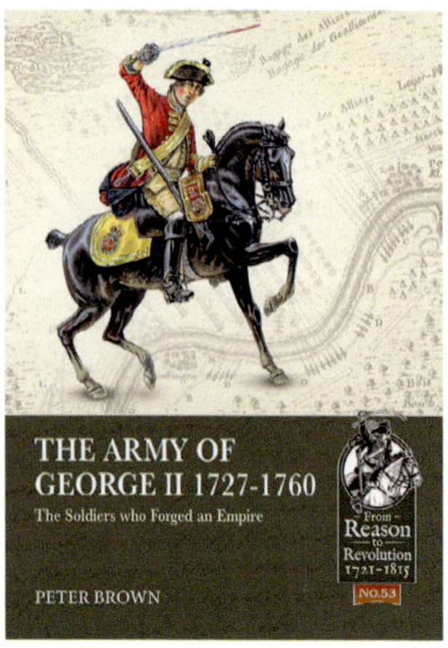

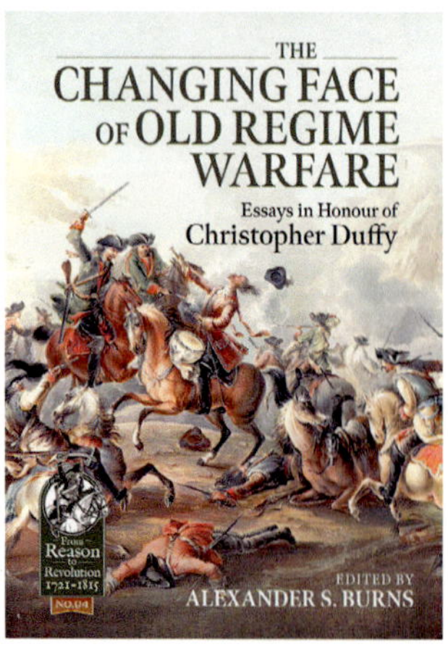

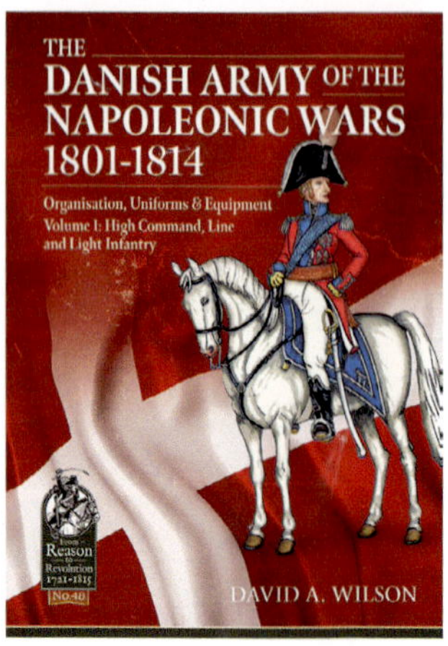